The Doha Blues

The Doha Blues

Institutional Crisis and Reform in the WTO

KENT JONES

OXFORD
UNIVERSITY PRESS
2010

OXFORD
UNIVERSITY PRESS

Oxford University Press, Inc., publishes works that further
Oxford University's objective of excellence
in research, scholarship, and education.

Oxford New York
Auckland Cape Town Dar es Salaam Hong Kong Karachi
Kuala Lumpur Madrid Melbourne Mexico City Nairobi
New Delhi Shanghai Taipei Toronto

With offices in
Argentina Austria Brazil Chile Czech Republic France Greece
Guatemala Hungary Italy Japan Poland Portugal Singapore
South Korea Switzerland Thailand Turkey Ukraine Vietnam

Copyright © 2010 by Oxford University Press, Inc.

Published by Oxford University Press, Inc.
198 Madison Avenue, New York, NY 10016

www.oup.com

Oxford is a registered trademark of Oxford University Press

Library of Congress Cataloging-in-Publication Data
Jones, Kent Albert.
The Doha blues : institutional crisis and reform in the WTO / by Kent Jones.
p. cm.
Includes bibliographical references and index.
ISBN 978-0-19-537882-5
1. World Trade Organization.   2. Doha Development Agenda (2001–)
3. Free trade.   4. International economic relations.   5. Globalization.
I. Title.
HF1385.J668 2010
382'.92—dc22   2009007212

An earlier version of chapter 3 was published as "The Political Economy
of WTO Accession: The Unfinished Business of Universal Membership."
World Trade Review 8 (2): 279–314.

1 3 5 7 9 8 6 4 2

Printed in the United States of America
on acid-free paper

In memory of my mother,
Sylvia Esther Phelps Jones
(1919–2008)

Preface

THE DOHA DEVELOPMENT ROUND TRADE NEGOTIATIONS COLLAPSED, once again, in July 2008; efforts to revive them in December of that year also failed. It was the second year in a row that efforts to restart the talks that had stalled in the summer of 2006 faltered, and the fourth time since they were launched in 2001 that formal negotiations came to a halt. The architects of the World Trade Organization (WTO), founded in 1995, established a more comprehensive system of trade rules and dispute settlement that was designed to improve on its predecessor, the General Agreement on Tariffs and Trade (GATT). Yet the new and improved trading system under the WTO has thus far failed to deliver a major multilateral trade agreement. The WTO, or more precisely the member countries of the WTO, have the "Doha Blues": they can't break the deadlock in the Doha Round. In the months following the 2006 debacle, WTO Director-General Pascal Lamy liked to joke that the negotiations were merely on a "coffee break," and could resume quickly if the parties agreed to it. Yet despite his efforts and those of the United States, European Union, Japan, India, Brazil, Australia, and other countries to meet since then, a final package of agreements has remained out of reach. In the meantime, critical political deadlines have come and gone, in particular the United States fast-track authority, needed to assure a direct up or down vote in the U.S. Congress, and the 2008 U.S. presidential elections, which ended the administration under which the Doha Round had begun. The appointment of a new European Commission and the general elections in India in 2009 also pointed to a further hiatus in the Doha Round negotiations.

While tough negotiations and stalled talks are nothing new in the WTO—or in its predecessor, the GATT—the Doha Round has been particularly frustrating. As was the case in many an earlier trade round deadlock, the main bone of contention in July 2008 was agricultural policy (although other issues also lurked in the background, unresolved). And yet there was a new twist this time. In earlier rounds, the United States and the European Union countries were the main combatants over agricultural trade issues. This time it was India, along with other developing countries, that declared the deal on the table to be unacceptable, signaling a new and more complicated process of reaching consensus on a global trade deal. The world economy had also become more complicated in recent years, as public anxiety over market globalization, terrorism, the environment, and the collapse in 2008 of global financial markets seemed to block the conclusion of a new global trade liberalization agreement. As the Doha Round stagnated, many countries eagerly sought bilateral and regional trade deals that could be negotiated relatively quickly, pursuing preferential rather than multilateral trade liberalization. Has the WTO run out of "juice," the attractions of trade opportunities and prospects of trade-driven economic growth that previously brought countries together in eight rounds of multilateral trade negotiations since 1947? Or are countries still poised to conclude a multilateral agreement, once conditions in the world economy become more favorable? In other words, are the Doha Blues a funeral march for the WTO, or merely a sad song over a lost love, negotiations that may yet return someday soon?

In fact there appear to be yet more refrains to write for the Doha Blues: the story does not end here, much as it would be tempting to declare the Doha Round dead. Despite the continuing string of setbacks, trade negotiators refuse to declare the round over, even as they acknowledge that the hiatus will be longer than Pascal Lamy's extended coffee break. There is a practical reason for this optimism. Trade officials have invested enormous amounts of time and effort to move the multilateral negotiations to their current position. While the talks are now suspended, each country's latest negotiating stance still provides a platform for progress in future talks. It is most important, in this regard, that countries not backslide on agreements previously achieved in the negotiations so far. In fact it seems that negotiators are already planning to "bookmark" their positions and pick up the Doha Round negotiations at a later date, after the political transitions in the United States and elsewhere have run their course (Schott 2008). It would make no sense, by this reasoning, to end the Doha Round and start from scratch. Indonesian Trade Minister Mari Pangestu summed up the situation: "Multilateral talks never fail, they just continue" (*Bridges Weekly*, July 28, 2008).

The main idea of this book is that the WTO faces the inevitable institutional problems of an organization buffeted by a growing and changing global economy, and it must change and adapt in order to overcome these problems. The problems come from the friction of existing institutional structures grinding against the changed requirements of achieving consensus in multilateral trade negotiations. These frictions originated in the Uruguay Round and have worsened over the course of the Doha Round as countries have tried to capture new gains from trade by renewing the cycle of multilateral trade liberalization that has become a regular feature of economic diplomacy since World War Two. Yet the circumstances, goals, and membership of the trading system have changed significantly since the GATT system was founded in 1947. The WTO must therefore also adapt and evolve. Across the decades, institutional conflict has often arisen in the trading system, and in fact the history of the trading system during this time is in many ways a study in institutional adaptation to expand and facilitate trade liberalization. The problems of the Doha Round are in this regard not unique. However, since the founding of the WTO in 1995, the expanding scope of trade negotiating topics, the changing requirements of representation in the negotiations, and the need for "coherence" between the WTO and other institutions have all run up against insufficient or outdated institutional structures that have hindered progress in the negotiations. The analysis will show that, in many ways, internal governance institutions in the WTO are in fact evolving in response to this challenge, and in some cases, external cooperation has spontaneously closed the coherence gap. But more directed WTO reforms may be necessary to put trade liberalization back on track, and new international institutions are necessary to deal with coherence issues. Domestic reforms in many WTO member countries will also play an important role in making progress on trade liberalization.

The Doha Round, and the GATT/WTO system in general, have been the subject of extensive and detailed study, focusing variously on the historical and political analysis of trade negotiations, the legal analysis of trade institutions, and the often technical economic analysis of bargaining strategies and the detailed welfare effects of trade. These wide-ranging approaches to WTO rules and negotiations illustrate the complexity of the institution and of a multisector multilateral trade negotiation such as the Doha Round. While drawing on many of these different sources of WTO analysis, this study proposes a simple and compelling reason for the constant adaptation of trade institutions to change: countries want and expect *gains from trade* from a successful negotiation. At the same time, they want to retain sovereign control over their domestic adjustment to the increase in trade, hence the importance of the WTO language of "concessions" balanced against foreign market access, the trophies brought home by a country's trade negotiators. Yet the fact that countries have continually returned to the negotiating table, against any and all adversities, highlights the significance of the gains from trade as a motivating force. It is a factor that is often seriously underestimated in the analysis of trade relations.

How can countries establish and maintain a workable system of global trade liberalization, an institutional structure that can continually deliver the widest possible geographical and sectoral scope of the gains from trade? The first chapter sets out to present possible roots of the problem, as well as a conceptual framework of the underlying institutional framework of the WTO, based on a set of mutually accepted goals, constitutive rules, mechanisms, and, importantly, trust. The plan for such an institution is simple: exchange trade concessions on a reciprocal basis, establish rules of trade policy and dispute settlement, and make decisions collectively as sovereign countries, on the basis of consensus. The second chapter addresses the institutional problems that have developed during the Uruguay Round and emerged during the Doha Round, in which the ambitions for achieving gains from trade in new areas have run up against some difficult rigidities in decision making, as well as inordinate expectations and an inherited distrust by many developing countries that emerged from their experience in the Uruguay Round. The analysis follows the development of this theme from the early years of the GATT through the completion of the Uruguay Round, followed by the disastrous Seattle Ministerial Meeting and the subsequent phases of crisis management during the Doha Round. Along the way, the negotiators have narrowed the agenda in order to improve the prospects for consensus, but ironically, the biggest potential gains have been sacrificed for lack of a flexible and workable bargaining framework. Developing new frameworks will be necessary in order to get trade liberalization back on track.

Chapter 3 deals with institutional aspects of the WTO accession process. The WTO is close to achieving its goal of achieving universal membership, with just a few large countries, notably the Russian Federation, outside the organization. However, the process of joining the WTO has become increasingly difficult as the rate at which countries are joining has slowed down, and each new member has, on average, taken longer to join than have previously acceding countries. In addition, existing WTO members appear to have learned to extract more concessions from new members, dragging out the process. The WTO purposely tightened the GATT's more open, "big tent" rules of accession in order to impose more discipline on new members. However, the one-sided negotiating power of the process, in which incumbent WTO members overwhelmingly have the upper hand, may be depriving new members of a sense of ownership in the organization, which is necessary to facilitate cooperation and consensus in trade negotiations, and it may be discouraging applicant countries. The trend in WTO accession casts doubt on its ability to bring the final 45 or so countries into the organization. It may be time for WTO members to reexamine the older and "softer" GATT approach as a way to move more quickly to effective universal participation in the global trading system.

Chapter 4 deals with the problem of representation in WTO decision making, focusing on the informal institution of "Green Room" meetings. Since decision making in the WTO is based on consensus, it is very difficult to deliberate on difficult issues in plenary sessions. With 153 members, it is clear that some system of small-group deliberations is necessary. The problem lies in how to provide representation for each member when the number of seats at the table is limited. Various proposals to establish an executive counsel or consultative board have never gained much traction, since they would require some combination of rotating seats and some kind of formalized regional or collective representation, an approach that is unacceptable to many members. In the meantime, WTO members have made increasing use of coalitions in defending their interests in the negotiations, which alleviates some of the problem of representation in the Green Room—as long as each coalition gains proper representation at the meeting. A more comprehensive approach might be to promote more formalized "platforms" in WTO deliberations, which would then be guaranteed representation in relevant Green Room meetings.

The problem of representation also lies at the heart of chapter 5, which examines the participation of developing countries in the WTO's dispute settlement understanding (DSU). In principle, all WTO members have equal access to the system. Yet among developing countries, only the larger ones have filed significant numbers of cases. Because the prosecution of a case requires extensive (and expensive) resources, the poorest countries have found it difficult to justify the expense. This is also in part because the large fixed cost of filing a case must be offset by a sufficiently large value of trade. Ironically, smaller and poorer countries also suffer from being too insignificant to be the targets of a case: it is through the discipline of DSU enforcement that countries open their markets and gain from import trade competition. Other problems may also make a "level playing field" between

large and small countries impossible, such as the system's reliance on contingent retaliation as an ultimate enforcement mechanism. Large countries
can pose a more credible retaliation threat than small countries, and may
also potentially use their political power as leverage in intimidating smaller
countries from filing cases. There is no easy answer to the problem of
achieving an equitable system of trade justice through the DSU, but some
system of transfers, pro bono legal support, and "small claims" procedures
would redress the imbalance of power in the prosecution of cases.

Chapter 6 turns to the general issue of coherence, which deals more
broadly with the problem of filling the gaps between rich and poor countries in the WTO. Many of the trade agreements in the Uruguay Round,
for example, imposed unfunded compliance costs on developing countries, notably the Trade-Related Aspects of Intellectual Property Rights
(TRIPS), Customs Valuation, and Sanitary and Phytosanitary (SPS) agreements. In many cases, developing countries are prevented from participating effectively in the global trading system because of a lack of "trade
capacity," including transportation, port, and communications infrastructure, competent government and administrative services, and expertise
in evaluating commercial trade and trade liberalization opportunities.
This chapter sets out to show that there are two analytical problems to be
overcome in establishing a workable institutional structure to build trade
capacity. The first is to find and build international organizations with institutional comparative advantage in particular aspects of trade capacity. The
second, and perhaps more difficult, task is to develop a system of coordination between and among the organizations, where the associated transaction cost often tends to be prohibitively high. In some, probably unusual,
cases, all participants benefit from the joint action directly, which reduces
the need for institutionalized coordination. With regard to WTO negotiations, the use of plurilateral financing agreements to cover compliance
costs may be a viable possibility. In general, establishing a reliable system
of coordinated governance to address crosscutting global issues is perhaps
one of the greatest challenges of our time.

The final chapter presents the prospects for reform and progress in liberalizing multilateral trade. Action items include domestic measures that
countries should take to facilitate trade liberalization, internal WTO measures to promote consensus in negotiations, and cooperative international
efforts to build global institutions. The reforms of most immediate importance are domestic measures to alleviate the trade adjustment problem,
which is probably best addressed through general adjustment measures.
Recommendations for internal WTO governance reforms include measures

to improve the "representation capacity" of WTO members and the terms of the accession process, to increase the transparency of deliberative processes, and in some cases to loosen the single undertaking requirement. Finally, the agenda for international institution building is long, but building the trade capacity of developing countries in conjunction with further trade liberalization should receive high priority. Also of high importance is the need for new global institutions to address global environmental and security problems. The unifying concept underlying all of these suggestions is that there are still potentially enormous gains from trade possible from broad multilateral trade liberalization, which, if captured, would be instrumental in promoting development, poverty reduction, and improved global economic growth. The gains would more than offset the transitional adjustment cost and investments in infrastructure required to make the liberalization happen.

In the end, gains from trade offer a compelling reason for trade negotiations, but the institutional framework for trade liberalization will typically define the scope of the gains. Countries will always have the incentive to bargain for trade liberalization, but without a strong set of rules and incentives to bargain multilaterally, countries will be left to their own devices and will submit to the natural preference to play favorites, usually in the form of bilateral or regional trade deals. Such arrangements may indeed increase welfare, especially if they pave the way for broader trade liberalization, but they also may divert trade and negotiating resources away from the larger prize of global liberalization, along with the benefits of a global trading system. Institutions, in other words, make a difference.

Acknowledgments

I WISH TO ACKNOWLEDGE THE CONTRIBUTIONS OF MANY COLLEAGUES, teachers, and mentors to my understanding of the global trading system. Foremost among these remains the late Jan Tumlir, Director of Research at the GATT from 1967 to 1985, who first impressed upon me the importance of institutional factors in trade relations. I am also grateful to Richard Blackhurst, former teacher and mentor, who continued to influence my thinking on trade throughout the years and sparked my interest in many of the topics in this book. For many comments and criticisms on earlier drafts of the papers contained in this volume, I am also thankful to the participants and discussants at the annual conferences at the Centre for the Study of International Institutions, University of Innsbruck (2004–2006), the Atlantic Economic Conferences in Berlin and Philadelphia (2006), and the WTO Symposium at the University of St. Petersburg, Russia (2007), to my colleagues Robert McAuliffe and Yunwei Gai, and to many trade officials involved with WTO negotiations, who prefer to remain anonymous. The author has also benefitted from conversations and correspondence with Andrew Stoler, David Walters, Dorothy Dwoskin, John Veroneau, Jeffrey Schott, Joel Trachtman, Scott Miller, and Gary Horlick, while any remaining errors are the responsibility of the author alone. The Babson College Faculty Research Fund and Glavin Fund provided generous support for this project, and I received the usual professional technical and clerical support of Linda Katz in the preparation of the many drafts that culminated in the final product.

Contents

Acronyms

AB	Appellate Body
ACWL	Advisory Centre on WTO Law
AD	Anti-Dumping
ADB	Asian Development Bank
AIDS	Acquired Immune Deficiency Syndrome
ASEAN	Association of Southeast Asian Nations
BATNA	Best Alternative to a Negotiated Agreement
CACM	Central American Common Market
CAFTA	Central American Free Trade Agreement
CP	Contracting Party (GATT)
D-G	Director-General
DSU	Dispute Settlement Understanding
EFTA	European Free Trade Association
EU	European Union
FDI	Foreign Direct Investment
FTA	Free Trade Area
GATS	General Agreement on Trade in Services
GATT	General Agreement on Tariffs and Trade
GDP	Gross Domestic Product
GSP	Generalized System of Preferences
IDB	Inter-American Development Bank
IF	Integrated Framework
ILO	International Labor Organization
IMF	International Monetary Fund

IP	Intellectual Property
IPR	Intellectual Property Rights
ITC	International Trade Center (WTO/UNCTAD)
ITO	International Trade Organization
LDC	Least Developed Country
LMG	Like Minded Group
MFA	Multifiber Agreement
MFN	Most-Favored Nation
MTN	Multilateral Trade Negotiation
PPA	Protocol of Provisional Application (GATT)
PTA	Preferential Trade Agreement
NAMA	Non-Agricultural Market Access
NGO	Non-Governmental Organization
OECD	Organization for Economic Cooperation and Development
OPEC	Organization of Petroleum Exporting Countries
RCA	Revealed Comparative Advantage (Index)
S&D	Special and Differential
SPS	Sanitary and Phytosanitary Measures
SSM	Special Safeguard Mechanism
TRIPS	Trade-Related Aspects of Intellectual Property Rights
UN	United Nations
UNCTAD	United Nations Conference on Trade and Development
UNDP	United Nations Development Program
WP	Working Party (WTO Accession)
WTO	World Trade Organization

The Doha Blues

1

The Problem and the Institutional Framework

What's Wrong with the WTO?

Founded with great fanfare in 1995, the WTO was touted as the new and improved version of the GATT, its predecessor. The GATT had been founded in 1947 as the surviving portion of the ill-fated International Trade Organization (ITO), but never achieved the status of a bona fide international organization itself; it was a "provisional agreement," with participation by "Contracting Parties" rather than members. Its trade promotion activities were limited for the most part to manufactured goods, and many of its agreements were in the form of codes adopted only by subsets of countries. The GATT dispute settlement system had built-in weaknesses, as decisions could be vetoed by the defendant in a case, and there were no formal enforcement provisions. Many GATT members, especially developing countries, had been admitted to the agreement without stringent requirements regarding market access and GATT rules compliance. The WTO was the new institution designed to incorporate and supersede the GATT as part of the Uruguay Round trade agreement. It was a true international organization, with a permanent structure and members. It tightened the rules on accession, redesigned the dispute settlement system so that decisions could only be vetoed with a unanimous vote of the members, and included enforcement provisions. WTO negotiations, following the Uruguay Round, included agriculture and services, as well as intellectual property and other behind-the-border issues, that is, domestic laws, regulations and practices that may have a differential and restrictive impact on imports. It made trade agreements comprehensive through the requirement of a "single under-taking" by all members. These were the new features of a new institution, designed to correct the shortcomings of the old one.

In the years since its founding, the WTO has fulfilled some, but not all, of these great expectations. It has established a comprehensive framework of rules and a successful system of dispute settlement. It has admitted 25 new members, and many others are still eager to join. It has created a net-work of day-to-day trade discussions at the committee level in Geneva that has kept the world trading system functioning smoothly. However, it has failed to deliver on what many consider to be its primary purpose: to act as a "trade liberalization machine" and generate new multilateral trade agree-ments. The first attempt to launch a new trade round, initially dubbed the Millennium Round, at the Third WTO Ministerial in Seattle, Washington, in 1999, ended in an embarrassing failure. Two years later, shortly after the events of September 11, 2001, the Doha Development Round was finally launched in Doha, Qatar, with what turned out to be a tenuous agreement on a negotiating agenda. Since then, the negotiations have lurched from crisis to crisis with rejuvenation in between, from stalemate to heightened expectations, from dramatic summit meetings to disappointment and col-lapse. The encouraging sign is that the negotiators don't want to give up; they keep coming back for another try at forging an agreement. Yet the disturbing question remains: why can't the WTO countries find a pathway to the successful conclusion of a global agreement, to carry on the record of success that the GATT showed in its eight completed trade rounds from 1947 to 1994?

This book is about the Doha Blues—the sense of malaise, frustration, and stalemate that has haunted the negotiations ever since they began in 2001. It will take a thematic approach to this issue and focus on the insti-tutional aspects of the problem, rather than giving a blow-by-blow account of the negotiations. There are in fact many insightful analyses of the Doha Round negotiations as they have progressed so far, including Das (2006), Bhaumik (2006), and Wilkinson (2006). There are also several observations and accounts of particular aspects of the problems of the Doha Round (Schott 2008, Finger 2007, Odell 2009, and Martin and Messerlin 2007, to name a few) and many more topical studies of Doha-related issues (Evenett and Hoekman 2006, Griller 2008).[1]

Why have the Doha negotiations been so painfully slow and unsuccess-ful so far? A review of recent commentary and analysis[2] seems to indicate that the difficulty has many roots, as shown by the following list of contrib-uting factors:

1. *Multilateral trade negotiations have become too unwieldy to manage effectively.* Membership in the GATT grew dramatically from the 1960s to the 1980s, and the WTO as of 2009 had 153 members, a large number to manage in a consensus-based decision process. In addition, the number of issues has grown with the expanded scope of the WTO coverage into agriculture, services, and "behind-the-border" trade issues.

2. *The single undertaking was a good idea in principle, but it doesn't work in practice.* In order to provide the widest possible scope of trade-offs that would provide each member with a stake in the negotiating outcome, and to avoid the fragmentation of the GATT system of codes, the WTO was founded on the principle that "there is no agreement until everything is agreed." In conjunction with the unwieldy scope of membership and agenda issues indicated in the first item above, some argue that forcing the negotiating outcome into a single, balanced package for all members is virtually unachievable.

3. *The balance of power in trade negotiations has shifted in favor of large developing countries.* The United States and the European Union had dominated trade negotiations for many years, and while they remain the world's leading traders (both in imports and exports), their relative importance in trade has diminished, and many faster-growing developing countries, such as India, Brazil, and China, are now asserting greater influence over the WTO negotiating process.

4. *The Doha Development Round was oversold as a trade negotiation to promote development.* Leading developed countries agreed to present the Doha negotiations as a "development" round in order to provide developing countries with a strong incentive to participate. Yet the WTO is not a development agency, even if trade plays an important part in development. It was impossible for the Doha Round to fulfill the expectations of a trade round presumably focused on development goals.

5. *Developing countries are "mad as hell" and won't take it anymore.* In conjunction with the previous item, many developing countries were disappointed in the outcome of the Uruguay Round, in which they expected large gains from liberalization of textile and clothing trade in exchange for commitments on the protection of developed countries' intellectual property and on other "behind the border issues." The delayed textile/clothing trade liberalization, in which China won the lion's share of gains, combined with potentially large

costs of intellectual property protection and the financial cost of compliance with new WTO commitments, led many developing countries to view the Doha Round as an entitlement to receive compensation for the raw deal they felt they got in the Uruguay Round, with few or no concessions on their part.

6. *Multilateral trade negotiations have run out of easy "fuel" and political support for reciprocal bargaining.* The trade negotiations previously depended largely on tariff bargaining, and the low-hanging fruit of high manufactured goods tariffs had already been harvested before the Doha Round. The natural political allies of such liberalization, industrial exporters, have subsequently lost the strong interest that often propelled the negotiations. Remaining bargaining issues in areas such as agriculture and services have much more intransigent domestic support for protection.

7. *Many countries are either economically or politically unprepared to benefit from trade liberalization.* Many developing countries suffer from a lack of sufficient market institutions, critical trade infrastructure, government capacity, and safety nets to promote adjustment to increased trade competition. These factors may be hindering the efficient allocation of resources and the ability to gain from trade. Many developed countries may also be suffering from a failure to deal with increasingly acute domestic adjustment pressures, which is usually a political prerequisite for achieving domestic consensus on trade liberalization.

8. *The world is distracted by other crises.* Global terrorism, global warming, and the financial crisis of 2008 have drawn attention and energy away from trade negotiations. In some quarters, these crises have even been cited as arguments against trade liberalization, presumably because trade contributes to these negative outcroppings of globalization.

9. *U.S. leadership in global trade liberalization has diminished.* During the cold war confrontation with the Soviet Union, the United States viewed the trading system as part of its economic bulwark against Communism, and the expanding U.S. economy provided a strong domestic political base for taking a leadership role in it. As U.S. economic growth has slowed in comparison to other countries, economic adjustment problems have arisen especially in its manufacturing sectors, the cold war threat has diminished, and the U.S. trade deficit has grown to unprecedented levels, so has U.S. enthusiasm and political support for trade liberalization declined. Another

take on this problem has appeared in the criticism of former president George W. Bush, whose foreign policies, particularly regarding the war in Iraq, were unpopular in most of the rest of the world and prevented the United States from taking a leadership role in the Doha negotiations.

10. *Business interests in global trade have shifted to regional supply chains.* For multinational corporations, the globalization of production has increased the importance of establishing smoothly functioning supply chains internationally through accommodating investment provisions and regulations in host countries. As far as these companies are concerned, the focal point of negotiations has therefore shifted toward bilateral investment treaties and preferential trade agreements that include investment provisions. The relative importance of tariffs and other WTO market access negotiations has declined.

This long list of factors working against the Doha Round is sobering, and might cause one to wonder how any global trade liberalization agreement could be achieved in the current economic and political environment. One could even add to the list by examining possible tactical missteps and strategic blunders made by the Doha Round negotiators themselves (see Schott 2008, Bhaumik 2006), although many of these mistakes have roots in the factors listed above. Furthermore, as Lawrence (2008) has argued, the success of the GATT in completing eight trade rounds has led, ironically, to a possible overreaching by the WTO, along the lines of the Peter Principle: successful institutions are eventually "promoted" into areas beyond their natural competence. Yet there is something missing in all this pessimism. If it is still possible to negotiate further gains from trade, why would any of the factors listed above, or even the tactical negotiating mistakes, ultimately block a new global trade agreement? In fact, one indicator of continued interest in trade expansion has been the proliferation in bilateral and regional trade agreements, driven partly by the lack of progress in the Doha Round.

The answer to this question is likely to lie in the institutional connection in each of the historical, political, and economic factors described above. For example, if the number of members or the scope of the agenda has become too large, why can't the organization adapt to this new reality and change the bargaining framework to a more efficient structure? If many developing countries were disappointed in the Uruguay Round, this should not deter them from negotiating vigorously for an agreement that will serve their interests. If the low-hanging fruit is already harvested, why not redouble the efforts to build ladders to reach the higher, but perhaps even sweeter, fruit? If internal decision making needs reform in order to generate consensus, there should be sufficient motivation, through the potential gains from trade, for countries to pursue these reforms. In this regard, the question of the WTO's underperformance comes down to an analysis of its institutional efficacy, which requires an understanding of the underlying conceptual framework of international economic institutions.

The WTO as an Institution: The Conceptual Framework

The WTO as an international economic institution sets out to reconcile the two counterpoised goals of its members: to gain from trade and at the same time to retain sovereign control of their trade policy, that is, the ability to restrict trade. The WTO is, in other words, a continuing and evolving study in the balancing act between progressive trade liberalization and residual trade restriction. On the one hand, it acknowledges the simple but compelling concept that trade liberalization is beneficial for all countries. On the other, it recognizes the political difficulty of opening one's own markets to imports. In this regard the powerful force of mercantilist tendencies is embedded in the WTO system and gives rise to the idiosyncratic nature of multilateral trade negotiations as a sort of zero-sum game. The prize for each player is foreign "market access" achieved on behalf of one's exporters; the price paid for your winnings is the grudging "concession" of reciprocal import market access to others. Such a dance of contradictory impulses requires an elaborate institutional structure of rules, norms, practices, and procedures that shape the process and the outcome of trade negotiations (Wilkinson 2006). Market access gains (for your exporters) and concessions (to imports) are carefully, and at times obsessively, weighed and measured in trade negotiations. Timetables for tariff reductions and trade reforms are the subject of detailed negotiation. Bargains must be struck on exceptions to market opening in order to secure political support at home, and the ability to retain control over imports of specific goods or in terms of specific procedures is a badge of national sovereignty. Rules within the institution related to market access are an important part of the system because they regulate your trading partner's behavior in living up to the negotiated commitment so as to prevent any backsliding. Agreements are closely monitored for violations ("nullification and impairment"), and violators can be hauled in front of a dispute panel to reclaim the benefits of lost benefits from the market opening measure. Yet at the end of a negotiation, a successful balance allows all members to return home victorious, each claiming it has pried open essential foreign markets while at the same time protecting essential domestic economic interests from dangerous foreign incursion. Such is the mercantilist logic of the WTO as an institution.

In its attempt to reconcile the gains from trade with the urge to protect domestic trade interests, it should be no surprise that the WTO strikes a delicate and often uneasy balance between the two. Countries on their own, even large ones, have found it very difficult to sustain a unilateral system that will secure broad, multilateral gains from trade. The WTO has emerged as a global trading system and thereby a global public good, overcoming the barriers to multilateral trade liberalization. For this very reason, the fundamental institutional structure of the WTO is of great importance. There must, for example, be a common goal, a set of shared objectives among its members, in order for such an international institution to exist. Rules, practices, and procedures must be developed in order to pursue the membership's goals. Some are formal, others informal. The architects of the institution typically have a significant impact on how the goals are achieved, at least at the beginning (Thelen and Steinmo 1992). History and experience shape traditional practice and expectations, for example, on how committees are run and negotiating drafts are prepared. Negotiators learn from their own experience and mistakes and those of others, they will vow to get back what may have been lost in an earlier negotiation. As circumstances change and the institution matures, so do the institutional needs of achieving the goals. In other words, the WTO is an institution that is constantly experiencing the tension between its existing institutional structures and its evolving environment. The institution may need to change in order to sustain its aspirations, for the delicate balance described above can break down if goals and structures are not aligned, or if they are not universally accepted.

Institutions, according to philosopher John Searle (1995), are "constructions of social reality" that are intended to serve a purpose. In order to understand the functioning of an institution, it helps to think of it in the following way. Your dog, according to Searle, can observe you kicking a soccer ball into the net, but your dog cannot observe you scoring a goal. It is only when the observer is conscious of the accepted symbolic meaning of the game (players, referees, rules, field of play, goals) and how the game is played that the observer can understand the outcome of the organized activity it entails. Institutions are the products of human interaction, and are constructed to impart status to the activities they organize and direct, the people that act as their agents, and the goals they set out to accomplish. In particular, status within an institution carries what Searle calls "deontic powers," that is, obligations and rights recognized by the collective participants. For the WTO, the main activity is trade negotiation, supported by dispute settlement and other forms of deliberation and information gathering. Representatives act on behalf of the governments of countries and territories having sovereign control over trade. The goal is to conclude market opening agreements and rules that regulate market access, that is, to bargain both for the gains from trade and for continued claims over certain areas of trade and domestic policy. By virtue of the WTO's institutional character, these agreements are given a status that creates reciprocal obligations and rights—in particular, reciprocal market access for members' traded products. Within this framework are the internal governance components of the institution, such as an organizational structure, procedural measures, and formal or informal practices related to deliberation and decision making.

The soccer analogy highlights the importance of knowing what the mutually recognized goals are in founding and joining the institution. Like other economically motivated institutions, the WTO exists because its participants (members) want it to exist and to perform functions that create benefits for them that cannot be created by the members acting alone. The necessary component is what Searle calls "collective intentionality," which is the basis of cooperative behavior. This feature of the institution points to the essential issue of motivation in the form of a least common denominator of interests, because the commitment of the participants in the institution will depend in large part on its focus on and credibility in achieving the collective goals. Just what are these benefits? Many commentators have focused on the political goals of trade, especially for hegemonic countries in the trading system: extending national power to other parts of the world, strengthening diplomatic influence, creating military alliances, establishing stability among trading partners, and so on. In fact, much of the motivation for trade agreements among governments has historically been overtly political (Finger 2008), and this dimension of trade relations is always of great importance. Much of the political analysis of the GATT/WTO system has focused on the strategic goals of the United States in shaping the trading system after the Second World War, particularly during the cold war. This analysis has extended to the details of governance, such as the consensus rule, dispute settlement, and "Green Room" (small group) deliberations, all as part of an institutional structure controlled by hegemonic trade powers.

Notwithstanding the value of a political analysis of the WTO's structure, there is a prior question that must be answered. What is the source of value that contributes to political power and is the object of control in trade relations? Put another way, what would motivate other countries, not just the hegemonic traders, to join a system that has allegedly succumbed to political capture? In other words, where's the beef in this institutional arrangement? The answer to these fundamental questions, which is essential to an understanding of the institutional development of the WTO and the course of the Doha Round, is simple but often vehemently challenged: *all countries stand to gain from trade*. Not just rich countries, advanced countries, and market-oriented countries, but also developing countries (indeed, least developed countries), transition economies, and centrally planned economies. Much of the commentary on, and especially the criticism of, the WTO and its institutional framework and problems misses this essential point. This is not to say that the gains from trade are equally or equitably shared among participants in trade liberalization, or even that a particular liberalization agreement will never reduce economic welfare, through terms-of-trade or foregone tariff revenue effects, for example. It also does not deny the political motivations that may lurk beneath the surface. But it does explain why the task of the negotiations for the entire membership—as well as the institution itself—is worth the candle. Whatever risks there are of some countries gaining more from the trade agreement, or of countries miscalculating the terms-of-trade effects, there is always a potential gain from trade liberalization. It is money that is on the table (or could be on the table), and countries are loath to give up the game and leave it there. Despite all the acrimonious negotiations, charges, countercharges, missed opportunities, and ministerial failures that have occurred in the WTO negotiations, and in the GATT negotiations that preceded them, one fact stands out: the countries always keep coming back to pick up the pieces and try again. Anyone who doubts the economic value of trade liberalization to the many and diverse WTO members should ponder the willingness of governments to persevere in the face of the many stops, starts, and challenges of a Tokyo, or an Uruguay, or a Doha, Round.

The gains from trade have many dimensions, and can only be summarized here briefly. WTO-sponsored trade liberalization operates on the principle of reciprocal market access opening. Increased trade through the opening of domestic markets compels countries to specialize their economic activity based on relative cost advantages, economies of scale, product differentiation, and other market opportunities, thereby improving the efficiency of production and expanding the exchange of exports for imports.[3] Yet beyond this basic proposition of specialization and efficiency, increased trade means access to goods and services of increased variety and quality, as well as to new technologies and the products of new technologies. Increased trade opens up new opportunities for both domestic and international investment, and allows companies to use international markets to make production more efficient throughout their supply chains. Trade typically increases competition and disciplines markets, providing an antidote to domestic monopolies. Because there are so many sources of the gains from trade, most trade negotiators have come to realize that, in any given trade negotiation, a valuable benefit from increased trade is waiting around every corner. New technologies, especially communications and information technology, have expanded the ability of firms to link markets globally and expand their markets. Global environmental concerns have created new markets for anti-pollution equipment and environmental services. The expansion of international transportation has increased tourism and made possible the movement of workers across borders. Whenever there are differences in the prices of goods and services across borders, there is typically an opportunity to gain from trade. The larger the gap, the greater the opportunity, and in services especially, the potential gains from trade are very large (see Hufbauer and Adler 2008). Whatever political constraints negotiators may feel, none of them wants to abandon the prospect of increasing trade opportunities for their economies.

The ability of an institution like the WTO to bring its members together into such reciprocal sacrifices of economic sovereignty depends also on its *legitimacy* among the members, and the ensuing *trust* that it inspires in the process of negotiations.[4] The WTO derives its fundamental legitimacy in part from a compelling human instinct for trading, what Adam Smith called the "propensity to truck, barter and exchange one thing for another... of which no further account can be given" (Smith 1776 [1976]). Bernstein (2008) and Irwin (1996), among others, have chronicled the long history of trade throughout recorded history, and there is growing evidence that trade developed in the earliest stages of civilization.[5] The functional legitimacy of the WTO as an economic institution is tied to the long-standing history of trade diplomacy, which has sought, through negotiated agreements among states across the millennia, to create frameworks that promote mutually beneficial international commerce. The presumption in any such negotiated agreement is that it will be of benefit to all parties, a principle that excludes the application of coercion against participants in the agreement. Legitimacy is therefore also based on a system of governance and decision making that is acceptable to all the participants. The cornerstone of the

WTO in this regard is the principle of consensus, which will receive much more attention in chapter 4. Yet consensus does not guarantee that all participants will have an equal voice or equal gains from trade, or that the process of decision making will always be inclusive, and it is in this context that the issue of trust arises.

Institutions that rely on negotiations depend on a level of trust among the participants that will make an agreement acceptable to them. To a certain extent, trust grows out of the rules themselves; for example, dispute resolution allows countries to take their trading partners before a panel for "nullifying and impairing" a negotiated (and in that sense guaranteed) market access benefit. This is especially important in the context of trade policy, since the parties to a negotiation must bargain under conditions of "bounded rationality"; that is, they cannot foresee all possible future contingencies that may affect the balance of concessions made at the time the agreement was made. Having recourse to third-party adjudication in the future provides a crucial measure of confidence in negotiating today, and is therefore an essential institutional element of an organization devoted to trade liberalization.

Regarding the negotiating process itself, there is a more subtle dimension of trust, however, which rests on the perceived fairness of the procedures and processes in the institution. The importance of trust in the WTO may appear puzzling in light of the general assumption that governments and their agents in trade negotiations will seek to maximize their utility regardless of the perceived motives or distribution of payoffs. The central idea of the GATT and WTO as institutions has always been that there are gains from trade for everybody. The gains at stake in the negotiation reside within the "lens of benefits" that is defined by the limits of the various countries' willingness to bargain on specific issues. A simple case is that country 1 is willing to lower its tariff on good X in exchange for a lower tariff in country 2 on product Y. The potential joint gains from trade for the world economy in such a situation would typically be maximized if both countries eliminated their tariffs. A country gains from trade both from lowering its own tariff and from the lower tariff in the other country.[6] Yet whatever the total gains are, they may not be shared equally; this depends on the degree of tariff cuts from both sides and on the market effects of the cuts. One side may walk away with the lion's share of the gains, while the other gains only a little. The hard economics of negotiations suggest that any gain at all is better than none, and that the country on the short end of the stick would still be willing to accept such a deal if there were no better alternative. Yet trust is in fact important in the WTO because negotiations, and the institutions that support them, rest ultimately on human interaction. Recent studies in behavioral economics have documented the importance of the "fair division" of bargains (see Carraro, Marchiori, and Sgobbi 2005), particularly in repeated games (Elms 2008). Trade negotiators, after all, are human beings, not disembodied automatons programmed to give their assent to a cold calculation of minimal welfare gains.

It is worth pursuing this point further. In practice, the fairness issue that arises out of bargaining power is shaped by mercantilist principles. Gains are typically measured in terms of new access to foreign markets, or rules and arrangements that benefit a country's exporting industries. Concessions consist of the additional market access granted to foreign exporters, or measures that reduce the country's sovereign regulatory control over its domestic market. The logic is political: more import competition entails the unpleasant adjustment process of layoffs and redeployment of resources, and furthermore endangers political support for trade liberalization through opposition by domestic protectionist lobbies. The ideal outcome by this mercantilist approach for an individual country would be for all of a country's trade partners to eliminate their tariffs, while the home country retains all its tariffs and other trade restrictions. The dispersion of bargaining power dictates a more balanced outcome, and most observers agree that bargaining power in the GATT/WTO has become progressively less concentrated over the years. Yet any imbalance in bargaining power may result in outcomes (using the mercantilist logic) tilted toward one country or group of countries. The upshot of asymmetrical bargaining power in the context of a repeated game, such as we have seen in the nine trade negotiations under the GATT and WTO, is that countries will constantly be seeking to improve their bargaining positions in the next negotiation, through influence in shaping the negotiating agenda and committee leadership, exploiting particular issues, and forming coalitions.

Bargaining asymmetry in itself therefore does not necessarily reduce the weaker countries' trust in the institution and its decision-making processes. It is, after all, a fact of life that experienced negotiators recognize, and they must adapt to it. If it undermined trust, then countries would be likely to withdraw from the organization, or refuse to negotiate altogether if it becomes evident that the benefits of the negotiations are not being shared equitably. It is noteworthy that withdrawals from the GATT were very rare and apparently unrelated to this issue, and there have been no withdrawals of membership from the WTO. Instead, there always seem to be opportunities to improve the outcome the next time. This general view among GATT and WTO participants, most of whom are more likely to express dissatisfaction than contentment with previous trade negotiations, appears to have propelled trade liberalization ever forward throughout the post–World War Two period. The institution will enjoy legitimacy among its participants to the extent that they see pathways toward their part of the collective goal in the future.

But there are potentially disruptive problems that can arise to threaten or challenge the foundation of trust that is necessary for the institution to be effective. One particular problem that the WTO has been grappling with is representation. In organizations whose activities are based on the principle of consensus, it is important that every member or participant that could block consensus have access to meaningful representation in the processes of deliberation, consultation, and dispute settlement. This is by no means an easy task in large organizations that require detailed bargaining. Individual representation for all countries in all meetings is not practical, and is physically impossible for countries with smaller delegations. Beyond that, smaller and poorer countries tend to have weaker trade policy infrastructure, including the capacity to analyze alternative trade proposals, engage in systematic domestic trade policy decision making, and have clear lines of authority in MTN bargaining. Chapter 4 will take up this issue in more detail, and will discuss the prospects for reform as the political environment of decision making has evolved.

Other problems that arise, particularly in the context of new and changing trade agendas, include asymmetric information and different levels of experience among negotiators. Negotiators, as mentioned above, must bargain on the basis of bounded rationality, judging alternative outcomes as best they can in the face of uncertainty. New areas of negotiation are particularly vulnerable to misjudgment. It may seem that countries would be very careful in their calculations of costs and benefits for their countries after many years of a high-stakes trade negotiation, but an agreement on new issues may contain unpleasant surprises and generate resentment. The upcoming discussion on the Uruguay Round "grand bargain" will show how damaging miscalculations and unexpected twists can undermine trust in the institution and come back to haunt later negotiations.

Scope of WTO Activity

One particularly important aspect of the WTO's institutional structure is the scope of its activities. This question has stimulated much debate. The original Marrakesh Agreement, which founded the WTO, states in article

III that "the WTO shall provide the common institutional framework for the conduct of trade relations among its Members in matters related to...this Agreement." This broad framework could potentially include any topic connected to "trade relations." Some areas do receive specific mention, but the agreement is careful not to undertake specific non-trade goals as part of its mandate. For example, the preamble acknowledges the goal of its members "both to protect and preserve the environment" but adds that they are free to pursue it "in a manner consistent with their respective needs and concerns at different levels of economic development." These anodyne statements do not commit WTO members to any specific non-trade goal. Yet there is nothing in the formal scope of WTO activities that would prevent the members from collectively setting new trade-related agendas not contained in any current trade agreements. This elastic provision leaves the door open, in principle, for possible WTO agreements on trade and labor rights, human rights, and/or the environment, for example. Similarly, the preamble recognizes the legitimacy of development goals, including sustainable development and the importance of trade in economic development. The WTO could thus potentially serve as the forum for negotiating a prescriptive distribution of the gains from trade away from rich countries and toward the poorest developing countries, for example. The fact that the WTO is unlikely to travel down these paths is the result of its central institutional constraint—the need for consensus—rather than the letter of its rules.

Indeed, many commentators have attempted to identify the proper scope for valid WTO negotiating topics, either by directly linking various new topics to trade policy, or by setting up rules or criteria to follow in evaluating a proposed negotiating topic. Lawrence (2006), for example, takes a "constructionist" view and argues that any new WTO rules must be consonant with the stated objectives in the Marrakesh Agreement that founded the WTO. At the other extreme, those in favor of using the WTO to pursue non-trade goals have proposed adding "social chapters" to the WTO, which would allow (or even mandate) member countries to impose trade restrictions on countries that refuse to comply with environmental, human rights, or labor rights standards. Maskus (2002) attempts a more systematic approach to the issue of negotiating new WTO rules by offering a set of economic and legal criteria, based on the following questions regarding the issue:

1. Is it trade-related?
2. Do current regulations impose externalities on other countries that multilateral rules can internalize?

3. Is unilateral action on the issue inadequate, suggesting the need for coordination among countries?
4. Is it possible to compute damages from failing to comply, thus facilitating dispute settlement?

An institutional view suggests that any extension of WTO obligations is likely to be marginal and anchored to its primary focus on trade liberalization. There are in fact many global issues that have some connection with trade, and whose solutions will also require cooperative or even collective action by the community of nations (see Mattoo and Subramanian 2008). However, the WTO does not have a constitution or autonomous enforcement powers, and therefore cannot legislate new rules and obligations for its members in the absence of consensus. Institutional change can and does occur, but it typically reflects the broad acknowledgment among the members of changing circumstances and the need to adapt to them in order to continue with the institution's primary goals.

The Process of Institutional Change

Major institutional change appears to require a major precipitating crisis, although incremental changes in the political and economic environment typically contribute to the impetus for reform. The 1846 repeal of the protectionist Corn Laws in England, for example, was the result both of major crop failures, including the Irish potato famine, and of economic structural change, including the transition from agriculture to manufacturing in British output and lower transportation costs in delivering grain. In the twentieth century, a major institutional reform was the passage of the Reciprocal Trade Agreements Act of 1934, championed by Secretary of State Cordell Hull, which authorized the executive branch, rather than Congress, to negotiate reciprocal tariff-cutting agreements and paved the way for multilateral trade liberalization under the GATT/WTO system. It was in part a response to the Smoot-Hawley tariffs passed by Congress four years earlier, but also to the accumulated "tariff fatigue" from trade restrictions and economic nationalism that had prevailed in the United States since 1922, along with the growing importance of expanding trade in the U.S. economy. These factors combined with the cataclysmic events of World War Two in the founding of the Bretton Woods system. The disastrous decline of global trade and finance during the Great Depression of the 1930s and the ensuing world war gave rise to a collective effort, led by the

United States and the United Kingdom, to establish a new global economic order. These efforts culminated in the founding of the International Monetary Fund, the International Bank for Reconstruction and Development (later known as the World Bank), and the GATT, a smaller version of what was originally a more ambitious institution, the International Trade Organization. Jan Tumlir, director of research at the GATT from 1967 to 1985, saw in the history of trade policy a "cycle of learning and unlearning," as governments would recognize the heavy cost of protection and liberalize, only to fall back into protectionism as domestic political forces harnessed fears of openness. The growing disillusionment with globalization, amplified by the global financial crisis that began in 2008, threatens to lead to yet another retreat from trade liberalization. These circumstances will surely test the durability of global trade institutions.

Kindleberger (1973, 1981) regarded the leadership of a single country to be essential in establishing and maintaining a stable global order, a role the United States came to fulfill in the postwar period of the GATT. Yet this notion of "hegemonic stability" has a serious drawback in that it tends to break down as the hegemon's influence declines. The effectiveness of an institution over time is dependent on its ability to adapt to new circumstances and challenges. For an international economic institution like the WTO, this process is bound to be difficult, because such an institution is typically founded in a particular political context, as Kindleberger suggests, with rules established or heavily influenced by the leading country at the time.

Change can also occur incrementally within the institution, and chapter 2 will show how the GATT developed institutional "fixes" to accommodate changes in the scope of negotiations and to facilitate agreement. The WTO itself was founded as an institutional response to perceived shortcomings in the GATT. Yet successful institutional change may require an entire complement of reinforcing measures throughout the institutional structure, and these changes may challenge the established order and meet resistance. A change in the scope of negotiations and rules that led to the WTO, for example, may remain incomplete if it is not accompanied by changes in decision making and the structure of negotiations. If Kindleberger and those who have chronicled the U.S. leadership role in the GATT/WTO system are correct (see Wilkinson 2006, for example) the hegemon may resist attempts at fundamental change in the institution, particularly with regard to decision making. If the United States is not in a position to assert its leadership in the global trading, it is doubtful that a single country could take its place.

Yet there is still reason for optimism that change can take place, based on the underlying motive for trade: there are real gains from trade still available in many manufacturing sectors, in agriculture, and especially in services. Within the existing structure of the WTO, which continues to enshrine this basic goal, what may be necessary is a new level of cooperation among the largest and most influential trading countries that will find ways, perhaps new institutional ways, to achieve consensus on significant trade liberalizing measures. This outcome is by no means certain. Countries may continue to muddle along with inconclusive multilateral negotiations, focusing instead on bilateral, regional, or other preferential trade agreements. Such piecemeal trade liberalization is less valuable than a comprehensive global agreement, and can play a constructive role mainly as a stepping-stone to larger multilateral agreements, not as an end in itself. There also remains the apparent need for a precipitating crisis sufficient to move the members to action. If they are not convinced that they are dangerously worse off in the absence of continued multilateral trade liberalization, the effort to reform the WTO will not be worthwhile to them.

Summary: An Institutional Sketch of the WTO

Figure 1.1 presents a conceptual view of the WTO as an institution, comprising an institutional core, internal operational institutions, and institutional output. The core is based on the collective intentionality of the members to seek the multilateral gains from trade, balanced against their individual national sovereignty over domestic trade policy. In essence, the WTO as an institution calls for its members to yield a sufficient amount of sovereignty over domestic import market access in order to secure reciprocal export market access. In this sense there is not a loss of sovereignty, on balance, but rather a trade-off of market access "sovereignty"—obligations to offer access to imports are balanced by the acquired right to market access for the country's exports. In pursuing gains from trade, the institution creates constitutive rules: principles guiding the relations among WTO members, such as MFN, national treatment, and reciprocal bargaining in negotiations; decision making and representation in the negotiating process; the scope of agreements that can be negotiated; and the differential status of members, according to special and differential treatment. From these rules flow the deontic powers associated with WTO rights and obligations, such as reciprocal market access and submission to a dispute resolution process. This framework is designed to deliver institutional output in the form of

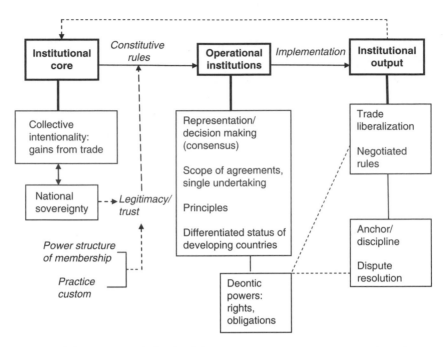

FIGURE 1.1 Institutional sketch of the WTO. Source: See text. Concept based on Searle (2005).

trade liberalization, satisfying the core gains-from-trade goal, and associated rules, which provide additional benefits in the form of an instrumental "anchor" to discipline and control domestic protectionist behavior and a dispute settlement system to protect members' gains from the opportunistic behavior of trading partners.

Since the institutional structure of the WTO is based on the specific goal of acquiring the gains from trade within the constraint of the domestic sovereignty of its constituent members, there is a feedback loop from output to the core institutional foundation. In other words, the WTO's sustainability as an economic institution depends on its ability to deliver the goods. Given the underlying ambition of the members to gain from trade, a failure by the institution to achieve trade liberalization may be traced back to weaknesses in internal institutional features. Note that the constitutive rules flow from the core institutional goal, but also from the context of custom, practice, and the existing power structure, for example. Thus historical and political, as well as economic, factors tend to shape the rules that govern negotiations. We can therefore speak about legitimacy and trust as important elements of the process of the WTO's negotiating framework. This means that changes in the negotiating environment may require internal institutional adjustments as well. For example, a change in power structure, in terms of bargaining strength among the members, or efforts to expand the scope of negotiations, may undermine the current structure of relationships that define the ability of the membership to reach consensus. Adaptation or reform may then be necessary to build a new framework for reaching consensus.

The institutional structure of the WTO provides a framework for understanding the challenges of pursuing trade liberalization in the twenty-first century. Many of the contributing factors in the Doha stalemate enumerated at the beginning of this chapter have a corresponding institutional dimension, which suggests that much of the real problem lies in institutional friction, the misalignment of negotiating goals with the frameworks for interaction to achieve them. And yet the problems of the Doha Round have roots in the negotiations that preceded them, the Uruguay Round, which led to the creation of the WTO. The discussion therefore turns to the evolution of the trading system during the postwar period, and how the legacy of GATT-era institutions challenged the new WTO system and hampered the Doha Round.

2

Institutional Friction in the Doha Development Round

The Legacy of the GATT

The WTO was founded in 1995 and continued the institutional tradition of the General Agreement on Tariffs and Trade, founded in 1947, to promote trade liberalization and regulate trade policy on the basis on non-discrimination. There were a number of formal institutional features of the GATT that were changed in the WTO: for example, the requirement of a single undertaking in negotiated multilateral trade agreements, the binding nature of dispute panel decisions, and the stricter requirements for new members to join. While these changes were explicitly designed to improve on the looser nature of GATT rules, they have created new and sometimes unexpected strains in the WTO's institutional structure as the members have adapted to the new regime. In addition, there were many informal processes established in the GATT that have created institutional stress, such as the "Green Room" process of small group deliberations. The negotiating environment has also changed, as reflected in the evolving role of developing countries in trade negotiations and an expanded bargaining agenda that came to include agriculture, services, and many "behind the border" measures. The WTO, in short, was intended to expand membership in the global trading system, broaden the scope of trade liberalization, and tighten members' commitments to the rules, but these changes have posed serious challenges to the negotiating process, which are described in this chapter as "institutional friction."

The GATT's institutional structure was a result of circumstances after World War Two, in which a larger, more comprehensive International Trade Organization (ITO) was actually negotiated but never came into being, because it failed to achieve the essential domestic legislative ratification from the United States. In its place, a portion of the agreement that formed the ITO, the General Agreement on Tariffs and Trade (GATT), was in fact put into operation, at first on a presumably temporary basis. Legally, it was not an international organization bound by treaty, but rather was bound by a contractual agreement among its participants, and thus it never required ratification by domestic legislatures. Its participants were in fact known as "Contracting Parties," not members. The United States, and to a lesser extent the United Kingdom, were the principal architects of the GATT.

The most important institutional aspect of GATT decision making, carried over into the WTO, is the requirement of consensus. Over the years, the functioning of the global trading system can be explained largely in terms of how building consensus evolved in trade negotiations. At the GATT's inception, with only 23 countries in the early postwar period, the United States dominated GATT activities, although the UK and other GATT members were also active in shaping negotiating issues. Later, the development of the European Common Market (the precursor of the European Union) presented a more potent counterweight to U.S. influence. By the time the last of the GATT trade negotiations, the Uruguay Round, was under way, the "Quad" (United States, European Union, Canada, and Japan) became the dominant force, but by that time, many other GATT participants, including several developing countries, had begun to play significant roles in the negotiations.

Achieving consensus has been the holy grail of negotiations in the GATT, and it remains so in the WTO. Theoretically, consensus means that every member has equal veto power over the negotiation. In practice, however, consensus is a process that typically begins with agreement on critical issues among a core group whose support is essential for the negotiations to be successful, and beyond that group it is necessary to acquire the assent of other members, to the point where the remaining members do not actively oppose the emerging agreement. Consensus, as chapter 4 will illustrate, does not necessarily imply unanimity, but rather the lack of active opposition by participating (or present) members. In the early years of the GATT, consensus began with the United States, which would negotiate bilaterally with the UK and then with other members. While this may seem like a formula for the United States to negotiate anything it wanted in the GATT, the consensus requirement did in fact "bite," and the United States, like other GATT participants, had to make concessions in order to secure final agreements. The number of countries in those early years was small, and some of the developing countries were not actively involved in the negotiations (and thus had no veto power to exercise). Wilkinson (2006, p. 56) notes that the number of GATT Contracting Parties grew only from 23 to 42 from 1947 to 1961, the end of the Dillon Round, and that only 22 of the 42 actually granted trade concessions in that round, including just five developing countries. In the first several GATT negotiations, the focus was on tariff reductions, which kept the consensus process simple, if not always easy.

In the early years of the GATT, tariffs were very high, and negotiations successfully liberalized trade through tariff cuts. Shortly after World War Two, average tariffs among major trading countries exceeded 40%, and in the United States the Smoot-Hawley tariffs had left average tariffs close to 60%. Most trade at the time was in manufactured goods, and the strong postwar efforts at reconstruction and economic expansion fueled a highly successful series of trade negotiations. Harvesting cuts in the low-hanging fruit of postwar tariffs in the GATT trade rounds had reduced average tariffs among participating GATT countries to about 5% at the end of the Uruguay Round. This signal achievement encouraged GATT participants, and later WTO members, to push the envelope further and extend trade liberalization into new areas such as agriculture and services, where there was fertile ground for reaping more gains from trade. And yet the institutional framework of trade liberalization over the past 200 years, and in the GATT/WTO system in particular, had focused on tariff reductions,[1] and extending it to the new areas has proven to be extremely challenging.

As postwar recovery in Europe progressed, the founding of the European Common Market in 1958 altered the dynamics of consensus building, because it bargained as a single unit for its member states, and it became increasingly powerful as a trading entity, with rapid economic growth and expanding trade in the 1960s. At the same time, the number of GATT Contracting Parties started to grow rapidly, reaching 76 in 1967. The scope of issues also began to grow beyond simple tariff cutting in the Kennedy Round (1964–67), although little progress was made on them at the time. Non-tariff issues continued to pile up, however, and during the Tokyo Round (1973–79) a series of "codes" on issues such as anti-dumping duties, subsidies and countervailing duties, customs valuation, government procurement, technical barriers to trade, and trade in civil aircraft was concluded. Significantly, these agreements were not part of the overall GATT multilateral agreement but were plurilateral agreements among subsets of Contracting Parties. This method of partitioning of the negotiating agenda allowed agreements to be concluded without the absolute constraint of the consensus rule. The drawback was that it weakened the very purpose of the GATT, which was to liberalize trade multilaterally for all participating countries.

The Tokyo Round introduced an important new feature for reaching consensus, the Green Room. Contracting Parties by the end of this round numbered 85, and although not all of them were actively engaged in the negotiations, it became necessary to structure the consensus building process with smaller group meetings, chaired by the Director-General, in order to hammer out provisional agreements that could be taken to other countries and finally to the plenary group for general approval. The Green Room became an informal but pervasive institutional fixture of subsequent GATT, and later WTO, negotiations. It is important to note here that the Green Room emerged as a practical way of dealing with the range of issues and participation level of the Tokyo Round. While the need for such an approach to decision making would continue, the decision-making environment would become much more challenging as the numbers of countries in the GATT and WTO would grow and the scope of negotiations would widen.

Two other important related elements of the GATT legacy help to explain the institutional frictions that have plagued the Doha Round: the exclusion of textiles and clothing, as well as most agricultural products, from GATT disciplines and the treatment and role of developing countries in GATT negotiations. The GATT, as noted earlier, was a smaller portion of the failed ITO agreement, and it focused mainly on manufactured goods. Trade in agricultural products was subject mainly to non-tariff barriers such as import quotas, subsidies, and other domestic support programs, which were largely exempt from GATT disciplines. This policy regime was the result of heavy protection of domestic agricultural interests among the developed countries, a situation that continues to this day. Trade liberalization in several agricultural products was of great interest to many developing countries, but the systematic exclusion of much of this sector from GATT disciplines represented a gap in the coverage of global trade rules that would have serious consequences in later negotiations.

An even more explicit carve-out occurred in the other major area of developing country interest: textiles and clothing. These sectors were also subject to heavy protection in industrialized countries, for the very reason that these were aging industries in which they were losing comparative advantage. GATT countries negotiated a series of restrictive quota agreements, first with Japan, then with most other textile- and clothing-producing countries, culminating in the series of cartel-like Multifiber Agreements (MFAs) from 1977 to 2005. It is in fact bizarre that the GATT, an institution devoted to MFN trade liberalization, lent its good offices to developing an agreement that was so overtly protectionist and discriminatory. These agreements rested on the political logic emanating from the United States and European countries that securing a predictable "trade peace" for their aging textile and clothing sectors was a necessary domestic measure that made it possible to proceed with more general trade liberalization in other industrial sectors. Since many of the thousands of bilateral quotas in the MFAs also established effective market shares for developing country exporters, many of them were in fact favorably disposed toward them. Yet there was always a sense that rich country control of market access in these sectors was a way of suppressing economic growth in the developing world, and the elimination of the MFAs became one of the key bargaining chips in the Uruguay Round that founded the WTO—with unexpected results.

The exclusion of agriculture, textiles, and clothing from most GATT disciplines was emblematic of the general problem of developing country participation in the GATT. The GATT was essentially a rich countries' club, despite the growing number of developing country Contracting Parties. With negotiating agendas dominated by the United States and European and other OECD countries, the primary focus was on items of cross-border trade within this group. At the same time, developing countries often faced high tariffs, tariff escalation, quotas, trade-distorting internal taxes, and domestic subsidies and other trade restrictions on their exports destined for the industrialized countries, as documented in the Haberler Report of 1958 (see Curzon 1965, pp. 225–226). Most of the developing countries of that time, for their part, had little bargaining power to negotiate away these barriers to trade. The industrialized countries, on the other hand, did not have any collective desire to eliminate these tariff barriers unilaterally, and the GATT, after all, was based on reciprocal bargaining. And so these barriers persisted for many years, in some cases continuing even to this day.

Ironically, the GATT itself emphasized the fact that developing countries were not equal partners by partially exempting them from GATT disciplines, especially in GATT article 18, which allowed tariffs and quotas for infant industries and to combat balance-of-payments problems (see Dam 1970, chap. 14). Later, as it became clear that developing countries were not benefitting much from GATT negotiations, the industrialized countries undertook to create more favorable trading terms for them, beginning with the addition of a development chapter, Part IV of the GATT, which included a formal exemption of developing countries from reciprocity. Otherwise, Part IV included highly qualified commitments such as giving "high priority" to reducing trade barriers of concern to developing countries. Yet the commitments had little political power or will behind them. GATT Part IV is rich in its symbolic acknowledgement of the problems of developing countries, an approach that would later be echoed in many Doha Round statements. What the GATT, and later the WTO, could not come to acknowledge in their declarations was that they were not, and never could be, development institutions, and therefore could not deliver on any specific development promises and commitments, aside from limited measures favoring trade from developing countries.

The industrialized countries in the GATT continued to endorse and develop methods to favor developing countries. The Generalized System of Preferences (GSP) was actually proposed by the United Nations Conference on Trade and Development (UNCTAD) in 1968, and sought to establish preferential treatment of developing country exports by the industrialized countries. The GATT countries endorsed this plan by granting it a waiver from MFN treatment, but in the end the entire GSP was voluntary and controlled by the individual industrialized countries themselves, which could determine which countries would receive the favorable treatment. The program thereby opened the way for non-trade issues to determine a country's access to the market access benefit, which products would be covered (thus allowing politically sensitive imports to be excluded from coverage), and what maximum volume of exports by a GSP country would be allowed before GSP treatment would be suspended. The principles of GSP treatment were extended and formalized in the Enabling Clause, a declaration adopted as part of the GATT's Tokyo Round negotiations in 1979. It provided for "special and differential treatment" toward developing countries in trade negotiations, including an exemption from GATT Article 24 rules restricting the formation of preferential trade agreements and the right not to sign Tokyo Round codes (see Hindley 1987, Finger and Winters 1998).

These efforts to provide a sort of "affirmative action" program for developing countries have had only limited success in increasing their gains from trade, notwithstanding their popularity among the developing countries themselves. Economically, discriminatory market access tends to misallocate resources, since the preference margins allow less efficient producers to remain viable in world markets. Since preferences are subject to political terms and conditions by the importing countries, they encouraged short-term perspectives rather than decision making based on long-term, rules-based MFN market access. They also created a perverse incentive structure for the recipients to maintain their preferences in the face of progressive trade liberalization, which would inevitably erode the preference margins. Finally, the ability of importing countries to exclude politically sensitive product limits from preferential coverage has reduced the ability of developing countries to gain from trade in their products of greatest comparative advantage.

There is an institutional dimension to this problem as well. The exclusion of developing countries from reciprocal tariff reductions reduced their participation in the crucial process of bargaining, which was the centerpiece of the trade liberalization process and the institutional foundation of the GATT. Experience has shown that economically significant market access is most likely to come from offering meaningful concessions in return. What developing countries are likely to get from the unilateral concessions of wealthier importing countries will always be subject to the latter countries' screening process of political acceptability, regarding both the affected domestic import-competing industries and the unilateral criteria used to determine the worthiness of the developing country in receiving the benefit. Furthermore, the opportunity to gain valuable experience was therefore lost for developing countries that did not participate actively in the early GATT trade negotiations. When developing countries later entered the Uruguay Round negotiations on the basis of reciprocal bargaining (but still with the assurance that they would not be expected to offer concessions inconsistent with their development plans), their expectations may have suffered from the false promises of past unilateral concessions, and they may have thought that somehow the system would favor them independently of their bargaining position.

Institutional Impact of the Uruguay Round

As an institution focused on trade liberalization and trade policy rule creation, the GATT had developed a pattern of bargaining and a set of practices in the several rounds of trade negotiations preceding the Uruguay Round:

1. A reliance largely on reciprocal tariff bargaining, first product by product, later on a linear-formula basis;
2. The relegation of negotiations on non-tariff barriers, which were more difficult to negotiate away multilaterally, to special agreements and plurilateral codes for subsets of participating Contracting Parties;

3. The lack of a formal requirement for GATT Contracting Parties to make their domestic trade regimes comply with the provisions of Part II of the GATT, resulting in a marked and chronic lack of progress in reducing agricultural protection;

4. The removal of textiles and clothing, which are politically sensitive in industrialized nations, from GATT disciplines through a series of multilateral trade restrictions;

5. The domination of industrialized countries in the trade negotiations, which focused reciprocal tariff reductions on manufactured goods of interest primarily to them;

6. The introduction of preferential terms for developing countries, including the exemption from reciprocal tariff cuts and the introduction of unilateral preferential market access, in an attempt to offset their weaker bargaining power and the fact that they had been gaining little from the existing GATT rules and negotiations.

This trajectory of GATT's progress (or lack thereof) in promoting trade liberalization put the developed and developing countries in the GATT on the road toward institutional conflict in the Uruguay Round. How that conflict was temporarily resolved in the conclusion of the Uruguay Round has shaped the resurgent institutional conflict in the WTO during the Doha Round.

The industrialized countries, led by the United States, the European Economic Community, and Japan, recognized the many shortcomings of the GATT and were eager to correct them. Gains from trade from tariff reductions were certainly still possible as the Uruguay Round began, but further progress in opening existing markets and finding new markets to open would require an agreement with a broader reach. Economic growth in developing countries had begun to accelerate, exceeding growth rates in the developed world and opening up new export market opportunities for trade (see tables 2.1 and 2.2). The United States, for example, saw opportunities for expanding its agricultural markets (while jealously guarding its own agricultural support programs) and for extending rules coverage into new areas such as intellectual property, foreign direct investment, and technical barriers to trade. The United States and Europe saw large potential gains from the virtually untouched area of services trade liberalization. Japan and other countries had become increasingly concerned with the lack of discipline in market access commitments by developing countries, because these countries were the subject of increasing interest as new export markets. It also eventually became clear that putting together such an ambitious package of new and diverse trade liberalizing measures would require a new and more comprehensive organization. In addition, an agreement would be needed requiring all countries to accept all elements of the package as a whole in order to establish a truly multilateral system of rules and market access. The developing countries, for their part, were becoming eager to play a significant role in the negotiations. Their numbers in the GATT were swelling, many of them were emerging as exporters of manufacturers, and export market access was replacing import substitution policies as a path toward economic development and growth (see table 2.3). The rich industrialized countries continued to block their import markets against products of interest to the developing world, not the least of which were textiles and clothing. Marginalized from a meaningful role in previous trade negotiations, many developing countries actively sought to establish a voice in the GATT that would assert their positions more forcefully.

The Uruguay Round (1986–1994) was indeed the most ambitious trade negotiation that had ever been attempted, and it was successful in concluding with an agreement covering a remarkably large range of trade liberalizing measures, innovative new rules, and the establishment of a new trade institution, the WTO. There were, to be sure, disappointments in the outcome, as many of the ambitions were left incomplete at the end of the round, and other shortcomings would certainly give rise to more trouble later. But at the time, there was a feeling of genuine accomplishment that overshadowed any doubts about the "new and improved" organization and the trade liberalizing measures that had been negotiated.

TABLE **2.1** GDP growth rates, annual average

	1965–73	1973–80	1980–91	1990–2000	2000–06
Low- and middle-income countries	6.6	4.8	3.3	3.6	5.7
High-income countries	4.6	3.0	2.9	2.4	2.3

Source: World Bank, *World Development Report*, various editions.

TABLE **2.2** Share of world imports (%)

	1963	1973	1983	1993	2003	2005
Developing countries	22	19	26	27	26	29
Developed countries	74	78	70	72	72	69

Source: WTO, *World Trade Report*, 2008a.

TABLE 2.3 Share (%) of developing economies in world
manufactures exports, 1983–2006

	1983	1990	1993	2000	2003	2006
Auto products	1	4	7	11	11	17
Chemicals	9	11	12	17	17	21
Iron/steel	10	15	19	22	22	31
Office/telecom	18	26	31	40	48	53
Textiles	30	34	40	45	45	55
Clothing	47	50	56	61	59	68
Manuf. total	12	17	21	28	28	32

Source: GATT, International Trade 1985 (for 1983); WTO, Statistical database (1993–2006).

In spite of these accomplishments, the Uruguay Round sowed the seeds of discord for the Doha Round. This is not to say that the Uruguay Round should therefore be considered a failure, or that it should not have been negotiated. Even the post–Uruguay Round calculations that have purported to identify large losses for developing countries do not adequately reflect the value of the innovations and new pathways forged in the new WTO, such as a more effective (if not perfect) dispute settlement system, the introduction of services onto the trade liberalization agenda, and the steps (baby steps though they were) toward agricultural trade liberalization. Developing countries had finally played a significant role in the negotiations, even if they would view the outcome as disappointing. The trading system could never turn back to the narrow, boxed-in constraints of the earlier rounds under the GATT. Uruguay Round naysayers fail to recognize that the realistic alternatives for developing countries at the time were probably much worse: either a "delinking" from the global trading system, which was actively debated in the years prior to the beginning of the Uruguay Round, or a continuation of modest GATT-like progress on a narrow range of products, with little change in the structure or coverage of trade being negotiated, a system that had fallen short in providing meaningful gains from trade to developing countries and was no longer providing an adequate bargaining framework for developed countries either.

Yet the advances made in the Uruguay Round toward a more comprehensive trading system are in fact closely tied to the institutional conflict that followed. For example, the agricultural, textile, and clothing sectors, previously excluded from most GATT disciplines, were opened for broader negotiation (or the beginnings of negotiation) in the Uruguay Round, in accordance with developing country—and some developed country—demands. However, there was no easy way to dismantle the institutional barriers to trade liberalization in these sectors. In agriculture, the positive step was taken of converting many existing non-tariff barriers to tariffs, which was intended to pave the way for later liberalization. At the end of the Uruguay Round, there was little actual progress in opening agricultural markets, reducing potential trade gains. In textiles and clothing, there was a major milestone in setting a timetable for phasing out the MFA quota system over ten years (1995–2005), but this arrangement turned out to be essentially a continuation of MFA quotas for most of the ten-year period, and special safeguard trade restrictions were set up in many importing countries to mitigate rapid export expansion that disrupted their domestic markets. Developing countries, therefore, were still left waiting, many years after the conclusion of the Uruguay Round, for open markets in the one manufacturing sector linked most closely with industrialization and growth. It should also be noted that most countries did not anticipate, even in the late stages of the Uruguay Round, the emergence of China as the dominant supplier of clothing on world markets, displacing many smaller countries and severely eroding their now unprotected market shares.

Another area of conflict came from the unanticipated costs of compliance with many of the "behind the border" measures negotiated in the Uruguay Round, including TRIPS, customs valuation, and sanitary/phytosanitary standards. The GATT had no institutional framework to aid countries financially in complying with negotiated obligations. Many developed countries, and even relatively advanced developing countries such as Mexico, had no system of enforcement for intellectual property protection, for example. Legal, administrative, and physical infrastructure was required to implement customs valuation reforms and to monitor sanitary standards. Subsequently, many countries did receive World Bank and other funding in support of WTO compliance projects such as these, but this aid was not systematically tied to the negotiated agreement, and it raised a serious question of efficiency. In view of the many development projects competing for support, were WTO compliance projects the best use of available funds for these countries? The institutional problem was how to promote further global trade liberalization without imposing undue financial burdens on poorer countries.

The most serious institutional conflict in the Uruguay Round occurred with regard to the introduction of the Trade-Related Aspects of Intellectual Property Rights (TRIPS) agreement into the WTO system. The problem lay not primarily in the merits of enforcing intellectual property rights (IPR) themselves in the global economy, although many economists have debated that point separately from the institutional issue. There is in fact a strong economic case for protecting intellectual property rights in terms of promoting technological innovation and improvements in product quality. Encouraging the development of new products and processes by imparting patent protection to the inventor also benefits consumers, who enjoy more varied and higher-quality products, and producers, who can manufacture more efficiently and less expensively as a result. Extending IPR globally also has the potential of closing the technology gap between rich and poor countries, especially insofar as such legal protection against counterfeiting and piracy of ideas and designs encourages greater transfer of technologies to developing countries through direct foreign investment (see Maskus 2002). There are strong international trade and investment issues involved with IPR, and for its advocates in the United States, Europe, and Japan especially, the TRIPS agreement would close the gap in enforcement that had created black markets for counterfeit products and dangerous and unsafe versions of pharmaceutical products.

Notwithstanding the economic and trade arguments for introducing TRIPS into the WTO, the institutional conflict resides in its incompatibility with the underlying negotiating premise of the GATT system. Since the first GATT trade negotiation, countries had exchanged market access "concessions" on a reciprocal basis or agreed on rules to regulate the market access "benefits" of negotiated agreements. The TRIPS, on the other hand, was not about the gains from trade per se, but rather the gains from exclusive proprietary claims on value. Compliance with the TRIPS, unlike compliance with traditional trade-opening measures, required countries to impose stricter regulations on economic activity rather than remove barriers and enhance economic activity, even if TRIPS proponents regarded the economic activity as illegal. This was also part of the problem stated earlier about TRIPS enforcement costs, which saddled developing countries with the legal and administrative cost of developing an IPR regime, often from scratch.

One can, to be sure, calculate the value of TRIPS as a concession for net intellectual property (IP) importers against the benefits of net IP exporters. Finger (2007) has calculated that this arithmetic reveals a lopsided transfer from poor to rich countries. TRIPS supporters might aver that this accounting understates the value of increased FDI induced by TRIPS, as well as significant future benefits resulting from the incentive structure favorable to innovation, including the development of exportable IP value from native music, art, and creative activities. Furthermore, it can be argued that the developing countries were willing to accept the TRIPS deal as part of a package that included textiles and clothing liberalization, the "grand bargain" mentioned by Sylvia Ostry, and that TRIPS should not be blamed if clothing trade didn't work out as expected by the developing world.

One must consider the institutional issue of the TRIPS in conjunction with the political dynamics of its negotiation. Despite its incompatibility with the GATT ethos of bargaining for market access, one can argue that the agreement is no less valid now that it has been accepted by the WTO members. There was strong political pressure on the developing countries to agree to it, for at least two reasons. First was the fact that the United States had already been imposing unilateral trade restrictions to protect its constituents' own IPR through "Special 301" measures, and these measures would surely have continued in the absence of TRIPS. In addition, a failure to agree on TRIPS would have blocked the elimination of the MFA regime as well as the promise for developing countries inherent in the establishment of the "new and improved" trade institution, the WTO. The institutional conflict that ensued from the TRIPS is therefore not necessarily an argument that it should not have been included in the Uruguay Round agreement. After all, parties to a trade agreement can, in the end, include anything they collectively deem relevant to getting the deal done.

Because of its incompatibility, however, one cannot escape the consequences of the TRIPS for subsequent events in the WTO. One measure of the institutional difficulty of the TRIPS was that strong opposition to its terms caused the agreement to be renegotiated in significant ways. The most important change was that the provisions limiting compulsory licensing were amended to remove the restrictions on importing generic drugs during serious disease outbreaks such as AIDS. In addition, the initial phase-in period for developing countries was extended further into the future. In short, patent-holding companies hoping to benefit from a tightly enforced global TRIPS regime were disappointed in their ability to collect on it. These developments certainly mitigated the effects of the TRIPS on developing countries, many of which adroitly managed the negotiations to amend the agreement in their favor in 2003.

Taking stock of the Uruguay Round institutional legacy, the negotiated agreements and the new and more comprehensive trade organization, the WTO, held great promise for expanding the reach of trade liberalization and the gains from trade into many new areas, especially in services and in other trade-related economic activities "behind the border," even though liberalization remained limited in many of them. The promised reform of the long-standing institutional framework for protection in agriculture and textiles/clothing, on the other hand, was more difficult to accomplish. The MFA system of quotas persisted to the bitter end on January 1, 2005, having delayed most trade liberalization until the late stages of the ten-year transition period, while tariffs on these products often remained at high levels. Agriculture negotiations resulted only in limited measures to liberalize markets, with the United States and EU playing the central roles in the agreement (Hoekman and Kostecki 2001, pp. 208–226).

The Uruguay Round was the first trade negotiation in which developing countries played a significant role in reciprocal bargaining, and for many of them it must have been a revelation. Previously they were relegated to a passive back seat at the talks, and they otherwise received unilateral concessions and preferential treatment, usually of limited value to them. In the Uruguay Round, the developing countries found that in matters of importance to them in the negotiations, there was to be no preferential treatment. Only limited market opening occurred in the important agricultural sector, and textile/clothing liberalization was delayed in such a way that its benefits were compromised, eroding further what market shares were left from the entry of China as a major supplier. Many of the new agreements carried unfunded compliance costs, and the TRIPS agreement implied significant outward transfers from developing to developed countries. Whatever gains the developing countries received—and a comprehensive analysis suggests that they were significant—they came away with the sense that they got less than they should have. What was touted as a "Grand Bargain" turned out, in the view of many developing countries and other observers, as a "Bum Deal" (Ostry 2007). In such circumstances, it is natural to focus on making up the difference at the next opportunity, which is what they did in the Doha Round. In addition, it was natural for those who considered themselves disadvantaged in the negotiations to focus on process issues within the new WTO, with the goal of correcting the informal institutions carried over from the GATT to the WTO, such as the Green Room consultations, the role and selection of the Director-General, the determination of the negotiating agenda, and so forth. These traditional arrangements had, after all, developed under the GATT "rich man's club," and many developing countries had come to regard them as subtle methods of excluding their views.

The WTO Stumbles toward Seattle

The new WTO therefore began to take up the business of generating trade negotiations with many institutional tensions unresolved. Wilkinson (2006) has noted that conflict and deadlock were not uncommon in the GATT, as

major negotiations have often ground to a halt over issues such as tariff formulas or (more commonly) agriculture; furthermore, these episodes were
part of a natural process that propelled the institution forward to meet the
challenges of adapting to an evolving negotiating environment. There was
every reason to believe that such crises would recur in subsequent trade
rounds. In the past, the main antagonists had been the United States and the
European Common Market (after 1992 the European Union). In the post–
Uruguay Round world of the WTO, with many more issues having entered
the negotiations and many more countries, especially from the developing
world, playing significant roles, the potential for conflict along both old and
new lines was increasing. The institutional tensions erupted not only in
the dramatic form of failed ministerial meetings, but also through ongoing
frictions and frustrations of procedure and representation.

Efforts to start a new trade round under the auspices of the WTO began
almost immediately, but were plagued by several elements of disarray that
appeared to accompany a new and unsettled institution. The only progress
in trade liberalization achieved during the first years of the WTO included
agreements in telecommunications and financial services concluded by 69
and 70 member countries, respectively (see WTO press releases, Feb. 17,
1997, and Dec. 15, 1997).[2] While one can argue that these were the only
countries that could have negotiated such agreements in a timely manner,
it also removed these issues from the upcoming multilateral trade agenda,
and therefore may have removed a set of bargaining chips from the bigger
game. The single undertaking of the WTO system needs a wide variety
of bargaining issues that can be traded off against each other, and also to
motivate exporting interests among WTO members to push for an overall
package. This is the political "oxygen" that typically feeds a negotiation.
Hindsight now suggests that an opportunity may have been lost by concluding these subagreements prematurely. In any case, negotiating these
agreements violated the new institutional principle of the WTO as a "single
undertaking," which was designed to avoid the à la carte approach of the
GATT codes.

There were also many distractions in the lead-up to the Seattle Ministerial that drew attention away from forging a broadly acceptable negotiating agenda. Much of the tension carried over from the frustrations of
the Uruguay Round among developing countries. The choice of the new
Director-General in 1999, for example, became a flashpoint for dissatisfaction among developing countries with the traditional rules of process
in the trading system. The position of executive secretary of the GATT
in its early years, and subsequently all GATT and WTO D-Gs until 1999,

were from the United Kingdom and Europe.[3] Developing countries had raised objections to this tradition in the Uruguay Round, and by 1999 were determined to have a larger role in the selection of the D-G. The resulting showdown was not strictly along a North-South divide, but the split was nearly even between the two finalists, Michael Moore (New Zealand) and Supachai Panitchpakdi (Thailand), and proved to have a crippling effect on preparations for the Seattle summit. The campaign lasted beyond the term of Renato Ruggiero, and left the WTO for four months with no sitting D-G. A compromise solution eventually emerged, giving Moore and Panitchpakdi each an equal three-year split of the D-G's term.

While the new D-G, Michael Moore, was scrambling to forge a consensus on an agenda for a new trade round, the lingering issues of the Uruguay Round were festering. Many developing countries were focusing on implementation issues from the Uruguay Round, such as delayed textiles/apparel liberalization, TRIPS compliance, and the costly development of new WTO-mandated institutions for intellectual property enforcement, customs valuation, and sanitary and phytosanitary measures in countries that might have difficulty in paying for them. Developing countries were particularly active in submitting comments on implementation issues in the months preceding the Seattle Ministerial, and many applied for extensions to compliance terms negotiated in the Uruguay Round. The overhang of unfinished Uruguay business, from many developing countries' point of view, added to the large number of new issues in the broadened scope of the WTO. The accompanying workload implied the need for even greater effort in preparing for the ministerial meeting, at a time when deliberations were lagging and many delegations were caught up in the D-G imbroglio. This was a painful lesson: the Seattle ministerial was in the view of many the most poorly prepared meeting of its type in the history of the GATT/WTO system, based on its ambition to launch a comprehensive new trade round.

As for the storied collapse of the Seattle Ministerial itself, poor preparation and mismanagement of the deliberations were primarily to blame (see Hoekman and Kostecki 2001, pp. 106–108; Jones 2004c, chap. 1). Nonetheless, underlying institutional conflict often provided the currents that brought many frustrations to the surface. For example, the basic debate over extending WTO rules to cover issues such as the environment and labor rights was represented on the street by the protestors, but also by U.S. President Clinton, who appeared in Seattle to advocate openly for an enforceable labor clause in trade negotiations. These protests and comments inflamed many developing country delegations, who regarded them as an attempt to justify new trade restrictions against developing countries that did not meet rich country standards in these areas. The disruption of the street protests added to the problems of representation, as many smaller delegations found that protestors often blocked their path to important negotiating group meetings, many of which were held concurrently (Wilkinson 2006). As the meeting was drawing to a close with no possibility of a ministerial declaration in sight, the chair and host of the Ministerial, United States Trade Representative Charlene Barshefsky, attempted to secure a last-minute communiqué from the WTO membership in an emergency Green Room session. Under the tense and acrimonious circumstances, this maneuver became the mother of all Green Room fiascos, a touchstone for subsequent efforts to reform this traditional method of small group deliberations, a topic that chapter 4 will pursue in more detail. There was, in the end, no consensus on a negotiating agenda, and the first formal attempt for the WTO to launch a new trade round ended in disarray, polarization, and failure.

The Doha Development Round

Institutions are important to the WTO because they establish the mutual purpose of cooperative interaction, the rules and terms of the interaction, and the legitimacy of the framework established to achieve the common goal. It is common to regard trade negotiations in terms of objective economic measures, such as tariff levels, trade volumes, and welfare gains, and political goals, such as the influence exercised by states on each other, forming alliances, or pursuing other foreign policy objectives. The economic and political factors are in fact usually decisive in the long run, but the institutional structures must be in place to facilitate the outcome. Yet, when the environment for trade negotiations changes in fundamental ways, the institutions must also adapt to them; otherwise, there will often be friction that will delay or even block progress on agreements. Negotiators, in the end, must represent their respective countries' interests in the negotiations, but they are also the flesh and blood that goes into and out of the negotiating room. Negotiators exert their influence on the basis of the representation they receive in the deliberations, the information they have, and the agenda placed before them at the table. As individuals, they can attend some meetings but usually not all, and they have access to information that is useful for establishing their negotiating positions only to the extent that it is available to them. Their positions are represented in negotiating texts if the chair of the negotiating group includes it. Negotiators have memories, they learn from experience, they talk to and share opinions with other delegates and their successors. If they decide that they did not receive adequate representation in deliberations, agenda setting, and working drafts in negotiations, or that they agreed to a deal that was only marginally acceptable or that resulted in unexpected consequences, they will be motivated to change the situation the next time around. As these experiences translate back into negotiating strategies, small or poor countries may not have power within such a large organization, but they will seek any available channels to assert their interests, fueled now with added anger or ambition.

In the case of the WTO, power—understood as the ability to influence outcomes of negotiations—derives from two principal sources. One is the degree of the country's economic and political influence independent of the WTO trade negotiations themselves. The other is the size of a country's import market, the bargaining chip of market access that is the target of potential exporters and the main subject of trade bargaining in general. The history of the global trading system since World War Two reveals the initial dominance of the United States on both counts, but with gradually declining influence. Its dominance of the postwar global economy helped it to shape the institutions of trade to pursue its economic and political goals, which through trade also garnered (sometimes grudging) support from all the other countries that voluntarily acceded to the system. U.S. hegemony could not remain undiminished, however, in an evolving trading system. The reemergence of Europe as a center of production and trade, together with the consolidation of centralized European bargaining power in the European Union, provided an increasingly powerful counterweight to U.S. influence. Other major trading partners also gained influence, leading to the central role of the "Quad" countries (United States, EU, Japan, and Canada) by the latter stages of the Uruguay Round. By the early years of the WTO, the world's economic center of gravity was shifting away from the rich countries toward large and rapidly growing countries such as China, India, and Brazil. In addition, the number of new WTO members continued to grow, mostly developing and transition economies. U.S. influence within the WTO remained strong, but it could no longer influence the negotiating agenda as powerfully as it did earlier. In such a time of institutional upheaval and discontent, it was not surprising that reactions to the Uruguay Round agreement arose. One was a challenge to the reciprocal negotiating process by one particular alliance of developing countries, the Like Minded Group. The other was a remarkable challenge to specific terms of the TRIPS agreement, which led in fact to significant amendments to it.

The Like Minded Group (LMG) emerged in the early years of the WTO as a coalition of developing countries led by India, whose original members also included Cuba, Egypt, Indonesia, Malaysia, Pakistan, Tanzania, and Uganda (Narlikar and Odell 2006, p. 120). Its membership expanded in the early years of the Doha Round negotiations to include the Dominican Republic, Honduras, Jamaica, Kenya, Mauritius, Sri Lanka, and Zimbabwe (Jawara and Kwa 2004, pp. 123–124). The original group organized itself in 1996 during the WTO's Singapore Ministerial Meeting and focused at that time largely on preventing labor standards from being included on the upcoming multilateral trade agenda. Later, as negotiations for a new round began to develop, the LMG set out to make resolution of Uruguay Round implementation issues for developing countries a condition for any progress in a new trade round. The LMG also protested against WTO negotiating procedures and processes, charging that many such traditional trade practices were nontransparent and undemocratic. In a lengthy official proposal to the WTO developed after the Seattle meeting and during the preparation of the Doha meeting in early 2001, the group promulgated a sort of manifesto that would reform the practices of the WTO Green Room and the drafting of agendas and negotiating texts, setting out new rules for preparatory processes in negotiations and processes at ministerial conferences.[1]

The LMG showed in this instance the reaction of some developing countries to both the Uruguay Round and the Seattle Ministerial by challenging the underlying institutions of representation. Their proposal had broad support among developing countries and even among a number of OECD countries. It was not adopted by the General Council, however, as other countries claimed it would set too rigid a framework for negotiating guidelines. In other words, the traditional way of conducting trade negotiations, often behind closed doors and sometimes with backroom deals and threats, was not pretty, but it was regarded as the only way that such negotiations could work at all. The LMG, for its part, was attempting to restrike the balance of negotiating power in the WTO in favor of the growing majority of developing countries by bringing the negotiating process more into the open, where the large and rich countries would have to leave their backroom machinations behind. The institutional question was whether such a radical departure from practice, not just in the GATT/WTO system but in most international trade negotiations as they had been practiced over the centuries, would be accepted as the way to move forward in the Doha Round. This was clearly not the case, but it should be noted that

WTO members, as well as D-G Mike Moore, acknowledged the issue, and because of the Seattle Green Room fiasco became much more sensitive to representation issues thereafter.

Yet the most radical idea of the LMG lay in its negotiating strategy. From 1998 to the Doha Ministerial in 2001, this coalition attempted to stonewall the start of the new trade round by demanding adjustments to offset the unanticipated costs and alleged unfairness of parts of the Uruguay Round that harmed developing countries. These included the contentious items mentioned in the earlier summary of the Uruguay Round: TRIPS, implementation costs of new measures, and the backloading of textile and clothing liberalization. More than offering just a list of complaints, the LMG strategy demanded detailed changes in the provisions of these Uruguay Round measures as conditions for entering into new trade talks. This aggressive negotiating strategy was the clearest expression of the institutional conflict that had developed in the WTO. While the LMG strategy did not prevail among developing countries, it signaled a level of resentment and frustration among them that continued to plague the negotiations.

As an attempt to challenge the dominance of the United States, the EU, and other OECD countries in the WTO, the LMG strategy ended in failure.[5] There were many reasons for their lack of success: the urgent collective mood to get a new round started in the wake of the 9–11 terrorist attacks, some partial concessions and side deals offered to some LMG members that peeled apart the group's solidarity, and the emergence of the "development round" theme that appeared to offer promise to developing countries for more extensive benefits this time around (Narlikar and Odell 2006). India was the last LMG member standing at the Doha Ministerial, and finally agreed to begin a new trade round without prior concessions. Other issues were papered over, in particular the Singapore issues, sowing the seeds for a future confrontation at the Cancún Ministerial (see below). However, the single most decisive weakness of the LMG strategy was that it amounted to an ultimatum challenging an essential element of the existing institutional structure of the WTO system: reciprocity. At the end of the Uruguay Round, the final deal had been completed, and there would be no renegotiation of it, with the exception of the TRIPS agreement to be highlighted below. But more than the fact that the previous trade round was ratified, signed, sealed, and delivered by the participating countries, it had also been paid for politically at home in all the participating countries, and these deals could not be reversed. Trying to reopen the Uruguay Round outcome was impossible because it was politically untenable. Domestic lobbies had counted their gains and losses, and looked forward to the next opportunity to bargain in a new trade round. That meant, by trade negotiating logic, that any new concessions made by a country would have to be paid for with new reciprocal concessions somewhere. This is part of the underlying social contract of the WTO.

While the LMG had failed as a coalition determined to wring unilateral concessions from the developed countries, developing countries were already pursuing coalition tactics on other issues that would be more successful. This was to become an important example of institutional adaptation to the WTO's system of representation. The Green Room disaster at Seattle and the collapse of the LMG showed the developing countries that they needed a viable strategy of joint action that would put pressure on the more powerful WTO members in order to achieve success. A coalition led by South Africa and the African Group of 41 countries, for example, scored a remarkable victory in amending the TRIPS agreement.[6] The pivotal issue was the AIDS epidemic, which had infected millions in sub-Saharan Africa and elsewhere in the developing world. The original TRIPS rules had made it extremely difficult for poor countries to acquire AIDS medicines cheaply, as there was no provision for the importation of patented drugs under compulsory licensing. This was the centerpiece of the move to amend it, and the large pharmaceutical companies, the driving force behind the TRIPS negotiations, were adamantly opposed to any such erosion of the intellectual property rights they thought they had secured in the Uruguay Round. As noted earlier, however, the TRIPS agreement did not fit into the institutional framework of the GATT/WTO system, and it is inconceivable that a traditional exchange of market access conditions would have led to such a renegotiation scenario.[7] By harnessing NGO support and public opinion in the United States, Europe, and other developed countries, the coalition managed to soften the impact of TRIPS on developing countries' access to less expensive drugs to fight AIDS and other diseases, first in the 2001 Doha Declaration on TRIPS and Public Health and later in the 2003 and 2005 General Council Decisions on TRIPS. Success in amending the TRIPS agreement, while limited and dependent on public support in developed countries, showed the growing ability of developing country coalitions to affect outcomes in the WTO.

Meanwhile, institutional conflict was creating fault lines in several dimensions of the Doha negotiations. The perennially intractable issue of agriculture revealed rifts along both North-North and North-South lines. Institutionally, this area remained difficult to penetrate with traditional methods of GATT/WTO reciprocal market concessions. Deeply embedded protectionist tendencies and numerous non-tariff trade barriers in many countries—both developed and developing—fostered a highly mercantilist approach to trade that left little room for significant global market opening. In fact, most potential gains from agricultural trade liberalization were estimated to occur domestically within the liberalizing countries, whose economies were often highly distorted by combinations of subsidies, price supports, tariffs, and quotas. Negotiators in key countries continued to set agriculture apart as a sector deserving special protection for reasons of national food security, of maintaining a desirable way of life and national traditions, or of preserving a subsistence rural economy in poor countries. While agriculture does not have a large share of global trade, it continued to be the tail that wags the dog in multilateral trade negotiations: progress in other sectors under discussions seemed all too often to depend on progress in agriculture. In all multilateral trade negotiations before the Doha Round, the agricultural agreements that have been concluded have been modest, at best, in terms of market opening. The Uruguay Round's accomplishment of converting quota barriers to tariffs held considerable promise for future liberalization, but progress was slow and fitful in the Doha Round.

There was also little momentum in the services negotiations, as liberalization in this area relied on reforms in many "behind the border" measures that were difficult to negotiate, even when countries were free to choose the areas of liberalization and to limit their commitments in any one services area. The General Agreement on Trade in Services (GATS) framework, established in the Uruguay Round, set up four modes of services under negotiation, based on the way the traded service is delivered: 1) cross-border supply (as of banking or telecommunications services transmitted electronically or by mail), 2) consumption abroad (as with tourists and medical patients), 3) commercial presence (such as foreign subsidiaries and hotel properties), and 4) the presence of natural persons (foreign workers entering the territory to conduct business).[8] Finding effective modalities for liberalizing services trade has been elusive, since countries have generally been very cautious in opening up domestic service markets that are subject to domestic regulation, certification, licensing, and standards, especially if they are unsure what impact new foreign competition will have in these sectors. Services now represent the largest and fastest-growing sector in the world economy, and also the fastest-growing sector in global trade over the last 20 years. The gains from services trade liberalization are potentially very large, and many developed countries in particular have been eager to gain new foreign market access. However, most countries have been reluctant to open up their services markets, and developing countries have had little participation in the negotiations. Ironically, what are estimated to be the single largest gains from trade negotiations for developing countries would come from mode 4 liberalization (movement of natural persons), that is, the temporary movement of workers across borders. Unfortunately, most countries are extremely reluctant to open their borders to significantly more labor migration, even if it is temporary.

While tariffs in manufactures have fallen steadily over the years, the Doha Round's non-agricultural market access (NAMA) negotiations still have room for significant liberalization, particularly with regard to trade among developing countries. In the Uruguay Round, developed countries lowered their manufactured goods tariffs from 6.3% to 3.8%. The developing countries' contribution focused on tariff bindings, the ceilings above which a WTO member cannot raise tariffs. Coverage of tariff bindings in manufactured goods as a proportion of tariff schedules increased from 21% to 74% in developing countries, but their overall bound tariff levels remained on average at 15%, much higher than those in developed countries. Based on the formulas under negotiation in the Doha Round, the reduced bound tariffs for most developing countries would still be higher than their applied tariffs, which would result in only a small amount of immediate market opening. This prospective outcome was disappointing to many exporters in the developed world, even though tariff bindings would aid liberalization by preventing large unilateral applied tariff increases by these countries in the future.[9] The NAMA negotiations would benefit from more ambitious strategies among the negotiators, perhaps setting up future stages of tariff cuts after the initial "down payment" of the more modest binding commitments.

Yet the reluctance of developing countries to commit to larger tariff cuts appeared to point to a pervasive skepticism about the benefits of trade liberalization from increased imports. While infant industry strategies may play a role in this attitude, their arguments in the Doha Round turned increasingly on their stated need for "policy space" in their development plans, suggesting an unwillingness to risk uncertain and possibly disruptive effects of trade adjustment in the context of domestic development strategies. There may also be fears in some cases that tariff reductions would result in uncompensated losses in tariff revenue. A lingering resentment over the disappointments of the Uruguay Round liberalization measures appears to play a role in the stalemate. The question is whether developing countries (and developed countries, for that matter) are willing in principle to sacrifice some amount of domestic policy space in order to gain the benefits of new export market access.[10] For example, a number of significant tariff peaks still exist among developed countries in clothing, footwear, and other items of interest to developing countries, and effective tariff rates on many processed goods are still high, which blocks the development of downstream industries in countries exporting commodities, a situation that applies in agricultural trade as well.[11]

Discord and Entropy

Despite many attempts to reenergize the negotiations, the Doha Round has suffered from a sort of entropy, a degradation of energy that has resulted from the continual conflict among hardened positions. At the Cancún Ministerial meeting in 2003, a newly formed coalition of developing countries led by Brazil and India, the G20, was frustrated at the continued intransigence of the position of the United States and EU on agriculture and proposed large cuts in their agricultural subsidies and tariffs, along with other reform measures.[12] A small group of African countries made U.S. cotton subsidies a focal point of this discussion. Another set of developing country coalitions formally protested the inclusion of the Singapore issues in the negotiations, which the EU and Korea had adamantly insisted upon and other developed countries had supported.[13] The developed countries agreed to drop three of the four Singapore issues (trade facilitation did remain on the agenda, and there was remarkable progress in this area, to be discussed in chapter 6). However, large numbers of developing countries insisted on reductions in agricultural subsidies by the United States and EU, which refused to budge on this issue. As a result, the Cancún meeting collapsed with no significant progress on the Doha agenda.

The Cancún Ministerial Meeting was a watershed event for at least two important reasons that are related to institutional conflict in the WTO. Bhaumik (2006), for example, described the sense of cathartic jubilation among many developing country delegations that accompanied the collapse of the negotiations. This reaction becomes understandable in view of the accumulated frustrations and disappointments experienced by these countries from the outcomes of the Uruguay Round and the Seattle and Doha ministerial meetings. Here, finally, developing countries had asserted their position in opposition to the dominant countries in the WTO and had prevailed, at least in terms of disrupting the agenda. The second and related significant institutional element was the emergence of effective developing country coalitions in a major WTO negotiation. Based on the experience of the LMG at the Doha Ministerial Conference, as well as many other unsuccessful attempts at coalition building, the developing countries had learned how to avoid many of the pitfalls and had maintained their cohesion despite pressures from the United States and EU to break ranks. The balance of power in the WTO was shifting, and although developing countries were unable to push through their own negotiating proposals, they showed that any final agreement would require their active participation and consent.

After Cancún, the WTO members had to downgrade expectations for a Doha agreement, based on the removal of Singapore issues from the table and the obviously large chasm between developing countries and the United States and EU regarding agricultural policies. Nonetheless, WTO members maintained the principle of the never-ending trade negotiation by patching up the Doha agenda at a special meeting in Geneva in July 2004 and restarting the talks, now with more modest expectations. Concerned about the acrimony that had attended the previous three ministerial meetings in Seattle, Doha, and Cancún, the WTO members then sought to keep the December 2005 ministerial meeting in Hong Kong free of major conflicts. In the event, the trimmed-down agenda in Hong Kong did not lead to any Cancún-like dramatic confrontations, but at the same time little progress was made toward a final agreement. The main accomplishment was an agreement, after much difficult bargaining with the EU, to end agricultural export subsidies by 2013. The United States pledged to remove cotton export subsidies earlier and to hasten the reduction of other cotton support programs, and rich countries assured the developing world of their readiness to increase aid for trade, but these promises lacked formal commitments. In the meantime, little progress was made on modalities for tariff reductions in agriculture and NAMA, or on new offers in the services negotiations.

Institutional friction appears to have led to a sort of rolling stalemate on the critical negotiating issues. In a new configuration of principal trading countries, the attempt by the G6 (United States, EU, Japan, Australia, India, and Brazil) to formulate modalities for agricultural trade liberalization foundered in July 2006, formally closing down the Doha negotiations for nearly a year (WTO 2006b). While the United States and EU blamed primarily each other for the collapse, it was clear that India, in particular, was also unwilling to negotiate further without major cuts in U.S. farm subsidies. The divide between the rich farm countries (United States and EU) and the leading developing countries (Brazil, India) became more apparent the following year, when attempts to move the negotiations failed once again. A third push to restart the talks involved considerably more preparatory work, and D-G Lamy got these countries to agree to a more extensive "mini-ministerial" meeting in July 2008 in Geneva.[14] The persistence of the negotiators again showed their eagerness to overcome remaining obstacles and conclude a comprehensive, if diminished, trade deal. This time, after nine days of marathon meetings, the talks finally broke down over the terms of the agricultural Special Surge Mechanism (SSM), which would have raised tariffs on food imports to India (and other developing countries) if volume surged by a certain amount. It was the surge point "trigger" that was the subject of irreconcilable differences.

There were in fact other issues left unresolved at the July 2008 mini-ministerial, although agriculture has always been the biggest single obstacle.[15] Blustein (2008) reports that the positions of the major negotiating powers had hardened on several issues, with little chance of a breakthrough. At this point, negotiators were debating over ever more arcane minutiae, and it was clear that any Doha deal would have been small compared to, for example, the big liberalizing package of the Uruguay Round. Still, the failure of major developed and developing countries to come to a meeting of the minds over agriculture revealed a continuing institutional gap in the structure of the negotiations. While the United States and EU had battled furiously over agriculture in previous rounds, they nonetheless spoke the same negotiating language in representing their respective farm lobbies and their policy entitlements. For developing countries, on the other hand, the stakes were different, as subsistence farming often dominated their agricultural sectors, with governments unwilling to take risks of a catastrophic displacement of farmers with few alternative modes of existence. Achieving a significant WTO agreement in agriculture that includes developing countries is therefore likely to require some combination of progress in agricultural productivity, domestic safety nets, new jobs programs, labor-intensive direct foreign investment, and foreign aid. Linkages to such inducements in the negotiations will require a new negotiating framework.

While the Doha Round stalled, other institutional issues also arose under the new WTO regime, with possible future impacts on trade negotiations. The accession of new members to the WTO introduced new procedures that raised the importance of bilateral negotiations with new members, apparently extending the accession negotiations. This topic will be the subject of chapter 3. In addition, the reformed dispute settlement understanding, which was intended to level the playing field among developed and developing countries, was not being used as much by the smaller and poorer countries, raising questions of the system's effectiveness, the subject of chapter 5. These issues, if unresolved, could also threaten to undermine the ability of WTO members to reach consensus in multilateral negotiations.

Summary

The Uruguay Round was truly innovative and ambitious, creating the WTO, with its tighter rules for dispute settlement and its extension of liberalization into new areas of trade. For many countries, the Uruguay Round agreement was a leap into the unknown, but the monumental nature of its new and expanded system of trade rules removed resistance to it: no country wanted to block the founding a new organization that promised so much to all its members. Unfortunately, its accomplishments have come at a high price. Table 2.4 summarizes the items of institutional friction that emerged during the transition from the GATT system during the Uruguay Round to the expanded and more ambitious WTO system. The WTO's institutional structures and procedures, inherited from the GATT, were inadequate to accommodate the challenges of trade coverage in new areas and a larger, more diverse membership subject to a shift in bargaining power. The unanticipated disappointments of the Uruguay Round for many developing countries created resentments regarding the WTO system that would surface in the Doha Round, making it extremely difficult to reach consensus on a new trade agreement. The developed countries in fact acknowledged their resentment at the outset by calling it the "development round," which, ironically, fostered unrealistic expectations among developing countries and only made matters worse.[16] Yet, in some ways, WTO members have adapted to the altered trade environment, especially in terms of a more open decision-making process and the formation of more effective coalitions. Further institutional problems remain, however.

The following chapters will examine four specific problems of the WTO that have grown out of this institutional friction. Chapter 3 will discuss the WTO's accession procedures, which reflect the original ambitions of the new organization in requiring comprehensive compliance with the broadened obligations of membership, but which have often included obligations that go beyond those of existing WTO members. Chapter 4 takes up the issue of Green Room procedures, which have been evolving but still raise serious concerns about the representation of all WTO members, and may require more systematic reforms. Chapter 5 will show that representation of developing countries is also an issue in the WTO's dispute settlement system, which is set up as an adversarial process that favors countries

TABLE 2.4 Institutional friction in the transition from Uruguay Round (UR) to WTO

New institutional development	Background	Unanticipated problems	Institutional friction
1. Active role of developing countries in UR negotiations	Need for expanded engagement in broadened UR agenda	Disappointment with UR outcome	Green Room backlash; reluctance to offer reciprocal concessions in Doha Round
2. Single undertaking	Need for organizational unity in new WTO	UR "Grand Bargain" → "Bum Deal"	Difficulty of assessing strategies, balancing diverse sectors
3. Textile/clothing negotiations	Draw developing countries into UR; end MFA	China domination of market; negative impact of backloaded liberalization	Built-in agenda; disillusionment with trade liberalization
4. New sector: services negotiations	Need to expand scope of trade bargaining in UR	GATS framework only; few commitments	GATS modalities gain little traction; reluctance to open sensitive sectors
5. Agricultural negotiations	Need to motivate developing countries to bargain in UR	Tariffication framework only; little liberalization	Domestic protectionism overwhelms negotiations framework
6. "Behind the border" measures	New source of gains from trade in UR	Funding of trade capacity requirements	No provision for funding coherence in WTO
7. TRIPS agreement	Piracy; U.S. unilateral measures	Unbalanced welfare effects; lack of trade capacity; AIDS medicine backlash	Misalignment with trade liberalization parameters, partial renegotiation required
8. Preference erosion	S&D treatment set up; downside of general liberalization	Need to compensate in negotiations	Inconsistency with MFN creates disincentive to liberalize trade
9. Tariff revenue	Poor countries sacrifice revenue; no alternative sources	Some poor countries may be net welfare losers in MTN	Monetary compensation may be necessary; not available through WTO
10. Dispute settlement	Need for enforceability, appeals process	Small/poor countries lack resources, can't benefit from cases	Inconsistency in correcting nullification/ impairment
11. Accession	Weak GATT obligations, esp. for developing countries	Bilaterals, increasingly lengthy accession negotiations	GATT-plus obligations, possible reluctance to bargain in future MTN

Source: See text.

with substantial legal resources and infrastructure. The coherence problem in the WTO is reviewed in chapter 6, which focuses on attempts to coordinate WTO goals and resources with those of other international economic organizations, such as the World Bank and the IMF. Together, these issues suggest the need for new institutional development both within the WTO and in the world economy, and a general review of reforms and efforts to improve the institutional structure and performance of the WTO will be the subject of the final chapter, "Getting Over the Doha Blues."

3

WTO Accession

The Hard Path to Universal Membership

THE WTO INTRODUCED NEW RULES FOR JOINING THE ORGANIZATION to replace those previously used by the GATT. This was part of an institutional overhaul intended to improve the discipline of membership in the global trading system, which had, according to prominent GATT members such as the United States and Japan, been too loose and weak to hold all members to the rules and to market access obligations. At the same time, in order to maximize the world gains from trade, the WTO has sought from its founding to achieve universal membership.[1] This chapter addresses the tension between these two goals and sets out to examine the political economy of the WTO accession process, focusing on the time it has taken for the first 25 new WTO members to accede, as well as the terms of their accession.[2] It begins with a review of the membership trends in the GATT and WTO and the benefits of membership. It then discusses the GATT rules of accession and why they were replaced in the WTO. There follows a presentation of a set of regression analyses on the length of time it takes to conclude an accession agreement and other related variables, with a discussion of the impact of learning and bargaining power by incumbent WTO members. The chapter concludes by considering the prospects for further accessions, as well as some possible reforms of the current WTO accession rules.

Overview of Current WTO Membership and Accession

As of early 2009, the WTO had 153 members, representing approximately 91% of the world's population, 98% of world GDP, and 96% of world trade.

Twenty-five of these countries have joined the organization through a formal accession process since it was founded in 1995. Twenty-six other countries, with a total population of 565 million, are currently under review for accession, most prominently the Russian Federation. In addition, there are, according to the United Nations membership rolls, 17 countries, with a total population of 64 million, that are neither members nor applicants for membership. The WTO founding membership comprises the 128 Contracting Parties (CPs) of the General Agreement on Tariffs and Trade (GATT) at the end of 1994. These countries negotiated and ratified the Uruguay Round trade agreement, which created a new and more comprehensive trade organization, the WTO.

The GATT had been founded in 1947 with 23 original CPs. GATT membership grew slowly at first, but expanded rapidly in the 1960s, as many newly independent countries joined, and surged again in the late 1980s and early 1990s, after the Uruguay Round was launched. Table 1A shows the GATT membership as it stood at the end of the Uruguay Round and founding of the WTO,[3] table 1B tabulates the 25 countries that had acceded to the WTO by 2008, table 2A shows the 26 countries that were in varying stages of the WTO accession process at that time, and table 2B reports the 17 countries listed as United Nations members that were not WTO member or applicant countries. After its founding in 1995, several countries carried over their requests for GATT membership to the newly formed WTO, and others started application procedures only after the new organization came into existence.

TABLE 3.1A Gatt CPs that became WTO founding members

Country	Date of membership	Mode
Australia	1-Jan-48	orig
Belgium	1-Jan-48	orig
Canada	1-Jan-48	orig
Cuba	1-Jan-48	orig
France	1-Jan-48	orig
Luxembourg	1-Jan-48	orig
Netherlands	1-Jan-48	orig
United Kingdom	1-Jan-48	orig
United States of America	1-Jan-48	orig
South Africa	13-Jun-48	orig
India	8-Jul-48	orig
Norway	10-Jul-48	orig
Zimbabwe (Rhodesia)	11-Jul-48	orig
Myanmar, Union of (Burma)	29-Jul-48	orig
Sri Lanka	29-Jul-48	orig
Brazil	30-Jul-48	orig

New Zealand	30-Jul-48	orig
Pakistan	30-Jul-48	orig
Chile	16-Mar-49	33
Haiti	1-Jan-50	33
Indonesia	24-Feb-50	26:5
Greece	1-Mar-50	33
Sweden	30-Apr-50	33
Dominican Republic	19-May-50	33
Finland	25-May-50	33
Denmark	28-May-50	33
Nicaragua	28-May-50	33
Italy	30-May-50	33
Germany	1-Oct-51	33
Peru	7-Oct-51	33
Turkey	17-Oct-51	33
Austria	19-Oct-51	33
Uruguay	6 Dec-53	33
Japan	10-Sep-55	33
Ghana	17-Oct-57	26:5
Malaysia	24-Oct-57	26:5
Nigeria	18-Nov-60	26:5
Sierra Leone	19-May-61	26:5
Tanzania	9-Dec-61	26:5
Portugal	6 May-62	33
Israel	5-Jul-62	33
Trinidad and Tobago	23-Oct-62	26:5
Uganda	23-Oct-62	26:5
Burkina Faso	3-May-63	26:5
Cameroon	3-May-63	26:5
Central African Republic	3 May-03	26:5
Congo, Republic of	3-May-63	26:5
Gabon	3-May-63	26:5
Kuwait	3-May-63	26:5
Chad	12-Jul-63	26:5
Cyprus	15-Jul-63	26:5
Spain	29-Aug-63	33
Benin	12-Sep-63	26:5
Senegal	27-Sep-63	26:5
Madagascar	30-Sep-63	26:5
Mauritania	30-Sep-63	26:5
Côte d'Ivoire	31-Dec-63	26:5
Jamaica	31-Dec-63	26:5
Niger	31-Dec-63	26:5
Kenya	5-Feb-64	26:5
Togo	20-Mar-64	26:5
Malawi	28-Aug-64	26:5
Malta	17-Nov-64	26:5
The Gambia	22-Feb-65	26:5
Burundi	13-Mar-65	26:5
Rwanda	1-Jan-66	26:5
Guyana	5-Jul-66	26:5
Switzerland	1-Aug-66	33
Yugoslavia	25-Aug-66	33

(continued)

TABLE 3.1A (continued)

Country	Date of membership	Mode
Korea, Republic of	14-Apr-67	33
Argentina	11-Oct-67	33
Poland	18-Oct-67	33
Ireland	22-Dec-67	33
Iceland	21-Apr-68	33
Egypt	9-May-70	33
Mauritius	2-Sep-70	26:5
Zaire	11-Sep-71	33
Romania	14-Nov-71	33
Bangladesh	16-Dec-72	33
Singapore	20-Aug-73	26:5
Hungary	9-Sep-73	33
Suriname	22-Mar-78	26:5
Philippines	27-Dec-79	33
Colombia	3-Oct-81	33
Zambia	10-Feb-82	26:5
Thailand	20-Nov-82	33
Maldives	19-Apr-83	26:5
Belize	7-Oct-83	26:5
Hong Kong	23-Apr-86	26:5
Mexico	24-Aug-86	33
Antigua and Barbuda	30-Mar-87	26:5
Morocco	17-Jun-87	33
Botswana	28-Aug-87	26:5
Lesotho	8-Jan-88	26:5
Tunisia	29-Aug-90	33
Venezuela	31-Aug-90	33
Bolivia	8-Sep-90	33
Costa Rica	24-Nov-90	33
Macao	11-Jan-91	26:5
El Salvador	22-May-91	33
Guatemala	10-Oct-91	33
Mozambique	27-Jul-92	26:5
Namibia	15-Sep-92	26:5
Mali	11-Jan-93	26:5
Swaziland, Kingdom of	8-Feb-93	26:5
Saint Lucia	13-Apr-93	26:5
Czech Republic	15-Apr-93	33
Slovak Republic	15-Apr-93	33
Dominica	20-Apr-93	26:5
Saint Vincent and the Grenadines	18-May-93	26:5
Fiji	16-Nov-93	26:5
Brunei Darussalam	9-Dec-93	26:5
Bahrain	13-Dec-93	26:5
Paraguay	6-Jan-94	33
Grenada	9-Feb-94	26:5
United Arab Emirates	8-Mar-94	26:5
Guinea Bissau	17-Mar-94	26:5
Saint Kitts and Nevis	24-Mar-94	26:5

Liechtenstein	29-Mar-94	26:5
Qatar	7-Apr-94	26:5
Angola	8-Apr-94	26:5
Honduras	10-Apr-94	33
Slovenia	30-Oct-94	33
Guinea	8-Dec-94	26:5
Djibouti	16-Dec-94	26:5
Papua New Guinea	16-Dec-94	26:5
Solomon Islands	28-Dec-94	26:5

Sources: Jackson (1969), Appendix D. GATT Documents Database, Stanford University, various.

TABLE 3.1B WTO accession countries (as of February 2009)

Country	Application	Accession	Months	Rule cmtmt	Ag tariff[wwA]	Nonag tariff[***]	Stability[**]
Ecuador	Sep-92	Jan-96	40	21	25.5	21.1	−0.83
Bulgaria	Sep-86	Dec-96	123	26	35.5	23.6	0.13
Mongolia	Jul-91	Jan-97	66	17	18.9	17.3	0.48
Panama	Aug-91	Sep-97	61	24	27.7	22.9	0.29
Kyrgyzstan	Feb-96	Dec-98	34	29	12.3	6.7	−0.91
Latvia	Nov-93	Feb-99	63	22	34.6	9.4	0.95
Estonia	Mar-94	Nov-99	68	24	17.5	7.3	0.92
Jordan	Jan-94	Apr-00	76	29	23.7	15.2	−0.12
Georgia	Jul-96	Jun-00	49	29	11.7	6.5	−1.26
Albania	Nov-92	Sep-00	94	29	9.4	6.6	−0.97
Oman	Apr-96	Nov-00	55	26	28	11.6	0.76
Croatia	Sep-93	Nov-00	86	27	9.4	5.5	0.35
Lithuania	Jan-94	May-01	89	28	15.2	8.4	0.85
Moldova	Nov-93	Jul-01	88	28	12.2	6	−0.62
China	Jul-86	Dec-01	185	82	15.8	9.1	−0.07
Taipei	Jan-92	Jan-02	120	63	15.3	4.8	0.52
Armenia	Nov-93	Feb-03	111	39	14.7	7.5	−0.51
FYROM	Dec-94	Apr-03	99	24	11.3	6.2	−1.04
Nepal*	May-89	Apr-04	179	25	41.4	23.7	−1.74
Cambodia*	Dec-94	Oct-04	118	29	28.1	17.7	−0.6
SaudiArabia	June-93	Dec-05	150	59	12.3	10.6	−0.6
Viet Nam	Jan-95	Feb-07	144	70	18.5	10.3	0.16
Tonga	June-95	July-07	145	29	19.2	17.3	0.72
Ukraine	Nov-93	May-08	174	63	10.7	5.0	0.16
CapeVerde*	Nov-99	July-08	104	26	19.0	15.0	1.01
Mean			*100.8*	*35*	*19.5*	*11.8*	*−0.08*
Std Dev			*43.5*	*17.5*	*8.8*	*6.3*	*0.78*

*Least Developed Country (WTO list)
**World Bank index of political stability, 2004–07
***Average bound tariff for category

Source: WTO (2005b), plus updates from WTO press releases (www.wto.org).

TABLE 3.2A Countries in WTO accession negotiations (February 2009)

Country	Application	Pop (mil)	GDP (bil)	Trade (bil)	Stability***
Afghanistan*	Nov-04	28.717	19.00	5.52	−2.03
Algeria	Jun-87	32.358	64.15	50.17	−1.42
Andorra	Jul-99	0.066	1.30	1.14	1.35
Azerbaijan	Jun-97	8.306	7.85	9.05	−1.52
Bahamas	May-01	0.319	4.82	2.29	0.94
Belarus	Sep-93	9.824	16.65	29.90	−0.24
Bhutan*	Sep-99	0.896	0.62	26.91	0.84
Bosnia/					
Herzegovina	May-99	3.909	5.50	8.74	−0.85
Ethiopia*	Jan-03	69.961	7.88	3.45	−0.98
Iran	Jul-96	67.006	126.32	81.04	−0.91
Iraq	Sep-04	24.683	19.15	38.17	−2.87
Kazakhstan	Jan-96	14.994	27.26	34.42	−0.11
Lao P.D.R.*	Jul-97	5.792	2.19	0.87	−0.76
Lebanese Rep.	Jan-99	3.54	19.85	1.75	−0.83
Libya	Jun-04	5.74	42.46	27.92	−0.02
Montenegro	Dec-04	**	**	**	**
Russian Fed.	Jun-93	143.85	328.81	289.54	−0.85
Samoa	Apr-98	0.184	0.25	0.18	0.89
Sao Tome &					
Principe*	Jan-05	0.153	0.05	0.04	0.08
Serbia	Dec-04	8.147	10.49	15.43	−0.97
Seychelles	May-95	0.084	0.56	0.72	0.84
Sudan*	Oct-94	35.523	15.41	7.36	−2.08
Tajikistan*	May-01	6.43	1.44	2.33	−1.19
Uzbekistan*	Dec-94	26.209	16.73	7.35	−1.37
Vanuatu	Jul-95	0.207	0.24	0.15	0.53
Yemen*	Apr-00	20.329	10.86	8.53	−1.48
Mean		*20.69*	*29.59*	*26.12*	*−0.59*
Std Dev		*32.15*	*67.88*	*58.29*	*1.06*
Total		517.23	749.8	652.5	
World		6,365	35,111.12	19,355	
% of World		8.1	2.1	3.4	
Total					

*Least Developed Country (World Bank list lowest quartile: 2005 GNI per cap < $825)
**Montenegro's data are included with Serbia's
***World Bank index of political stability, 2004
Population, GDP, and trade figures are for 2004

Sources: WTO (2005b); World Bank WDI database, World Bank Governance Index database.

TABLE 3.2B Remaining countries not yet applying for WTO membership

Country	Pop (mil)	GDP (bil)	Trade (bil)	Stability
Comoros*	0.59	0.22	0.08	−0.13
Equatorial Guinea	0.49	2.02	6.12	−0.3
Eritrea*	4.23	0.73	0.60	−0.14
Kiribati	0.10	0.05	0.12	0.77
Korea PDR				
(North)*	22.38	18.80	3.56	−0.67
Liberia*	3.24	0.42	0.37	−2.2
Marshall Islands	0.06	0.10	0.06	0.66
Micronesia	0.11	0.22	0.07	0.83
Monaco	0.03	0.87	**	1.13
Nauru	0.01	0.06	0.05	0.66
Palau	0.02	0.13	0.12	0.66
San Marino	0.03	0.94	***	1.22
Somalia*	7.96	4.36	0.76	−2.39
Syrian Arab Rep.	18.58	20.73	14.52	−0.66
Timor-Leste*	0.92	0.33	0.25	−0.62
Turkmenistan	4.77	5.80	7.62	−0.92
Tuvalu	0.01	0.01	0.08	0.86
Mean				*−0.072*
Totals	63.55	55.80	34.13	
World Total	6,365.00	35,111.12	19,354.96	
% of World Total	1.00	0.16	0.18	

*Least Developed Country (World Bank list lowest quartile: 2005 GNI per cap < $825)

**Trade figures not separable from France's

***Trade figures not separable from Italy's

Sources: UN Membership database, World Bank WDI database; World Bank Governance Index database.

Benefits of WTO Membership

As described in chapter 1, countries will gain from trade through their own unilateral trade liberalization efforts, so it is not immediately evident that membership in the WTO adds to a member country's economic welfare.[4] However, the revealed preferences of 128 founding member countries, in addition to 25 new members and 26 applicants that have been willing to endure a lengthy accession process, show a strong perception among these countries that membership in the WTO system is beneficial. Its value in fact derives principally from the institutional elements of a rules-based organizational network. Despite the gains from unilateral free trade policies, most countries' governments find it difficult to overcome mercantilist tendencies, embedded in entrenched protectionist lobbying of import-competing industries, potential terms-of-trade gains from tariffs in large countries, and nationalist economic ideologies. WTO membership requires each member to commit to a set of trade policy rules regarding imports (principally MFN and national treatment), reciprocity in trade negotiations, and orderly dispute settlement. These measures provide an external anchor that helps to prevent submission to domestic protectionist interests, and also suggest that the rigors of WTO accession may improve a country's economic performance and growth, especially among countries that began from a position of weak governance (see Tang and Wei 2008). In addition, the commitment element of membership among a country's trading partners provides an important additional benefit by reducing the risk of arbitrary market access barriers or closure that each country's export and import sectors would otherwise face in international trade. This commitment in turn encourages domestic and foreign direct investments in trade-related activities. For many smaller countries, WTO market access rules are particularly important, since they would have great difficulty bargaining for such broad market access provisions on their own. An additional benefit for all members comes from the multilateral bargaining network of WTO negotiations, which tends to reduce the transaction costs of trade-opening agreements for each individual member. Global trade liberalization would otherwise have to proceed on the basis of hundreds or thousands of bilateral or regional agreements, which would furthermore be likely to create conflict and discrimination in trade relations and inefficiency in welfare.[5] Finally, the dispute resolution mechanism provides third-party adjudication of alleged rules violations, thereby protecting and securing members' negotiated gains from trade liberalization.

In summary, WTO membership makes it possible for its members to gain from trade through its ability to improve market access for its members, to commit its membership to trade policy rules, and to protect the benefits of negotiated agreements through dispute settlement. The main difficulty of joining the WTO lies in the adjustment and compliance costs—political, social, and economic—that accompany trade liberalization and deregulation. Some of these costs are incurred because a number of institutional elements of WTO membership require expenditures to develop legal and regulatory systems, such as intellectual property protection, customs valuation, and product standards compliance. For poorer countries, external aid may be required to finance these expenditures. In addition, liberalization measures may entail disruption or displacement of local import-competing industries as part of the process of the reallocation of domestic resources, a situation often made worse by factor immobility and other market rigidities. Internal market reforms and (in wealthier countries) adjustment assistance to workers may be necessary to smooth the process of adjustment that is necessary to move resources into more competitive industries, and may therefore shape the domestic policy agenda as part of joining the WTO. Poor countries in particular typically have deficient internal adjustment mechanisms, including a lack of infrastructure, weak market institutions, and insufficient trade capacity. Yet the benefits of a rules-based agreement guaranteeing nondiscriminatory market access terms and dispute resolution provide the potential for increased trade and economic growth, and therefore also a strong argument for joining. As an institution, the WTO provides the public good of trade liberalization, allowing each member to garner larger gains from trade with greater certainty and lower transaction cost than the alternatives of bilateral or regional trade agreements.

A related and more difficult question arises regarding the value of new membership to the incumbent WTO members and how this factor may affect accession terms and the length of accession negotiations. Theoretically, it is clear that each additional member to the WTO brings the world economy closer to the ideal of fully liberalized global trade, and thereby increases economic welfare for all WTO members. However, the economic gains for the existing membership will be marginal if the country is small, and even when the applicant country is large, the stakes may be small relative to the volume of world trade. Many applicant countries have already opened their economies to a certain degree, and the additional openness of WTO membership may be significant for them as individual countries but less significant to the collective WTO membership, which is therefore less motivated to grant them admission to the organization quickly. Incumbent member countries also look at new WTO members in terms of their implications for future dispute settlement cases. Whatever gains from trade the new member may bring to the trading system, a country with unresolved compliance issues may create acrimonious dispute cases. For this reason, wary WTO members, especially those anticipating increased trade flows with the applicant country, will take a slower and more deliberate approach to the accession process. Finally, the incumbent countries may see the accession negotiations as an opportunity to extract concessions from the applicant country without having to offer reciprocal concessions.

The GATT System's Accession Process

Accession to the GATT from 1948 to 1994 was in many ways easier and more open than the WTO process that followed it. The GATT was a more limited agreement and of more modest scope, covering primarily trade in manufactured goods. As a condition of admission, an applicant country's compliance with the GATT was therefore easier to negotiate. In addition, since the GATT was originally conceived as a temporary organization, GATT membership was based on a Protocol of Provisional Application (PPA), which reduced an applicant's requirements to implement certain articles of the GATT, depending on the country's existing legislation (Jackson 1969, pp. 39–41; Lanoszka 2001, pp. 580–581).[6]

GATT accession procedures were governed by GATT articles 33 and 26. In the early years of the GATT, countries applying for membership under Article 33 typically entered into organized tariff negotiations (the 1949 Annecy and 1951 Torquay Trade Rounds), which upon ratification effectively granted membership to the new participant-signatories. Fourteen new members joined the GATT in this way, without separate protocols of accession. Subsequently, under Article 33 a country could negotiate an individual protocol of accession, under the terms of the PPA described above, requiring a two-thirds majority vote of the existing CPs. From 1955 to 1994, 32 countries joined the GATT through Article 33 protocols of accession. This was the pathway to GATT membership for countries that had not recently gained independence from a colonial power (see below). As the liberalizing measures of GATT negotiations accumulated over time, the "ticket of admission" into the GATT increased commensurately. Yet the waiver provisions of the PPA allowed for considerable flexibility in some negotiations for membership, such as those for Poland, Romania, Hungary, and Yugoslavia, which had Communist political systems and varying degrees of nonmarket and mixed economies.[7] In addition, countries anticipating accession under Article 33 could make a declaration of "provisional accession," which would allow the country to enjoy GATT (particularly MFN) treatment in its trade relationships with GATT members that sign on to the declaration (Jackson 1969, p. 94).

The other pathway to formal GATT membership was through Article 26: 5(c), which applied to those countries that had previously been colonies of existing GATT members but had gained national independence. If the colony had previously been treated as a customs territory under GATT rules, it was allowed to join the GATT, under sponsorship of the former colonial power. This was a simple and straightforward process under which 64 newly independent countries from Africa, the Caribbean, and Asian-Pacific areas became GATT members. In addition, the benefits of GATT membership were also extended to many countries that did not in fact have full GATT membership. Former colonies eligible for Article 26: 5(c) accession enjoyed "de facto application" of GATT treatment during the

interim period before they became full members, as long as they recipro-
cated with GATT treatment toward its existing membership (Jackson 1969,
pp. 97–98).

In short, GATT membership was subject to varying terms of accession, and included various levels of participation. The underlying concept
of GATT participation, based on its broadly inclusive nature, was to create
a "big tent" in order to spread the application of GATT treatment as widely
as possible. This state of affairs appeared to generate increasing difficulties
over time. In the absence of detailed protocols of accession, it was often
unclear exactly what obligations many countries had under the GATT,
especially those that had entered under Article 26: 5(c). The United States
and Japan, in particular, complained in the GATT about the lack of concession schedules for countries entering under Article 26: 5(c) (see GATT
1993). Eventually, all GATT countries were required to submit schedules
of concessions (as they would have under a normal accession protocol) in
order to join the newly formed WTO in 1995 (see GATT 1994).

Accession Rules in the WTO System

Compared to the GATT procedures for accession, the WTO is a much more
legalistic organization. This is because it broadened the scope of trade
negotiations into many new areas and thereby increased the stakes—and
rewards—of membership. No longer limited primarily to tariff negotiations in manufactures, the WTO may reach into each member's agricultural subsidy, trade-related investment, intellectual property, services trade,
customs valuation, and phytosanitary policies. All new WTO members
must therefore comply with the obligations of the sum of all WTO agreements at the time they join, a much larger set of commitments than existed
under the GATT. No "provisional accession," "special protocols" (as for
nonmarket economies), or "de facto application" of membership is possible in the WTO. In addition, WTO membership subjects its members to
the discipline (and protection) of a dispute settlement system that is now
subject only to a "negative consensus." This means that all WTO members
must together veto a dispute settlement decision in order to overturn it, in
contrast to the ability of any member under the GATT (including the defendant country) to veto a decision. In principle, the goal of the new WTO
approach was to define more precisely each member's rights and obligations and to hold everyone more strictly to account in terms of abiding by
the rules. In order to avoid dispute settlement cases, new members must

TABLE 3.3 Accession procedures in chronological order

Step	Procedure	
1	The applicant sends a communication to the Director-General of the WTO indicating its desire to accede to the WTO under Article XII.	
2	The communication is circulated to all WTO members.	
3	A Working Party (WP) is established and a chairperson is appointed.	
4	The WTO Secretariat informs applicant about procedures to be followed.	
5	The applicant submits a Memorandum on its foreign trade regime for circulation to all WTO members.	
6	The WTO Secretariat checks the consistency of the Memorandum with the outline format (Annex I) and informs the applicant and the members of the WP of its views.	
7	WP members submit questions on the Memorandum and the applicant answers. (Repeat 7 if necessary.)	
8	The WP meets.	
9	WP members submit and the applicant answers more questions on the Memorandum.	Bilateral negotiations between the applicant and interested WP members on concessions and commitments on market access for goods and services (as well as on the other specific terms of accession) are undertaken.
10	WP meets again.	
11	Repeat steps 9 and 10, until 12.	
12	The examination of the Memorandum is complete.	
13	Terms and conditions (including commitments to observe WTO rules and disciplines upon accession and transitional periods required to make any legislative or structural changes where necessary to implement these commitments) are agreed.	Concessions and commitments on market access for goods and services (as well as on the other specific terms of accession) are agreed.
14	A WP Report is prepared.	The Schedule of Concession and Commitments to GATT 1994 and the Schedule of Specific Commitments to the GATS is prepared.
15	A draft Decision and a draft Protocol of Accession (containing commitments listed in the WP Report and the Schedule of Concessions and Commitments to GATT 1994 and the Schedule of Specific Commitments ot the GATS) is prepared.	
16	The WP adopts the "accession package."	
17	The General Council/Ministerial Conference approves the "accession package."	
18	The applicant formally accepts the "accession package."	
19	The applicant notifies the WTO Secretariat of its formal acceptance.	
20	30 days after step 19, the applicant becomes a member of the WTO.	

Source: World Trade Organization, Accessions page, http://www.wto.org/english/thewto_e/acc_e/acc_e.htm.

therefore be in compliance with WTO obligations across a wide spectrum of policies, which increases the burden of accession negotiations.

The WTO accession process itself is also much more formal than it was under the GATT. The provisions of WTO Article 12 state simply that countries may accede "on terms to be agreed between it and the WTO," with approval by a two-thirds majority of the existing WTO membership (WTO 1995), although votes are rarely taken. The complexity of the negotiations is revealed in the 20-step procedure for accession that has developed (see WTO 2006a), summarized in table 3.3. The negotiations broadly follow two overlapping stages, the preparation of a potential member's "memorandum of the foreign trade regime" (see below) and bilateral negotiations with Working Party (WP) members. As a practical matter, WTO accession decisions are driven ultimately by the approval of the members, who have not delegated any formal negotiating role to the WTO Secretariat. Accession negotiations therefore take place between the applicant and the WTO membership. All interested WTO members can take part in the WP that presides over the accession process, and each incumbent member has the right to engage in bilateral negotiations with the applicant regarding specific issues.[8] Individual WTO member countries, even small ones, can potentially stall or block progress in any given case.

Additional guidelines for accession are found in the Doha Declaration, in which the WTO members state that they

> ...attach great importance to concluding accession proceedings as quickly as possible. In particular, we are committed to accelerating the accession of least-developed countries (art. 9)...Accession of LDCs remains a priority for the Membership. We agree to work to facilitate and accelerate negotiations with acceding LDCs... (art. 46).[9]

The hortatory language in the Doha Declaration, however, provided no guarantee of quick accessions, as the record has shown.

What Determines the Length of WTO Accession Negotiations?

It was common under the GATT system to refer to the terms of an accession protocol as the "ticket of admission" to the organization. In practice, the price of admission to the GATT was often quite low, as described earlier in the discussion of waivers, Article 26: 5(c) accessions, and various intermediate levels of participation. Yet the later accessions to the GATT did reflect an acknowledgement of the increasing cost of joining, in terms of tariff concessions and obligations, after several rounds of trade negotiations had continued to lower trade barriers (see Smith 1996). Still, the average length of time from application to accession for the 30 countries joining the GATT under individual Article 33 protocols was 62 months (note that Article 33 accessions during the Annecy and Torquay rounds did not require individual protocols). Some accession negotiations dragged on for many years, but even then the applicant country often enjoyed provisional GATT membership status, as was the case with Switzerland, Egypt, Philippines, Thailand, Costa Rica, and El Salvador. Most other countries joined the GATT more quickly, and often had de facto GATT status in most of their trade relations before officially joining.

In contrast, the WTO accession process is framed by two demanding institutional factors. The first is the applicant's preparation of the Memorandum of the Foreign Trade Regime, followed by its review and evaluation by the WP. In the Memorandum, the applicant country must identify all aspects of its legislation and administration that have a bearing on trade policy and WTO obligations. This document is then subjected to exhaustive scrutiny by the WP, which must ultimately be satisfied that the applicant's trade regime is in conformance with the requirements of WTO membership (see table 3.3, steps 5–12). Members of the WP typically submit questions or challenges to the applicant's Memorandum; the applicant is obliged to respond to these, and to undertake corrections needed to come into compliance with WTO obligations. This process may go through much iteration, lasting from several months to several years. The second institutional factor is the right of any existing WTO member to negotiate a bilateral agreement with the applicant country regarding additional rules and concessions, which would then become part of a final MFN application in the WTO protocol of accession. Depending on the specific interests of an applicant's trading partners, an applicant may need to complete several bilateral agreements, and these negotiations may be detailed and acrimonious, leading to further delays in the accession process.

Negotiations to join the WTO are therefore potentially lengthy. The elapsed time for WTO accessions among the first 25 new members averaged 101 months, and table 3.1B shows that the length of the accession process has increased over time, from the relatively short negotiations of early joiners Ecuador and the Kyrgyz Republic (40 and 34 months, respectively) to the typically longer negotiations of later joiners such as China (185 months), Nepal (179 months), and Ukraine (174 months). Current applicants to the WTO as of February 2009 had already been negotiating for an average of 121 months (the sample includes recent applications), as shown in Table 3.2a. While some cases appeared to be near completion (Russia, Vanuatu), others had been dragging on since the pre-WTO period with no end in sight (Algeria, Belarus, Sudan, Uzbekistan). One reason for the longer accession process is that the concept of the "price of admission" has become much more important, in view of the fact that the WTO has built upon 48 years of prior GATT-sponsored trade liberalization, in addition to the wider scope of agreements (and thus obligations) that all WTO members must accept. In joining the WTO, a new member benefits from the sum of all previously negotiated liberalization measures, and current members typically demand that the applicant make all the appropriate market access concessions and adjustments to its economy that are commensurate with WTO membership. These concessions include not only tariff reductions and the elimination of traditional trade barriers but also offers of market access in services sectors, as well as compliance of national laws and regulations with the requirements of the TRIPS agreement, sanitary/phytosanitary standards, and technical barriers to trade. A legislative action plan to bring the legal and regulatory framework into line with WTO obligations is required. Kavass (2007) notes that many applicant countries do not realize the nature and extent of reforms that will be required until after the detailed negotiations begin.

The WTO accession process can therefore be lengthy, complicated, and costly, especially for governments that do not have a well-established framework for regulating trade, intellectual property, and other trade-related activities. Many developing and transition economies, burdened with a legacy of central planning and/or weak legal and policy institutions, have difficulty just determining where all the elements of trade policy are located in their own governmental structure. Poor countries may lack the capability of analyzing the impact of WTO membership on their economies, and may also suffer from a lack of commitment by the government, as the trade ministry competes with other governmental sectors for limited resources and priority in the country's policy agenda. There may also be internal political battles as domestic interests resist exposure to import competition. These difficulties are likely to add to the time it takes to negotiate an accession agreement. As mentioned earlier, the lengthiness of the accession process may also be the result of the desire of incumbent WTO members to assure that all major WTO compliance issues have been laid to rest, so that the danger of acrimonious WTO disputes is minimized. According to this view, it makes little sense to rush the accession negotiations if the result is that many outstanding issues of contention remain with the new member regarding intellectual property, market access, and other policies affecting trade.

Perhaps the most controversial element of WTO accession is the fact that bargaining power lies squarely with the incumbent WTO members, especially the large and politically powerful countries, and these countries may have increased their exploitation of this power with each successive accession negotiation.[10] Odell (2006, pp. 9–11, 22–23) argues that any new bargaining situation forces negotiators to act on the basis of bounded rationality—in other words, to make the best decision given incomplete information and uncertainty about the outcome.[11] Additional experience in accession negotiations, however, allows incumbent members to recognize the extent of their own bargaining power, leading to strategies that can win additional concessions from subsequent applicants. The hypothesis is that WTO members involved in accession WPs began in 1995 with a new and unfamiliar negotiating situation, and then in the course of several negotiations learned progressively to impose increasingly demanding terms on applicants.[12] The bargaining asymmetry is reinforced by the fact that the applicant alone is asked to adjust its trade regime for the purposes of joining; no reciprocal concessions come from the incumbent members, who have "paid" for their WTO benefits in earlier trade negotiations. This imbalance applies particularly to small applicant countries, which have few means of leverage or influence on WTO members in general, and can only appeal to moral suasion or plead their lack of resources to fulfill costly obligations. Even large countries, such as China and Russia, have had little room for deflecting demands for concessions in the bilateral stage of negotiations, although one can argue that China, with its large potential import market, was able to bargain for longer transition periods for some of its obligations. Russia, for its part, has appeared to be using what leverage it had in domestic energy market development to try to reach more favorable terms of WTO accession.[13]

The record of WTO accessions so far has also revealed that new members must often make additional "rule commitments," and often accept "WTO-plus" terms of accession—that is, they must make concessions that go beyond the existing WTO obligations of members at comparable levels of development.[14] The number of negotiated rule commitments is shown in table 3.1B. The number of these commitments has also generally grown with each new accession, especially in the most recent cases, but more importantly, details of some of these commitments show that they go beyond WTO obligations for existing members. Evenett and Primo Braga (2005) report, for example, that Jordan agreed to give WTO treaties precedence over other international treaties, beyond the requirements of customary international law, that Ecuador agreed to eliminate all subsidies before its accession date, and that China agreed to transitional safeguard provisions that do not apply to any other WTO member.[15] Adhikari and Dahal (2003) report that Cambodia gave up its right to agricultural export subsidies and agreed to submit to additional TRIPS measures. In the services sector, most acceding countries ended up making commitments to open trade in many more subsectors than were agreed to by their peer WTO incumbents during the Uruguay Round (Evenett and Prima Braga 2005, Adhikari and Dahal 2003).[16] While Kennett (2005, pp. 50–53) observes that not all rule commitments involve "WTO-plus" provisions, the number of such commitments may be taken as a rough measure of the degree to which applicants have had to agree to special obligations of interest to incumbent WTO members.[17]

In addition, applicants may be required to lower tariffs to levels below those of incumbent WTO members. For example, Anderson and Martin (2005) calculated that the average bound agricultural tariff for all existing WTO developing country members was 48%, while the average for the first 25 newly acceding WTO members was about 20% (table 3.1B), most of which are developing or transition countries. For LDCs that were already members of the WTO, the average bound agricultural tariff was 78%, but the average for the three new LDC members, Nepal, Cambodia, and Cape Verde, was 29.5%, well below the overall developing country average. Most new WTO members therefore reduced their tariffs, by substantial margins, to levels lower than their incumbent WTO member counterparts, indicating that the new members have had to submit to more demanding (from a mercantilist perspective) obligations than existing members. In addition, the pattern shows a general decline in the bound tariff rate as the total number of completed accessions increased (a trend to be examined in more detail below).

Despite the view of some legal scholars denouncing WTO-plus measures and extra tariff concessions (see for example Broude 1998, p. 164), the asymmetrical distribution of bargaining power has become a strongly embedded feature of the accession process. There is strong evidence that many WTO members are keen to press this advantage, based on a "consolidationist" approach to the trading system (Smith 1996, p. 173). As indicated in the earlier discussion of the GATT's rather loose membership criteria and the frustration it caused in some members, one major motivation for negotiating a new trading system was to establish a more specific set of legal obligations that could be adjudicated in dispute settlement cases. This approach to the WTO trading system's accession process implies that new members with poorly developed market and trade institutions should be required to make concrete commitments to bring their economies into compliance with the norms of an open trading system. The "big tent" of the earlier GATT accession conditions therefore gives way to the "narrow gateway" through which new WTO members must pass.

Regression Analysis

What factors have contributed to the lengthy accession process and to the terms of accession? It is difficult to generalize, since each country's negotiations are unique. However, it may be reasonable to hypothesize that certain factors have played a systematic role. Four OLS regression equations were tested, with the following dependent variables: 1) the elapsed time from WTO application to final accession; 2) the number of special WTO rule commitments agreed to by the acceding country; 3) the final bound average nonagricultural and 4) agricultural tariff of the acceding country. Based on the institutional provisions of the accession process discussed above, one type of explanatory variable would try to capture the extent to which there is a gap between the applicant's current trade regime and the required WTO-compatible trade regime, such as development or transitional economy status, or measures of total or per capita GDP. A greater gap would imply a longer negotiating process. These and additional explanatory variables may also indicate the extent to which the applicant country is important enough to target for additional concessions (and lengthier negotiations), such as those measuring market share in WTO members' markets and other economic profile statistics. Trade and political profile variables may suggest either longer or shorter negotiations, based on the tendency for the applicant country's exports to attract antidumping cases, for the country to have high pre-WTO tariffs, or to exhibit strong governance characteristics (a possible indication that the country will agree to quick negotiations in order to establish the "anchor" benefits of WTO membership for its economy). Finally, explanatory variables regarding the negotiating circumstances, such as how many completed accessions have preceded the applicant's WP report or whether the original application occurred before the WTO was founded in 1995, may indicate the importance of learning by incumbent WTO members involved in the negotiations, and how they view carryover applications from the GATT era.

Regression Results

Elapsed Time

The detailed results of the regressions are included in table 3.5 in the appendix and are summarized in this section. The first set of regressions uses *elapsed time* from application to final WTO accession as the dependent variable. It is difficult to establish a specific behavioral model of time-to-accession, because each case is subject to individual circumstances, and delays can arise from both sides of the negotiations. The linear regression model and the limited availability of common data for all counties may therefore suggest statistical correlations rather than a cause-and-effect relationship. With these caveats, the results provide support for the hypothesis that the accession negotiations have become longer as the total number of WTO accessions has increased, at least for the first 25 completed accession cases. The variable *Accessions* represents the accumulated number of WTO accessions that had been completed before the final Working Party report for a given applicant country was issued. Thus, for the first new WTO acceding member, Ecuador, this number was 0, and for the acceding member with the latest WP report in the sample, Ukraine, the number was 24.[18] The results indicate that for each additional WTO accession completed before this stage in an applicant's accession negotiations, the elapsed time from application to formal accession increased by approximately 3.3 to 4.4 months, other things being equal, with consistently strong statistical significance. The implication, based on the earlier discussion of asymmetrical negotiating strength and consolidationism, is that the Working Party has accumulated negotiating experience and has increasingly exercised its bargaining power for each case under review, leading to an increasingly lengthy accession process. It is also possible that incumbent bargaining power is enhanced by the network externality of WTO membership, a factor that would be consistent with these results. As more and more countries join the WTO, the cost of remaining outside the network increases for nonmembers, lending increasing bargaining power to existing members, which dictate terms of accession. Thus, increasing exploitation of bargaining power through learning is perhaps compounded by the inherent increase in bargaining power through the network externality as more countries join.

The variables for post-Marrakesh application and pre-WTO tariff levels exhibited somewhat statistically weaker results, but nonetheless had the expected signs. Filing an application after launch of the WTO on January 1, 1995 (WTO App) reduced elapsed time by 21 to 31 months, with 95%

significance in most of the regression variants in which it appears. The implication is that those "legacy" membership applications left incomplete when the GATT period ended may have been systematically more problematical.[19] Higher pre-WTO tariffs implied longer accessions, but the results were not consistent across the variants tested. The trade policy profile variable, AD Index (showing AD cases filed against the applicant in years prior to and during the negotiations), indicated an increase of nine to ten months for each unit increase in the index, suggesting that countries targeted by anti-dumping investigations will face longer negotiations.[20]

Among the economic profile variables, real GDP (RGDP) and the applicant's share in five key WTO import markets (CoreMktSh) were highly correlated with each other.[21] All had a positive coefficient and were in some cases significant at the 10% level or better. For example, an increase in an applicant's total import market share in the aggregated "core" WTO countries (United States, EU, Australia, Japan, Switzerland) by one percentage point increases the candidate country's elapsed time by 15 to 21.5 months as reported in three variants, suggesting that the greater the country's importance as an exporter, the longer the bargaining becomes. An applicant country's size and economic "footprint," based on these various measures, all suggest that larger countries take somewhat longer to negotiate accession.

In principle, the impact of an applicant country's bargaining power, based for example on its GDP or the size of its import market, appears at first to be ambiguous. Larger countries may be able to dictate better terms (and perhaps quicker accessions) than small countries, based on the supposed eagerness of incumbents to add a larger contributor to world trade to their ranks. However, a larger country that bargains harder could also lengthen the negotiations. In addition, small countries may agree more quickly to the incumbents' terms if their goal, for example, is to link in to the policy anchor of WTO membership. In the regressions, the economic profile variables all exhibit a positive impact on elapsed time. This suggests that either the applicant's additional bargaining power (if any) tends to lengthen the negotiations or the applicant's size increases the stakes for the incumbents and thereby encourages them to bargain harder to strike WTO entry terms favorable to them. Smaller countries may be insignificant enough to warrant quicker approval.[22]

WTO Rule Commitments

An important part of the negotiating agenda is the set of rule commitments that applicant countries agree to in their terms of accession, which is part of the "price of admission" to the WTO. As noted earlier, rule commitments vary in terms of their severity, and no attempt has been made to categorize or weight them in the regression data. The regression results for the number of rule commitments by an applicant confirm the informal observations of Evenett and Primo Braga (2005) that applicant concessions have increased as the number of accessions has increased. The accessions coefficient was positive and highly significant in most regression variants, indicating an increase in the number of rule commitments by 0.6 to 1.1 for each additional accession completed prior to an applicant country's working party report. Among the applicant status and trade policy profile variables, the results were weaker, with some unusual results. An increase by 1 in the AD index resulted in three to five additional rule commitments, with 10% or better statistical significance in four out of five variants. LDC status resulted in 10 to 14 fewer rule commitments, with 10% or better significance in the four variants tested. This result is consistent with the official WTO proclamation to facilitate LDC accession.

The economic and political profile variables, in contrast, showed much more significant results. A one percentage point increase in import market share among key WTO members increased the number of rule commitments by 12 to 14.5, for example. A particularly interesting result was that a one-unit increase in the government accountability index resulted in five to seven fewer rule commitments, with 10% or better significance in the four variants tested. The World Bank accountability index focuses on measures of political participation, transparency, and openness, such as freedom of the press. This result suggests that applicant countries exhibiting greater accountability may have been regarded as potentially less disruptive in terms of their trade practices, thereby requiring fewer constraining special rule commitments. Looking at it from a negative perspective, the lower the accountability rating, the more the incumbent WTO members may have thought it necessary to bind the new member with special constraining rules.[23]

Tariff Commitments

In these regressions, lower tariff bindings represent a tougher bargain for applicants and tighter WTO commitments. The results show consistently that additional WTO accessions by other countries tighten subsequent applicants' tariff bindings, with statistical significance at the 5% level or better. For nonagricultural tariff bindings, each additional accession lowers (tightens) the average bound tariff by approximately 0.4 percentage points; for agricultural tariff bindings, it tightens the tariff by 0.5 to 0.6 percentage points.

LDC status generally allows for less stringent tariff bindings. Final bound nonagricultural tariffs for LDCs were higher by 7 to 8 percentage points, with 5% or better statistical significance. For agricultural tariff bindings, the LDC effect was also strong statistically, raising them by 14 to 16 percentage points, with 1% statistical significance in most cases. One interesting result is that transition country status is most significant for nonagricultural tariff bindings, and actually *tightens* them by an additional 7 to 8.5 percentage points. The transition economy dummy coefficient for agricultural tariff bindings was also negative, but much less significant. There is informal evidence that several transition countries accepted lower, more stringent tariff bindings in manufactures as part of their strategy to adjust their economies and integrate more quickly into the world trading system (see Drabek and Bacchetta 2004). Along similar lines, the World Bank government effectiveness measure was highly significant in some regression variants, lowering the negotiated nonagricultural tariff by 5 percentage points, but was insignificant in explaining agricultural tariffs.[24] More effective and efficient governments tended to agree to tighter tariff bindings, perhaps again as part of an "anchor" strategy that welcomed WTO discipline. Higher overall pre-WTO applied tariffs, on the other hand, indicated somewhat higher final tariff bindings for nonagricultural goods, but not for agricultural goods.

Among economic profile variables, manufacturing imports per capita and real GDP per capita were statistically significant at the 5% level or better, but only in the nonagricultural tariff regressions. An increase in an applicant's annual per capita manufactures imports by $100 decreased the negotiated average nonagricultural tariff by about 0.1 percentage point, and an increase in real GDP per capita of $100 decreased this tariff by about 0.06 percentage points. An interpretation of this result that is consistent with WTO incumbent bargaining power would be that tariff negotiations were tougher on applicant countries with more manufactures imports and higher GDP per capita, since the market access stakes were higher for WTO incumbents.

Outstanding Accession Cases in 2009

In early 2009 there were 26 countries under review for WTO accession. Together these countries represented about 8% of the world's population, 2% of world GDP, and 3% of world trade. By far the largest was the Russian Federation, but there were other countries of significant population and/or GDP, such as Iran, Iraq, and Algeria. There were also very small applicants in this group, including Andorra, Bahamas, Bhutan, Samoa, São Tomé and Príncipe, Seychelles, and Vanuatu. Some had submitted applications for WTO membership shortly before this time, but others were still in the group of legacy applicants from the GATT, including the Russian Federation, Algeria, Belarus, Sudan, and Uzbekistan. As noted earlier, the average elapsed time since application to February 2009 for this group was over 121 months, already significantly longer than the average for the first 25 WTO members to join (101 months). Eleven countries were in transition from nonmarket to market economies, and nine had LDC status. Several were currently suffering from ongoing civil wars or insurgencies (Afghanistan, Iraq, Ethiopia, Sudan) and many others also exhibited questionable political stability.[25] Two appeared on the U.S. list of "countries of concern," formerly described as "rogue states" sponsoring terrorism (Sudan, Iran).[26] This group was therefore, on average, poorer, smaller, less stable, and less likely to receive full support from WTO incumbents than the sample of 25 new WTO members. Based on the foregoing analysis, one would expect that their WTO accession negotiations would be lengthy. As for the group of 17 nonmember, nonapplicant countries, it also contained several LDCs and several politically difficult cases, such as North Korea, Liberia, and Somalia. Most of the nonapplicant group did not even have observer status at the WTO, and so had not shown interest in joining.

These applicants were continuing their negotiations in uncertain and in many ways more pessimistic times. As noted in chapter 2, the Doha Round, launched so hopefully in October 2001, has suffered through a long and still inconclusive period of negotiations. Trade pessimism was rising in the United States and EU at this time, making these WTO members more likely to drive a hard bargain in accession negotiations, since they may have come to see these negotiations as an opportunity to wring concessions from new members that could not be won multilaterally in the Doha round. As for the applicants, while most were likely to see the "static" advantages of WTO membership, based on MFN treatment and protection of gains under dispute settlement, some may have come to question the ability of the WTO to deliver dynamic gains through progressive trade liberalization. For this reason, the WTO accession process should be subject to a thorough review, with an eye toward possible reforms.

Three Concerns, Three Proposals

The WTO system is required by its institutional mandate to strike a balance between openness to new members and discipline in maintaining adherence to its rules and norms. Thus, long accession negotiations can be defended as the necessary price for maintaining the integrity of the organization, as well as defending national economic interests. In addition, the comprehensive reforms in a country's administrative and policy-making practices that accompany a WTO accession negotiation typically have the salutary effect of establishing an integrated and coherent national trade strategy. It is also clear, however, that WTO accession negotiations have often led to "WTO-plus" requirements for new members. This is the inevitable result of a process that gives most of the bargaining power to incumbent members, with no formal guidelines on terms of accession. From the consolidationist point of view, one could argue that stricter entry requirements, even beyond the obligations of current members, serve to enhance the liberal trade order. Furthermore, some countries have apparently accepted WTO-plus terms as politically useful external anchors for internal reforms. Yet the WTO accession process as it has developed reveals three potentially serious concerns.

Opportunity Cost of Delayed Accession

The first problem is that delays in accession entail an opportunity cost of foregone trade and foregone participation in the WTO system. The longer countries remain outside the WTO system, the less the gains from trade for them and their (potential) trading partners. The counterargument is that shorter accession times imply less comprehensive compliance and more disputes, perhaps crippling trade relations and decreasing the gains from trade down the road. How might the accession process be shortened without undermining the integrity of the trading system? One possible remedy would be to partition WTO benefits and corresponding obligations with a program of graduated membership, more like the ideas of provisional membership and special protocols of accession under the previous GATT system. Countries could partially join the WTO with initial commitments to more liberal trade in goods, followed by concessions in TRIPS and other areas later on. Existing WTO members could similarly withhold WTO benefits in terms of adjusted tariff treatment, for example, with timetables for ramping up to full benefits that are commensurate with the applicant's schedule of increasing WTO compliance. The key to this approach lies in relaxing the accession principle of full compliance with existing WTO agreements, at least in terms of WTO accession.[27] It is true that partial membership would complicate WTO relations within the organization, but a reformed system could use strict timetables and quid pro quo concessions and benefits to promote it and encourage it as a transitional arrangement.

A simpler and more modest alternative would be to formally introduce special and differential (S&D) treatment into WTO accessions, especially for LDCs but perhaps on a graduated basis for more advanced developing countries as well. The WTO General Council did in fact issue a decision (WTO 2002) that "[n]egotiations for the accession of LDCs to the WTO be facilitated and accelerated through simplified and streamlined accession procedures," declaring that "WTO members shall exercise restraint in seeking concessions and commitments" and grant special and differential treatment in terms of transition periods for compliance."[28] Charnovitz (2007, p. 18) has noted, however, that the subsequent protocols of accession for two LDCs, Cambodia and Nepal, did not contain any indication that such S&D treatment was applied. The evidence from the regression study in this chapter suggests that the WPs applied milder requirements on LDC accessions informally, in terms of the number of rule commitments and the level of tariff bindings. A formal provision in accession rules and protocols that specifies S&D treatment and extends it to include transition periods would establish the desired framework for more flexibility and perhaps faster negotiations. However, implementing formal, specific S&D requirements is likely to be difficult, since WTO members would thereby be conceding significant bargaining power.[29]

The informal nature of WTO incumbent negotiating flexibility is also evident in certain aspects of China's protocol of accession, which included several transitional provisions. A large country with attractive market access prospects for incumbent WTO members may have enough leverage to negotiate more favorable terms, but in general, no applicant country can count on any negotiated easing of accession terms. To ease the general rules requiring comprehensive WTO obligations upon accession, more systematic WTO guidelines for the accession WP would be required, and as Lacey (2007) has noted, WTO members are unlikely to yield their powerful negotiating leverage. The problem is made more difficult because applicant countries themselves, due to the political difficulties of domestic reform and inefficiencies in governance, may also be responsible for delays in accession. Yet as a practical matter, in view of the list of remaining applicant and other nonmember countries, some additional flexibility in WTO accession requirements to most of the remaining and future applicants, based on an extension of the General Council decision discussed above (WTO 2002), would allow the admission of new members more quickly into the WTO system.

Financial and Technical Requirements for
Meeting WTO Obligations

The second objection relates to the resource capacity of many new and potential WTO members to adjust to the requirements of membership. Many WTO rule commitments require government expenditures and capacity building that may be costly to fulfill. Finger and Schuler (2000) documented the costly nature of certain Uruguay Round commitments, including TRIPS, customs valuation, trade facilitation, and sanitary/phytosanitary standards. In the absence of systematic aid and technical assistance, these requirements represent unfunded mandates that many poorer countries cannot afford, or that would divert scarce resources from more productive use in those countries. In poor countries, with undeveloped markets and institutions, the burden of adjustment can be great. The solution to this problem lies in building more coherence in WTO relations with the World Bank, IMF, regional development banks, and other international institutions and agencies, a topic that will be discussed in more detail in chapter 6. The WTO, along with several other international organizations, has in fact sponsored an "Integrated Framework" (IF) program for helping the LDCs, the poorest of the developing countries, to build the necessary institutional capacity and expertise to take part in the world trading system, including WTO accession.[30] However, these efforts have not appeared to reduce significantly the time-to-accession.[31] For other developing countries with income levels above the LDC category, IF aid is currently not available, although the World Bank has stepped up efforts to support WTO accession countries (Auboin 2007, p. 16). In the absence of IF assistance, trade negotiators from the rich countries do not come to the bargaining table with capacity-building budgets to sweeten the pot, and are not inherently qualified to negotiate the terms of their use (see Finger and Wilson 2007). Better coordination of financial compensation to offset the costs of WTO rule commitments and other access obligations for all (not just LDC) developing country and transition economy applicants could not only speed the accession process but also facilitate a more rapid integration into the WTO system. The key is that *temporary, transitional* subsidies could be used in this manner to secure *permanent* liberalizing measures and gains from trade.

Consequences of Lopsided Bargaining in Accessions

The third objection is largely political, but with potentially serious economic consequences. In the absence of guidelines on the terms of accession, the lopsided negotiations format, pitting the collective WTO incumbent membership against a single applicant, tends to be discriminatory in what it can demand from the acceding country. In response to this objection, it is reasonable to observe that stricter WTO-plus commitments and tariff bindings by applicants to levels below those of existing WTO members do in principle contribute to a more open trading system, and may even help those countries secure internal reform programs. Yet to the extent that the outcome is the result of power politics, the ends may not justify the means. In general, within the WTO consensus-based system, a certain amount of arm-twisting, threats, and bullying is bound to take place behind closed doors, and one must acknowledge such practices by the large countries as a fact of life in global trade relations.[32] Yet if the deck is stacked too heavily against the applicant countries, it will be difficult for many of them to achieve a sense of participation in the WTO as a trade forum. The risk is that heavy-handed treatment in accession talks may poison the well of future trade negotiations. One possible solution to this particular problem could begin with an understanding among incumbent WTO members restraining the use of WTO-plus demands, again along the lines of the 2002 General Council decision described earlier (WTO 2002). For example, the process could establish benchmarks for expected entry concessions on the part of the applicant, based on the obligations of current members of similar size and development status. In the absence of formal guidelines for the accession WPs, it would, however, be much more difficult to establish the practice of restraint, given the pattern of demands shown by existing members toward WTO applicants so far.

Conclusion

Many observers have complained about the length of WTO accession negotiations and about the increasingly demanding concessions that incumbent members have been extracting from new members. This chapter has provided some statistical confirmation of the patterns of elapsed time in the negotiations and of the terms of accession. The regression results show a link between cumulative accessions and increasing length of time until a country's accession is complete, suggesting that incumbent WTO members have learned to assert their bargaining power more and more in each new accession negotiation. The number of WTO rule commitments has increased for each new accession completed, and the final average bound tariffs in agriculture and in nonagricultural goods have been tightened for each successive acceding country. For LDCs, the preliminary result (based on the cases of Cambodia, Nepal, and Cape Verde) is that the accession negotiations are not significantly shorter, despite the intention of the Doha agenda to expedite the process, although their terms of accession have been somewhat less demanding. Still, the prospects for the group of 26 current WTO applicants are not encouraging. Many have already been negotiating longer than those countries that have acceded to the WTO, and many may face delays for various political reasons.

The WTO remains arguably the most successful international organization of its kind, bringing significant economic benefits to its members through a system of rules, a forum for dispute settlement, and a framework for further trade liberalization. It has indeed moved closer to universal membership, but many of the remaining accession cases are likely to be extremely difficult. The accession process has become excessively lengthy and burdensome for applicants, delaying the gains from trade and a more inclusive trading system, imposing heavy financial costs on new members, and potentially creating lingering resentment from the one-sided negotiations. WTO members could improve the accession process by introducing more flexibility in transition periods, improving the coordination of aid to fund mandated internal reforms, and limiting the demand for WTO-plus concessions from applicants. Some of these provisions are already in place, formally or informally, for LDC applicants, through the IF facility and the 2002 General Council decision on LDC accessions. A formal implementation of these reforms and their extension to applicants with incomes above the LDC level, perhaps on a graduated basis, could contribute significantly to achieving the goal of universal membership.

Carrying the logic of the goal of universal membership further, WTO members should seriously consider the potential benefits of bringing even the hardest-core pariah nations into the WTO, perhaps, at the beginning, with a form of entry-level membership, as described above. For example, from a political perspective it was indeed inconceivable to consider the entry of the People's Republic of China into the world trading system until the late 1980s. Most countries regarded its accession to the WTO in 2001 as an important milestone in integrating the country into the world economy and the community of nations, despite continued concerns with human rights and political repression. While the great potential of China in terms of trade and international investment probably tipped the balance in favor of its acceptance as a WTO member, it may still serve as an example of the ability of a "big tent" approach to promote more stable and peaceful political, as well as economic, relations. This principle has not been applied more broadly to outcast, troublemaking, and allegedly terrorist states, which might be induced to consider WTO membership with the promise of greater access to trade and investment, technical assistance, and potentially higher GDP growth. With an appropriate set of incentives, WTO membership negotiations could be part of a larger strategy to draw such countries into the community of nations. After all, the WTO is an institution committed to trade liberalization, a goal with political as well as economic benefits, and membership could be instrumental in changing a country's corresponding internal structures.

Yet this chapter has shown that WTO rules have imparted to its members superior bargaining power in accession negotiations, which they have learned to exploit, all the more so in response to the stalled Doha Round. They are unlikely to give up their superior bargaining power easily, but perhaps the best prospect would lie in an effort to revive the GATT-based approach of getting everyone inside the tent first through a broader application of S&D treatment in accessions, supported by redoubled efforts to revive multilateral trade liberalization. As a consensus-based organization, the WTO may in fact find it easier to promote multilateral trade liberalization in future years by easing up on the draconian accession process now, thereby promoting a more viable system of participation and "ownership" by its new members, and moving toward its stated goal of universal membership.

Appendix

TABLE 3.4 Independent variables and expected signs of coefficients

Accessions (+ elapsed time, rule commitments; - bound tariffs): The number of prior WTO accessions already completed when the current candidate's working party report is issued.

Accountability (? elapsed time): World Bank index based on the country's citizens' ability to participate in selecting their government, as well as freedom of expression, freedom of association, and a free media (measured on scale from −3 to +3).

ADIndex (+ rule commitments): Index of antidumping cases filed against the applicant country in five years prior to WTO application. Coded 0 = 0 cases; 1 = 1–3 cases; 2 = 4–10 cases; 3 = more than 10 cases

Ag%GDP (− bound ag tariff): Agricultural output as a percentage of GDP

AgEmpl (− bound ag tariff): Percentage of the workforce employed in agriculture

AgIm percap (− bound ag tariff): Annual agricultural imports per capita

CoreMktSh (+ elapsed time, rule commitments): Market share of applicant country's exports in the five WTO "core" accession-reviewing countries: United States, EU, Japan, Switzerland, and Australia. Expected sign is positive, as greater exporting activity indicates higher stakes of gaining WTO status and tougher bargaining by existing major WTO member countries.

GovtEffctv (? bound non-ag tariff): World Bank index of government effectiveness of the applicant country (measured on scale from −3 to +3).

LDC (? all regressions): dummy variable, showing 1 if country is officially listed by WTO as "least developed" and 0 if not.

MnfMpercap (− bound non-ag tariff): Real manufacturing imports per capita of acceding country.

Pre-Tariff (+ elapsed time): the level of the applicant country's average applied tariff just before application to join.

RGDP (+ elapsed time): real GDP of applicant country. Expected sign is positive, as the stakes for admitting economically larger countries are higher, and more valuable concessions are possible.

RGDPcap (– bound non-ag tariff): real GDP per capita of applicant country.

Transition (? bound tariffs): dummy variable, showing 1 if the country is a transition country (former communist/centrally planned economy), 0 otherwise.

WTOapp (– elapsed time; ? rule commitments): dummy variable showing 1 if the country originally applied after founding of the WTO in 1995, 0 if application predated 1995.

TABLE 3.5A Regression results: elapsed time to accession

	1	2	3	4	5	6	7
Intercept	39.48***	35.70***	46.92***	45.90***	53.33***	53.66***	43.94***
	(10.25)	(9.63)	(9.32)	(9.46)	(8.24)	(8.51)	(9.80)
Accessions	3.33***	3.42***	4.11***	4.07***	4.40***	4.31***	4.12***
	(0.70)	(0.70)	(0.65)	(0.66)	(0.62)	(0.71)	(0.69)
WTO App	−24.58**	−21.48*	−28.83**	−27.81**	−28.89**	−28.76**	−31.74**
	(11.53)	(11.18)	(10.65)	(11.01)	(10.87)	(11.13)	(11.24)
Pre-Tariff	1.38**	1.57***	0.81	0.93			1.35**
	(0.54)	(0.52)	(0.59)	(0.58)			(0.56)
LDC						4.54	
						(15.81)	
CoreMkSh			15.83*		21.02***	21.48**	
			(8.07)		(7.28)	(7.61)	
RGDP				0.05			
				(0.03)			
ADIndex	9.17*	10.05**					
	(4.44)	(4.38)					
Acctabilty	−8.09						
	(7.66)						
AdjR-sq	0.762	0.761	0.747	0.736	0.736	.724	0.712
SER	21.24	21.30	21.92	22.38	22.38	22.89	23.36

* Significance at 10% level, **5% level; ***1% level

Note: Dependent variable: elapsed time to accession. N = 25 (standard errors in parentheses).

Data sources: CIA Handbook; IMF listing of transition economies; United Nations, Comtrade database; World Bank Governance Index database; World Bank WDI database; WTO Web site, pages for Accessions, Antidumping, Developing Countries; WTO trade statistics page; WTO (2004). See bibliography, "Databases and Web Sites," for URL information.

TABLE 3.5B Regression results: rule commitments

	1	2	3	4	5
Intercept	18.22***	18.17***	17.99***	18.58***	17.22***
	(2.78)	(2.81)	(2.99)	(2.98)	(2.98)
Accessions	0.85***	0.90***	0.88***	0.60**	1.14***
	(0.27)	(0.27)	(0.29)	(0.23)	(0.28)

(continued)

TABLE 3.5B (continued)

	1	2	3	4	5
LDC	−9.96*	−11.00*	−10.77*		−14.11**
	(5.61)	(5.69)	(5.93)		(5.90)
ADIndex	3.85**	3.59*	3.76*	5.06***	2.85
	(1.74)	(1.80)	(2.00)	(1.74)	(1.90)
CoreMktSh		12.93***	12.91***	12.31***	14.52***
		(2.90)	(2.97)	(3.07)	(3.00)
RGDP	0.04***				
	(0.01)				
Accountability	−6.13**	−5.34*	−5.25*	−6.70**	
	(2.55)	(2.62)	(2.72)	(2.69)	
AdjR-sq	0.830	0.826	0.817	0.802	0.800
SER	7.23	7.31	7.50	7.78	7.86

* Significance at 10% level; **5% level; ***1% level

Note: Dependent variable: rule commitments. N = 25 (standard errors in parentheses)

Data sources: CIA Handbook; IMF listing of transition economies; United Nations, Comtrade database; World Bank Governance Index database; World Bank WDI database; WTO Web site, pages for Accessions, Anti-dumping, Developing Countries; WTO trade statistics page; WTO (2004). See bibliography, "Databases and Web Sites," for URL information.

TABLE 3.5C Regression results: non-agricultural tariff

	1	2	3	4	5
Intercept	19.76***	17.43***	21.82***	22.57***	19.89***
	(1.77)	(2.08)	(2.22)	(2.54)	(2.68)
Accessions	−0.39***	−0.36***	−0.39***	−0.38***	−0.35***
	(0.11)	(0.11)	(0.12)	(0.12)	(0.12)
Pre-Tariff		0.26**			0.22*
		(0.09)			(0.11)
LDC	8.33***		7.44**	6.97**	
	(2.56)		(2.89)	(3.10)	
Transition	−7.63***	−8.36***	−7.34***	−8.51***	−8.01***
	(1.68)	(1.73)	(1.85)	(2.17)	(2.10)
RGDPcap				-0.0006**	
				(0.0002)	
MnfMpercap		-0.001***			-0.001***
		(0.0004)			(0.0004)
GovEffctvnss	−5.09***	−5.14***			
	(1.35)	(1.42)			
AdjRsq	0.662	0.623	0.594	0.562	0.552
SER	3.671	3.85	4.02	4.18	4.22

* Significance at 10% level; **5% level; ***1% level

Note: Dependent variable: non-ag tariff. N = 25 (standard errors in parentheses)

Data sources: CIA Handbook; IMF listing of transition economies; United Nations, Comtrade database; World Bank Governance Index database; World Bank WDI database; WTO Web site, pages for Accessions, Anti-dumping, Developing Countries; WTO trade statistics page; WTO (2004). See bibliography, "Databases and Web Sites," for URL information.

TABLE 3.5D Regression results: agricultural tariff

	1	2	3	4
Intercept	30.41***	27.49***	30.53***	27.95***
	(4.11)	(3.32)	(4.22)	(3.65)
Accessions	−0.53**	−0.58**	−0.52**	−0.58**
	(0.21)	(0.21)	(0.21)	(0.21)
WTO App			-1.16	
			(3.46)	
LDC	13.92***	15.09***	13.90***	15.91**
	(4.88)	(4.02)	(4.99)	(5.48)
Transition	−6.95*	−5.04	−7.03*	−4.55
	(3.21)	(3.00)	(3.42)	(3.38)
Ag%GDP				−0.05
				(0.14)
AgIm percap	−0.02		−0.02	
	(0.01)		(0.01)	
AdjRsq	0.388	0.376	0.359	0.349
SER	6.92	6.98	7.08	7.14

* Significance at 10% level; **5% level; ***1% level

Note: Dependent variable: ag tariff. N = 25 (standard errors in parentheses)

Data sources: CIA Handbook; IMF listing of transition economies; United Nations, Comtrade database; World Bank Governance Index database; World Bank WDI database; WTO Web site, pages for Accessions, Anti-dumping, Developing Countries; WTO trade statistics page; WTO (2004). See bibliography, "Databases and Web Sites," for URL information.

4

The WTO Green Room, Coalitions, and the Problem of Representation

THE CENTRAL INSTITUTIONAL FEATURE OF WTO DECISION MAKING is that final agreement is based on *consensus,* and in such a large organization, attaining consensus is difficult. Managing the process of WTO deliberations has involved in the use of small-group "Green Room" meetings of representatives of select countries, a convention inherited from the GATT, designed to form the basis for consensus among the entire membership. Yet, as described in chapter 2, the process of WTO decision making has come under increasing stress in recent years, especially in the wake of high-profile breakdowns in negotiations at the Seattle and Cancún ministerial meetings, the subsequent suspension of the Doha Round in July 2006, and the failure to restart the negotiations at the ministerial level in 2007 and 2008. This chapter sets out to examine the possible role of the Green Room in this problem, and to investigate efforts and proposals to improve representation and decision making in the organization. The chapter begins with a description of the conceptual framework for understanding the political economy of Green Room decisions. After a brief discussion of the background of the Green Room system, it presents an account of the factors that have contributed to a progressive weakening of the ability of Green Room negotiations to form the basis for consensus. There follows a discussion of the use of coalitions to streamline the negotiating process and an assessment of one particular proposal to establish formally structured regional representation through a consultative board. The last section presents the author's proposal for introducing a system of coalitions and platforms within the Green Room structure and concludes with an outlook on future governance reform in the WTO.

The Meaning of Consensus and the Origins of the Green Room

In its reliance on consensus, the WTO is unlike other international institutions, especially those designed for a global membership. United Nations deliberations,[1] if they entail critical political or security issues, are always subject to the veto power of the Security Council. Among the WTO's "Bretton Woods" sister institutions, the International Monetary Fund (IMF) maintains an executive board and the World Bank has a board of executive directors, with decision making in both cases determined by a system of weighted voting by countries. The weights are determined by a country's GDP, current account transactions, and official reserves.[2] While in principle each WTO member has equal voting rights, in practice voting rarely takes place in the WTO. Article IX of the Agreement Establishing the World Trade Organization indicates that "the WTO shall continue the practice of decision-making by consensus followed under GATT 1947." Neither the GATT nor the WTO defines consensus explicitly. Kenworthy (2000) and Hoekman and Kostecki (2001) note that consensus is regarded in diplomatic practice as "the absence of dissent," which presumably represents agreement that is weaker than unanimity. The practice of Green Room–based decision making, as the following accounts will show, certainly indicates that "consensus" in the WTO typically represents a state of acceptance by all members to an agreement that is superior to any practical alternative. Members may not like the decision, but they are nonetheless willing to join the consensus if they believe it is the best outcome available to them. Finding the basis for consensus among the WTO membership is therefore the holy grail of any WTO multilateral deliberation, since no final agreement is possible without it. The critical question is whether the current system of informal consultations is the best way to achieve this goal.

Given the accomplishments of the GATT/WTO system over the years, including the completion of eight major multilateral rounds of trade negotiations since 1947,[3] it is perhaps surprising that a system of consensus-based decision making has been so successful. Leadership was important during this period, as the United States, alone at first and later together with the European Union, came to dominate the global trading system. However, they still had to work with other countries to achieve consensus on multilateral trade deals. The pattern established under the GATT, which continued until the Uruguay Round agreement, was that any multilateral trade agreement had to begin with the agreement of these two parties. Since the inception of the WTO in 1994, however, a U.S.-EU agreement alone has not been enough to provide the basis for a consensus among all WTO members, even though agreement between the two giants is still necessary before any negotiated WTO agreement can be achieved.

The WTO currently has 153 members,[4] and each one of them theoretically has veto power over any agreement. The path to negotiated agreements has often been slow and painful, marked by periodic stalemates, walkouts, and negotiating brinkmanship, features that have also characterized the Doha Round. The ability of the WTO membership to avoid the gridlock that such a method of decision making might generate is due in part to a system of trade negotiations that uses efficient bargaining procedures. For example, the first step is to establish a broad and inclusive approach to formulating the agenda, in order to accommodate as many countries' trade interests as possible. Following the principles of Most-Favored Nation treatment and reciprocity, individual negotiating groups then rely on "principal supplier" and "multilateral balancing" rules in moving from bilateral to multilateral bargaining in market opening discussions.[5] In order to move toward a final agreement, the WTO Director-General (D-G) will often employ an informal Green Room system of meetings at critical stages of the negotiating process, in which a small group of countries meets to bargain over particularly difficult or sensitive issues upon which progress in the negotiations depends. This practice began in the GATT system during the Tokyo Round (1973–79).

The WTO has continued the practice of Green Room deliberations. It is managed by the D-G, who calls meetings and determines who will be invited.[6] During Ministerial conferences, the Green Room meetings are often comanaged by the Conference chair, and on other occasions the Chairman of the WTO General Council presides.[7] Such meetings often occur in a crisis atmosphere. Participation in Green Rooms is by invitation from the D-G or chair only. The United States and European Union are by all accounts always present, and until the Doha Round were typically (but not always) joined by their "Quad" partners, Japan and Canada. Over the course of the Doha Round, the core group has included the United States, EU, and some combination of Brazil, Japan, India, and Australia. Depending on the issue and the scope of national interests involved, the D-G will also invite other developed and developing countries. Formal minutes are not taken and deliberations are officially off the record, although attempts have been made in recent years to communicate the substance of meetings to nonparticipants. These informal meetings are typically designed to make possible a frank discussion of issues within a group that is small enough to allow meaningful dialogue, but inclusive enough to assure that an emerging consensus can be taken to the larger WTO membership as the basis for an agreement. Thus, even though the Green Room meeting is an informal arrangement, the deliberations have a quasi-official character and are meant to provide a credible basis for approval by the general WTO membership. This model of decision making is based on the experience of many trade negotiators that once the number of active participants in a debate reaches 25–30, progress becomes increasingly difficult. Blackhurst (2001) describes this arrangement as a "concentric circles" model of decision making, in which the smaller group is needed to assure a practical process of negotiation on behalf of the larger group.

Yet in recent years it has been increasingly difficult for the Green Room meetings to form the basis for a viable consensus in the entire WTO membership. The tension in the Green Room process comes in part from the lack of transparency that is linked to its informal, off-the-record discussions. In addition, if participation is not sufficiently inclusive, there is a danger that critical deals may be concluded without meaningful input from other interested WTO members. If such a deal is struck, excluded members may have little opportunity to affect the rest of the negotiations, as they are faced with a "take it or leave it" package that may include few benefits for them. Even if the D-G has taken pains to be as inclusive as possible, the underlying constraint of limited participation may stir resentment among those who are not invited. This situation may arise especially in crisis situations that arise suddenly and involve crosscutting issues, in which it is difficult to identify (or impossible to include) all parties that have a strong stake in the discussion. Forming a consensus on broad multilateral trade issues became a major cause for concern after the spectacular failure of the Seattle Ministerial in 1999 to launch a new trade round. Despite the eventual launch of the Doha Trade Round in 2001, negotiations have bogged down, and in some cases broken down completely, as they did at the September 2003 Cancún Ministerial meeting. There is increasing concern that decision making within the WTO has become a prisoner to overpowering gridlock. Has this problem arisen despite the Green Room system, or because of it?

Conceptual Framework

The political structure of GATT/WTO decision making follows a hegemonic trade model, with the United States dominating from the inception of the GATT in 1947 throughout the 1960s but declining in relative importance since then. The United States and the European Union remain the two dominant players in the WTO, although this is a necessary but not sufficient basis for consensus. Despite the nominal reliance on broad-based consensus, bargaining power in the WTO is determined by a combination of population, wealth, and trade volume (particularly through high per capita GDP and the volume of imports it can support), since trade flows determine what Odell (2000) calls the "best alternative to negotiated agreement" (BATNA).[8] One measure of bargaining power in this regard is a country's share of world trade. Trade between the United States and the EU and their respective trading partners alone accounts for more than half of all world trade, and these countries are therefore in a position to negotiate bilateral agreements among themselves and with selected trading partners that affect a significant amount of world trade.[9] Using this measurement, it is possible to establish a rough ranking of bargaining power according to trade and GDP, with the EU and United States at the top, followed by Organization for Economic Cooperation (OECD) countries and the larger developing countries such as India, Brazil, and China, with the poorest developing countries at the bottom.[10] However, the distribution of bargaining power continues to evolve, with India and Brazil, along with China and some other developing countries, having rapidly increased their role in global trade, in part because of their own increasing role in international trade, in part because they have taken a leadership role in representing many of the smaller developing countries. Kindleberger (1981) emphasizes the importance of hegemonic leadership in creating stability for international economic systems, and this factor is relevant to WTO negotiations, whose progress typically follows initiatives by the large and powerful countries. At the same time, Cohn (2002) observes that hegemonic leadership does not always guarantee absolute progress toward trade liberalization, based on observations regarding textile, steel, and automobile trade protectionism, for example. To the extent that power-based bargaining determines the process of forming a consensus in the WTO, Steinberg (2002) has described the system as "organized hypocrisy." It is important to recognize, however, that the large countries, acting on their own, cannot completely control WTO negotiations, which offer benefits beyond those available under preferential trade agreements. Gains from multilateral trade in an organization with near-universal representation are thus still subject to the constraints of final agreement based on consensus (at least in the form of non-opposition) of the entire membership. As noted in chapter 1, mutual gains from trade provide the institutional foundation of the WTO and the primary motive for the WTO membership to persevere through long negotiations to reach an agreement.

Bagwell and Staiger (2002) have formalized and synthesized such a theory of trade negotiations in the GATT/WTO system, and Odell (2000) has provided a political framework for understanding international economic negotiations in general. The Bagwell/Staiger model sets out to analyze the logic of rules-based bargaining for market access, and allows all member countries to move from the lower welfare levels of unilateral tariff-setting, as represented by an uncooperative Nash equilibrium, to higher welfare levels of reciprocal tariff reductions. While the rules of the trading system tend to even out the differences in negotiated welfare gains between small and large countries, it is clear that the "zone of agreement" of possible negotiated outcomes leaves room for disproportionate sharing of the economic and/or political gains from trade.[11] Thus, both parties may indeed benefit from the negotiated tariff reduction, but the gains may not be shared equally. A small country would, according to welfare economic analysis, be willing to accept a lesser share of the gains as long as it represents a superior outcome to the next best alternative, such as the uncooperative Nash equilibrium tariff or the (presumably inferior) status quo. In considering the role of power-based bargaining, it is noteworthy that large countries theoretically have more advantageous bargaining alternatives (BATNA), such as separate bilateral or other preferential trade arrangements, which are not, however, superior to a system of multilateral cooperative tariffs.[12] These considerations shape the political economy of Green Room–based decision making.

In this context the Green Room talks enter the negotiating model as a potential way for larger and more powerful countries to maintain limited control over a sequential bargaining process. Hamilton and Whalley (1989) have identified three stages of multilateral negotiations: agenda setting, proposal development, and subsequent end-game bargaining. It is typically assumed in the bargaining model that countries seek a "political optimum" in their bargaining, in which government preferences may favor income distribution in favor of certain groups.[13] By controlling the agenda, at least in its later stages, and leaving other participants outside the Green Room with a "take it or leave it" decision, those in control of the process may be able to avoid the more difficult political sacrifices that a "balanced" agenda would otherwise impose on them. They may then move toward their politically optimal outcome, perhaps at the expense of weaker participants. Weaker countries, in turn, would then be expected to try to protect or enhance their interests in various ways, for example, by: 1) insinuating themselves into the Green Room as full participants; 2) forming an alliance with a Green Room participant that can effectively represent their interests; or 3) forming an effective alliance among other "outsiders" that can collectively increase their bargaining power vis-à-vis the Green Room. In forming an effective alliance, weaker countries may enhance their bargaining power by presenting a credible threat of defection from the overall, consensus-driven bargain. The drawback is that this strategy raises the stakes by putting all possible negotiated gains at risk.

It is important to recognize a number of specific Green Room factors in completing our understanding of the conceptual framework. First, the incentives for all WTO members, including those outside the Green Room, to agree to a trade liberalization agreement have apparently been extremely compelling, at least until recently. In addition to the immediate gains from trade liberalization, small as they may be for some participants, there are systemic gains from taking part in the WTO system (see Birdsall and Lawrence 1999). For smaller and weaker countries especially, the rules-based system offers protection for all previously won gains from trade, as well as any future gains from trade, through the dispute settlement process (Yarbrough and Yarbrough 1992). Nonparticipation in the negotiations by one country is likely to diminish its own welfare, not only for the present but also perhaps in the future. An explicit recognition of future benefits would formally require a present-value calculation of future net WTO benefits to participating countries. Nonparticipation by a larger number of countries, or by one or more of the large countries, could be even worse if it were to undermine the rules-based system itself. This is the downside risk of a coordinated boycott or walkout, which countries would have to weigh against the possible gains of forcing a renegotiation more favorable to them.

The second point is that the traditional bargaining model assumes straightforward tariff negotiations, and one of the critical complications of recent WTO negotiations is the increasingly wide range of disparate issues that countries must somehow balance in a negotiated "single undertaking" package. The uncertainty of economic gains and political costs from liberalizing non-tariff barriers, especially behind-the-border measures that may be very difficult to quantify, such as domestic subsidies and regulations, will tend to make the optimization problem more difficult to assess. McMillan (1988) notes that trade negotiations typically have multiple equilibria based on the large set of various liberalization measures that are welfare-improving, which will require a coordination of expectations (through leadership of some participants, for example) in order to generate a focal point and one particular equilibrium as an outcome. Bargaining is therefore

"path-dependent," in the sense that particular historical and political con-
texts, not to mention personalities of WTO officials and negotiators, may
play significant roles in the negotiating agenda and its outcome. More
importantly, this complication may reduce the efficiency of the Green
Room process in allowing the stronger countries to anticipate correctly the
negotiating resistance points of those countries outside the Green Room.
This process may be further complicated by the emergence of a new power
structure in the negotiations, in which a basic agreement among the leading countries may be difficult to establish. There have been increasing signs
of this sort of impasse in the Doha Round in the significant gaps between
the United States and European Union, on the one hand, and India and
Brazil, on the other, with regard to issues such as agricultural subsidies and
contingency protection for subsistence farmers.

To the extent that the Green Room system is important in allowing a
country's interests to influence the negotiations, it also sets up an insider-
outsider problem. Those who have access to the Green Room can presumably assert their own interests more readily and achieve a more favorable
outcome on the negotiating zone of agreement. If the seats at the Green
Room table are limited, then reforms that include new Green Room members may entail displacing current participants, so that a potential zero-sum
welfare trap is created. Overcoming the pitfalls of the zero-sum solution
would therefore require either a compensatory scheme for the losers or
other reforms (for example, some way of expanding Green Room participation) in order to avoid the veto of the displaced participants.

Finally, it is necessary to consider a contrarian position: that the Green
Room itself does not really matter in terms of allocating the gains from
negotiated outcomes. Some trade officials with Green Room experience,
for example, insist that powerful countries cannot control the negotiating agenda or outcome any more through the Green Room than they
otherwise do in the WTO system, since the D-G calls the meetings, sets
the meeting agenda, and invites the participants. Satisfaction among the
strong countries with Green Room processes and negotiating drafts that
arise from them is not guaranteed. In this view, the bargaining power and
representation of weaker countries in the WTO depends on their ability to
form effective coalitions rather than on their access to the Green Room.[14]
These observations stand in sharp contrast with many Third World cri-
tiques of WTO governance (Jawara and Kwa 2004, Sharma 2003), which
see the Green Room as a tool for rich country bullying and dominance
over poor countries. Since the Green Room represents an informal process
controlled by the D-G, these conflicting views suggest that its effectiveness

may depend at least in part on the personality, leadership, and competence of the D-G, as well as the D-G's ability (or lack thereof) to remain neutral in granting Green Room representation to different points of view. Dissatisfaction among some countries with the Green Room may also merely reflect more important underlying problems of WTO representation, such as the lack of adequate staff in many developing country delegations to attend multiple meetings and the lack of resources to adequately assess alternative negotiating positions and trade-offs.

Evolution of the Green Room Process

Historically, the dominance of the United States in the early years of the GATT led to decision making that relied principally on U.S. initiatives and on bilateral consultations between the United States and other GATT members or small groups of members. Green Room sessions were not needed to forge a consensus at that time. It was only later, as the European Union (founded in 1958 as the European Common Market) gained importance in world trade, the GATT membership expanded, and the complexity of issues increased, that the need for a more structured system of consultation developed. The earliest reported Green Room meetings took place during the Tokyo Round. They acquired their nickname from the green décor of the GATT D-G's meeting room in Geneva. Early Green Room meetings during the Tokyo Round tended to be small, with fewer than eight member countries represented, but since the Uruguay Round the meetings have generally included 25–30 or more countries (Cohn 2002, p. 16). The list of participating countries in the Green Room talks depends on the issue.[15] While developed country interests continue to be well represented in the Green Room, large developing countries, especially Brazil and India, have increasingly asserted strong bargaining positions as representatives of large groups of developing countries, such as the G20 group of developing countries at the Cancún Ministerial Meeting. At the same time, it is important to remember that one country can speak for others only on issues of strong common interest; neither the developed nor the developing world has a unified bargaining position on most WTO issues.

The evolution of the world trading system has made the informal and ad hoc nature of the Green Room process increasingly difficult to manage. One significant problem is that the membership has expanded greatly in recent years. The GATT began with 23 countries; the WTO now has 153 members and continues to grow. The increasing membership alone makes negotiations more and more unwieldy and a Green Room process less and less likely to capture all the critical differences among the members. Another difficulty with the Green Room bargaining process is that the scope of negotiation issues has also expanded. In the early years of the GATT, the focus of negotiations was the tariff, and broad bargaining schemes of tariff reductions were relatively easy to devise because they provided transparent, quantitative measures of liberalization.[16] Beginning with the Kennedy Round (1963–67), the trade agenda has turned increasingly to non-tariff and "behind the border" barriers to trade, which are much more difficult to negotiate. In the Uruguay Round (1986–94), the scope of negotiations expanded to include hitherto untouched areas in agriculture, intellectual property protection, and reform of the dispute settlement process, among other issues.[17] The proliferation of trade topics has complicated the negotiating process, as shown by the increasing amount of time over the years it has been taking to conclude each successive trade round.[18] The Green Room process has increasingly been called upon to resolve a wide range of complicated trade-offs that each WTO member must consider. Achieving a viable consensus within the Green Room that will also be acceptable to a much larger membership has correspondingly become more difficult.

Related to the problem of increasing complexity is the requirement that all WTO members in the final trade agreement must now accept a "single undertaking," the entire package of negotiated outcomes, with no partial opt-outs, a feature introduced in the Uruguay Round. Earlier negotiations in the Kennedy and Tokyo rounds had allowed à la carte treatment on some issues, making it much easier to partition the negotiations and forge a Green Room consensus on a more limited number of core topics. In contrast, the Green Room meetings now must deal with the implications of each element of a wide-ranging agenda debate and interim agreement for a final package. Cross-sector linkages, in which progress in one negotiating group may depend on progress in another, can further complicate the process of reaching final agreement.

Aside from the constraints of a single undertaking, the WTO's dispute settlement understanding (DSU) has further increased the stakes of the negotiations. The reformed DSU has made WTO dispute panel decisions virtually impossible to veto, in contrast with the earlier GATT system, which allowed any member to veto a decision. Thus, countries can no longer ignore a dispute settlement decision that goes against them, and must anticipate the possibility of future challenges to their national trade policies and practices in any negotiation. Combined with the other factors described above, the upshot for Green Room meetings is that it has become much more difficult to achieve the minimal terms of consensus for the entire WTO membership, now that vetoing a dispute settlement case has been effectively eliminated.

Green Room politics have also changed as a result of the evolving role of developing countries in the world trading system. In earlier, tariff-focused negotiations under the terms of Part IV of the GATT and "special and differential treatment" introduced in the Tokyo Round, developing countries were allowed to take a largely passive role, with no requirement for reciprocity in market-opening proposals. Ironically, this aspect of developing country participation in the GATT tended to marginalize their role in the negotiations, and later came to clash with the trend toward a broader trade agenda in which their interests were greatly affected. Whereas the stakes for developing countries in earlier Green Room tariff discussions were not particularly high, more recent trade talks include items with potentially high costs or benefits for them, including intellectual property protection, trade facilitation, textiles and apparel, and developed country agricultural subsidies, to name a few.[19] The arithmetic of Green Room representation also tells a story. Nearly all of the new members that have joined the GATT/WTO since the very early years have been developing countries, and now the vast majority of the WTO membership—approximately 75%—consists of either developing or transition economies. At the same time, the Green Room's capacity to accommodate the specific interests of the WTO's growing developing country membership has not increased. There is, in addition, a lingering sense of unfairness among some WTO members regarding the outcome of the Uruguay Round, which they regard as the result of Green Room manipulations by rich countries to ram proposals such as TRIPS down the throats of the poor countries while protecting their own interests in agricultural and textiles trade barriers (Jawara and Kwa 2004, pp. 44–46). As noted in chapter 2, this factor appears to have contributed to the difficulty of reaching consensus in the Doha Round. In the wake of increasing complexity in the negotiations and a growing sense of unfairness by some WTO members regarding the frequent lack of transparency and the exclusivity of the Green Room process, polarizing issues can quickly erode the political good will necessary to reach consensus among the WTO membership. Nongovernmental organization (NGO) advocacy groups are now closely watching WTO negotiations and often encouraging developing countries, already angered by Green Room governance, to take a hard line on particular issues. Under these circumstances, fruitful negotiations toward common ground become more elusive.

Dissatisfaction with the Green Room process increased in the early years of the WTO. Blackhurst and Hartridge (2004) report an illustrative example of the asymmetrical bargaining process that was already showing significant signs of stress:

> The December 1996 Singapore Ministerial Declaration was based on a draft prepared in Geneva containing agreed text on all but certain sensitive issues. In Singapore, an "inner circle" [Green Room] composed of ministers from thirty-four of the WTO's then 128 members took responsibility for arriving at agreed text on the remaining issues. At the late evening session devoted to getting a consensus on the draft declaration, most of the other 90 or so WTO members with delegations in Singapore took the floor in turn, each making virtually identical interventions consisting of three points: first they thanked the thirty-four members of the inner circle for their hard work; second that although they had some reservations on certain points, they could join the consensus in favor of the draft declaration; and third, that the way in which the draft declaration had been prepared was undemocratic, unfair and disgraceful, that they were no longer willing to accept a decision-making process that always presented them with *faits accomplis,* and that they attached the highest priority to fundamentally revising the way important decisions are arrived at in the WTO.

Smaller developing countries, in particular, have long railed against the Green Room process, and against other elements of WTO governance that allegedly diminish their ability to influence the course of trade negotiations. As the account of the Singapore Ministerial above points out, however, until recently, at least, the developing countries had been willing to accept the asymmetric bargaining model. Three types of problems might upset the model's sustainability, however: 1) the perceived lowering of expected net benefits by individual or groups of developing countries below the bargaining resistance points; 2) the formation of bargaining cartels by developing countries, especially with larger and more influential countries, that could hold hostage important trade benefits to the dominant countries; and 3) polarizing situations or issues that undermine the credibility of the Green Room system and motivate a slowdown or stalling of the negotiations. The relevant WTO governance issue thus becomes this: at what point would the smaller WTO members credibly refuse to accept a Green Room bargain made in their absence?

Steinberg (2002) describes WTO consensus-based decision making as a bifurcated process. "Law-based" bargaining is based on procedural rules and prevails at the early stages of a negotiation in order to provide a broad basis of welfare-enhancing negotiating issues for the widest possible membership. Thus, the beginning agenda for trade negotiations tends to be wide-ranging and ambitious. Any measures to prevent the inclusion of issues deemed important by significant WTO member countries (or groups of countries) would threaten the launch of the trade round. Steinberg contrasts this accommodating approach to consensus building in the early stages with the asymmetrical "power-based" bargaining that tends to prevail in the latter stages of the negotiations, when the large trading powers assert their leverage to conclude the negotiations on terms favorable to themselves. However, power-based bargaining may also take place at early stages if the agenda itself is the subject of controversy, as it was at the Doha and Cancún ministerial meetings.

As noted in chapter 2, it was the Green Room crisis at the Seattle Ministerial in 1999 that became a watershed for Green Room criticism. Poor preparation had resulted in a failure to agree on the agenda for a new trade round, and in last-minute desperation, U.S. Trade Representative Charlene Barshevsky resorted to what seemed to be the only method left to forge a face-saving communiqué: a Green Room meeting among the Quad and a select group of countries. The Green Room negotiations themselves failed to forge an agreement, and even if it had, there was a strong likelihood that the rest of the membership would have rejected it. Perhaps more important was the perception among WTO delegates from many developing countries that they had been openly neglected and marginalized in the attempt to forge a "WTO consensus" in their absence.[20]

The growing strains on WTO decision making, as noted above, have created a difficult bargaining environment in the Doha Round. Odell (2001) noted that WTO decision making had deadlocked on most significant multilateral trade issues since the end of the Uruguay Round in 1994. While WTO members did successfully launch the Doha Round in November 2001, it was under considerable pressure to redress the failure of the 1999 Seattle Ministerial and to provide a united front in support of global trade in the wake of the September 11 terrorist attacks in the United States. The Doha meeting was indeed saved at the last minute by behind-the-scenes bargaining by the EU and the United States with India (with considerable obfuscation of the resulting agenda). The exceptional circumstances of the Doha Ministerial could not, however, prevent the subsequent failure of the subsequent Cancún Ministerial, in which a backlash against Green Room procedures by developing countries played a significant role. The Quad countries had made preparations for Cancún in the traditional manner, through a series of Green Room, "mini-lateral" and bilateral meetings, which had also included larger developing countries such as India and Brazil. There were, however, numerous issues of contention that remained as the Cancún meeting began, including a number of divisive issues that had been papered over in the Doha Declaration. The EU and the United States, in particular, attempted to use Green Room bargaining to emphasize certain agenda items of special interest to them, while minimizing progress on issues that were politically sensitive to them at home. Now that serious negotiations had begun, countries were applying their own interpretation of the Doha text regarding concrete negotiating commitments, and these interpretations diverged significantly. The Green Room process had therefore not achieved internal consensus even among its participants, but many countries had hoped that differences could be addressed and overcome in the Cancún Ministerial meeting. Many developing countries were expressing growing disillusionment with the Doha agenda, and many joined together to form the G20 alliance, including large countries such as China, India, Brazil, and Indonesia.[21] They came to the meeting demanding more concessions from the Quad countries on farm trade. A small group of African countries demanded reductions in U.S. cotton subsidies. On these and other agricultural issues, the United States in particular was taking a hard position, and the EU, for its part, insisted until very late in the Cancún meeting on including the Singapore issues, which many developing countries adamantly refused to consider. An interim Cancún text reflected Quad intransigence on these issues. As the meeting proceeded, many participants hardened their positions, and as the political will for compromise failed to materialize, the meeting collapsed. While there were many contributing factors that led to the failure of the Cancún Ministerial, it appeared that Green Room procedures, at least in the traditional "one country, one voice" format, had become ineffective as a process of identifying and achieving compromise on the many critical negotiating "resistance points" among various participants. Subsequent efforts to reignite the Doha negotiations in Geneva (July 2004) and at the Hong Kong Ministerial (December 2005) could not prevent a suspension of the negotiations in July 2006, followed by yet more failures to revive the talks in June 2007 and July and December 2008.

Representation through Coalitions

The "large group" problem of representation in the WTO has sparked interest in the use of coalitions to streamline the negotiating process, spurred on by the apparent success of developing countries in forming coalitions for purposes of joint bargaining, especially at the Cancún Ministerial Meeting.[22] A coalition in the WTO may form if its value in terms of the joint trade negotiations payoff for its members is potentially greater than the sum of payoffs for each potential coalition member acting separately, assuming that transfers are possible to compensate individual losers with proceeds from the coalitional strategy. Payoffs are measured in terms of additional market access (in the form of increased export volume), the minimization of import concessions,[23] and/or the avoidance of implementation costs imposed by trade agreements (Finger and Schuler 2000, Finger 2005a). Using the terminology of Rivera-Batiz and Oliva (2003), we can define the characteristic function as the expected total payoff for all participating countries in a trade negotiation, to be divided in some manner among the players. Potential coalition partners will attempt to determine if the total expected joint value of the coalition's bargaining strategy is greater than the sum of individual values of the *non*-coalitional game. The incentive for a group of WTO member countries to form a coalition therefore rests on a "power transformation" scenario in game theory (see Selten 1987). The power of the coalition is that it enhances the joint payoff made possible by coordinated action while also allowing for an acceptable distribution of the economic gains from the coalition among the members.

Coalitions in the WTO can take various forms (Narlikar 2003, chaps 1–2), and the distinctions are important in understanding how they affect the issue of representation in WTO decision making. Many coalitions form around particular trade issues, such as agriculture and services. Costantini et al. (2007) take up this issue by focusing on the economic structure of countries that exhibited similar bargaining preferences in agricultural trade negotiations. Using cluster analysis, these authors identified "natural bargaining coalitions" in agricultural negotiations that matched up well with many of the actual coalitions that emerged in the Doha Round. In this case, representation is focused narrowly on a single (albeit important) issue. When a coalition forms along a single dimension, joint representation will be similarly circumscribed. Such coalitions generally reflect what Drahos (2003) calls "exchange trust," a calculation of net benefits of the coalition based on a focused negotiating objective, as represented in the game theoretical framework described above. The Cairns Group, for example, is a coalition of countries that have agreed to adopt joint or similar positions on a particular range of WTO agricultural issues, so that a single view within the group is likely to prevail only on these issues.[24] It is much more difficult to identify a set of stable partners in joint representation across a broader set of negotiating issues within the WTO. For example, a regional or ideological coalition typically requires both exchange trust and a broader basis of "social identity trust" (Drahos 2003), which comes from common values, culture, history, economic/legal/political structures, and experience, a situation that has apparently been absent from most attempts at such coalitions in the GATT/WTO system (Narlikar 2003, chap. 7).

Achieving the requisite level of trust to maintain a coalition and provide for joint representation is also difficult because of the uncertain nature of bargaining processes and outcomes. WTO members must negotiate on the basis of *bounded rationality*; that is, they intend to maximize utility, but their decisions are subject to limited information and computational capacity.[25] Uncertainties often apply not only to the future "state of nature" in the trading environment but also to the reliability and true interests of their potential coalition partners. Thus it is difficult to calculate payoffs in advance, especially for small and poor countries without the resources needed to process the available information. Coalition partners may not be able to anticipate the nature and magnitude of transfers needed to complete the coalitional deal, based on the "reservation values" of each others' positions, and there must be a foundation of trust among them, bringing specific negotiators' personalities into the equation. In the absence of trust, there will always be suspicions that a partner will defect, lured away perhaps by a side deal with a more powerful player outside the coalition. One possible way to overcome some of these problems would be to improve the quality and availability of information and trade analysis, especially for developing countries.

Regional Representation and the "Consultative Board" Proposal

In practical terms, the WTO problem of representation lies in finding some straightforward way to accommodate the interests of all members in the organization, a goal that has led to a growing interest in a formal structure of *regional* representation. The critical question is whether regional coalitions can effectively provide joint representation for their members through a bargaining agent that acts on behalf of constituent principals. The EU now represents 27 member countries as the single voice of that group in all WTO negotiations. This is because the extent of integration among EU countries allows internal transfers and a unified decision-making structure for trade policy.[26] For all other WTO members, each sovereign country's trade-related welfare is exposed and "on the table" in a multilateral trade negotiation, and therefore each country has to be careful to monitor closely the costs and benefits of the bargaining outcomes. Allowing a coalition partner to represent one's own economic interests in this context requires a significant level of confidence in the principal-agent relationship, since it is very difficult to collect compensation in cases of defection or incompetence. At a Green Room meeting, for example, a country holding another country's voting proxy would not only have to present the interests of that country, but would also have to advocate and bargain actively on its behalf. For this reason, many WTO countries are wary of a system of Green Room representation by proxy, since common interests do not necessarily establish the basis for joint representation. At a minimum, a formal representation structure for the entire WTO membership through a smaller body would require a close correspondence of trade interests between the proxy-holding country and its constituents.

There is a certain irony in proposals to use regional economic interests as a framework for coalition bargaining in the WTO. The *Future of the WTO* report (Sutherland et al. 2005, chap. 2), for example, strongly criticizes preferential trade agreements (PTAs) because of their discriminatory nature.[27] If WTO members decided, on the other hand, to encourage more regional trade integration to encourage coalitions and bargaining efficiency, then the proliferation of PTAs could undermine the central MFN principle of the WTO. It is important to note that regional WTO representation would not necessarily lead to a proliferation of discriminatory trading blocs, and none of the proposals under consideration in this study has proposed such an arrangement. However, closer integration, including PTAs, would in many cases be consistent with a coalition strategy to internalize cross-partner transfers. For example, countries A and B may agree to form a coalition and support each other's WTO market access agenda in conjunction with reciprocal and preferential market access among themselves. Tighter control over the use and discriminatory effects of PTAs—or else greater acceptance of such arrangements—may therefore be required in order to facilitate formal regional representation in the WTO.

The tension between the GATT/WTO system's nondiscriminatory principle and the proliferation of PTAs since the early 1990s has sparked renewed interest in the study of economic integration and its consequences for trade negotiations. While traditional trade theory has focused on such arrangements as "second-best" policy choices with regard to trade liberalization, Fratianni and Pattison (2001) highlight the advantages of smaller-group "clubs" within a larger organization such as the WTO in terms of bargaining toward consensus. Herrmann-Pillath (2006) presents an institutional model of regionalism in which countries gravitate naturally toward PTAs with each other based on social networks, economic structure, and stable market access expectations. Given the strong tendency toward PTAs, the question for WTO governance is how such country-to-country relationships could be harnessed to simplify the problem of representation in multilateral negotiations. During the Doha Round, interest grew in developing a comprehensive system of formal representation in a smaller executive committee that could hold small-group meetings or act as a steering group for the WTO as a whole. Sutherland et al. (2005) proposed such a committee of WTO members based on regional representation. Schott and Watal (2002) have proposed in a more detailed manner a revised Green Room arrangement based on the executive board model of the IMF and World Bank. Blackhurst (2001) has proposed a similar "inner circle" model. The executive board model has received support among senior WTO officials and some major countries.[28] It would retain the basic negotiating purpose of the Green Room and would formalize the guaranteed representation of all regions of WTO membership.

The proposal by Schott and Watal (2000) includes a system of regional groupings for a WTO consultative board with 20 seats, some for individual countries and the EU, the others rotating seats for regional constituencies. Representation on the board would be based on a country's relative weight in world trade volume, but in addition, there would be guaranteed seats for each geographical region of the WTO world membership, with some form of rotating participation among each group. The purpose would be to assure the widest possible representation of WTO members in the deliberations, with improved transparency and a continued requirement for consensus among the entire WTO membership for major decisions or negotiations. The following presentation sets out to examine whether regional coalitions in the WTO are possible, based on similar trade patterns, trade-to-GDP ratios, GDP per capita, and trade policy structure. While there may be cultural, linguistic, or other similarities among the countries within the regions, the data do not take these factors specifically into account. Table 4.1 presents one possible regional representation plan described by Schott and Watal, with some modifications based on the expansion of the EU and of WTO membership since it was first proposed and the insertion of most other WTO members into the proposed regional groupings. In their original presentation, Schott and Watal qualify this configuration as but one of many possibilities, but the general rule would be that the groupings must combine a significant share of world trade with regional representation. Smaller countries would have an incentive to join the strongest possible regional association, while most of the largest countries would still retain separate seats, as they do in the current Green Room system.

In the configuration shown in table 4.1, the United States, Japan, Canada, Republic of Korea, Mexico, Israel, South Africa, Taipei (Taiwan), and the EU all qualify for separate seats. The rest of the seats represent new regional groupings: China/Hong Kong, ASEAN, EFTA, Australia/ New Zealand, the transition (former Communist) economies not aligned with the EU, North Africa and the Middle East, the South Asian subcontinent, Mercosur, the Andean Community, two separate African groups, and the CACM/Caricom region.[29] Table 4.1 gives a brief economic and trade profile of the members of each group, including GDP per capita, an "openness" ratio of trade (imports plus exports) to GDP, and a series of seven revealed comparative advantage (RCA) indexes for goods categories. For each regional group, the mean and standard deviation of these measures has been calculated, in order to capture the dispersion of these measures among members in the group.[30]

There are some loose pieces of the global puzzle to deal with in this particular configuration of regional representation. Many smaller countries have been inserted into the groupings by virtue of their location, but they may be outside the primary regional association. This is the case for smaller Asian countries in the ASEAN group and for the Dominican Republic in CACM/Caricom. Large countries, such as India, are included in the same group along with much smaller countries, such as the Maldives, even though large disparities in size could complicate regional representation. A large country like India may be happy to represent its broader constituent region—on its own terms—but would be unlikely to allow other countries to represent it in a WTO forum, and would probably demand its own seat. Chile is another example of problematic fit; table 4.1 places it with the Andean Community, based on its location and on the difficulty of placing it elsewhere. Other countries would have a hard time fitting in with any regional grouping, such as Cuba, and its WTO activities have focused on issue-based alliances with other developing countries, such as the Like Minded Group.[31] Other groupings have less of a regional character, such as EFTA-plus-Turkey and the transition economies, but in the end it is virtually impossible to group the entire WTO membership along regional lines.

If such a system were to function at all, however, each group would need to show an alignment of interests in trade matters and the political will to work together with its partner countries. Looking at the EU countries in table 4.1 as a point of reference, it is clear that a customs union

TABLE 4.1 GDP per capita, trade openness and RCA calculations for proposed WTO regional groupings[a]

Country	GDP/ cap[b]	Trade/ gdp%	RCA calculations[c]						
			Ag	Fuel/ min	Iron/Stl	Chem	Mchn	Txtl	Clthg
1 United States	35566	19	1.18	0.31	0.39	1.20	1.27	0.67	0.26
2 Japan	38222	20	0.11	0.13	1.58	0.79	1.74	0.61	0.04
3 Canada	24222	60	1.38	1.61	0.52	0.60	0.93	0.37	0.24
4 Korea, Republic of	12232	62	0.24	0.37	1.54	0.83	1.71	2.33	0.62
5 Mexico	5792	55	0.68	0.98	0.49	0.34	1.49	0.57	1.48
6 Israel	17298	62	0.64	0.13	0.09	1.38	0.70	0.86	0.51
7 South Africa	3026	49	0.99	1.92	4.31	0.61	0.46	0.36	0.28
8 Taipei, China (Taiwan)	23400	N/A	0.28	0.27	1.62	0.77	1.46	2.76	0.47
9 European Union									
Austria	24217	77	0.93	0.38	1.75	0.94	1.14	0.98	0.56
Belgium	22544	172	1.13	0.59	1.64	2.69	0.62	1.21	0.70
Bulgaria	1835	93	1.40	1.26	3.07	0.72	0.34	1.44	6.65
Cyprus	12647	47	3.27	1.00	0.04	1.08	0.79	1.03	0.96
Czech Republic	5866	111	0.60	0.36	1.64	0.56	1.31	1.51	0.50
Denmark	30262	59	2.51	0.65	0.49	1.53	0.72	0.75	1.11
Estonia	4841	149	2.18	0.52	1.04	0.60	0.77	1.75	1.67
Finland	24225	59	0.91	0.53	2.30	0.58	1.11	0.34	0.15
France	22723	44	1.31	0.31	1.24	1.44	1.17	0.80	0.59
Germany	22868	56	0.55	0.25	0.94	1.10	1.34	0.71	0.43
Greece	11449	33	2.71	1.20	1.12	1.16	0.33	2.01	4.20
Hungary	5103	109	0.89	0.26	0.44	0.63	1.59	0.56	1.12
Ireland	27932	95	0.99	0.10	0.03	4.31	0.74	0.18	0.13
Italy	19090	40	0.82	0.27	1.18	0.97	0.95	2.02	1.81
Latvia	4116	73	4.02	0.42	2.74	0.58	0.24	2.40	2.80
Lithuania	4078	94	1.76	1.63	0.24	0.71	0.68	1.77	3.05
Luxembourg	46067	N/A	0.76	0.27	6.12	0.43	1.14	1.51	0.31
Netherlands	22973	109	2.13	0.90	0.69	1.28	0.85	0.47	0.42
Poland	4634	58	1.04	0.63	1.04	0.60	0.97	0.94	1.29
Portugal	10284	52	1.10	0.31	0.55	0.51	0.93	2.54	3.40
Romania	1963	73	0.71	0.85	3.07	0.45	0.56	1.12	7.71
Slovak Republic	4235	137	0.52	0.59	3.31	0.49	1.22	0.96	1.07
Slovenia	10411	96	0.53	0.40	1.27	1.29	0.95	1.36	0.90
Spain	14691	42	1.83	0.42	1.17	1.00	1.07	1.02	0.71
Sweden	27998	61	0.87	0.43	1.95	1.29	1.10	0.41	0.27
United Kingdom	25742	39	0.74	0.83	0.74	1.62	1.10	0.70	0.48
Mean	*17843*	*56*	*1.39*	*0.59*	*1.53*	*1.10*	*0.91*	*1.17*	*1.65*
Std Dev.	*11330*	*37*	*0.91*	*0.37*	*1.32*	*0.82*	*0.33*	*0.63*	*1.95*

(Insufficient data for Malta)

10	China Group									
	China	1067	60	0.57	0.32	0.46	0.42	1.12	2.73	3.97
	Hong Kong, China	25633	295	0.23	0.11	0.40	0.45	1.20	2.55	3.38
	Macao, China	N/A	N/A	0.25	0.13	0.01	0.10	0.13	5.23	23.73
	Mean	*1200*	*84*	*0.35*	*0.19*	*0.29*	*0.32*	*0.81*	*3.50*	*10.36*
	Std Dev.	*17370*	*166*	*0.19*	*0.12*	*0.24*	*0.20*	*0.60*	*1.50*	*11.58*
11	ASEAN–Plus									
	Brunei Daruss	N/A	N/A	0.01	6.90	0.05	0.01	0.14	0.03	1.76
	Cambodia	313	81	0.00	0.00	0.00	0.00	0.00	0.00	26.12
	Fiji	2328	82	4.21	0.02	0.14	0.10	0.01	0.39	6.50
	Indonesia	781	45	1.82	2.47	0.36	0.53	0.42	2.13	2.25
	Malaysia	4011	175	1.18	0.83	0.48	0.49	1.48	0.43	0.65
	Papua N. Guinea	645	109	2.55	5.44	0.02	0.01	0.08	0.00	0.00
	Philippines	1047	94	0.67	0.24	0.02	0.11	1.14	0.33	2.43
	Singapore	21941	298	0.25	0.75	0.18	1.11	1.59	0.22	0.41
	Thailand	2276	109	2.10	0.29	0.54	0.62	1.14	1.20	1.50
	Viet Nam	470	115	N/A	N/A	N/A	N/A	N/A	N/A	5.88
	Mean	*1297*	*128*	*1.42*	*1.88*	*0.20*	*0.33*	*0.67*	*0.53*	*4.75*
	Std Dev.	*6924*	*74*	*1.40*	*2.57*	*0.21*	*0.38*	*0.66*	*0.71*	*7.82*
	(Insufficient data for Solomon Islands)									
12	EFTA–Plus									
	Iceland	30952	49	7.19	1.51	1.37	0.34	0.10	0.27	0.03
	Norway	40482	48	0.74	5.30	0.51	0.53	0.29	0.12	0.04
	Switzerland	33765	61	0.34	0.27	0.43	3.22	0.69	0.65	0.36
	Turkey	2977	48	1.20	0.31	2.89	0.35	0.68	4.94	7.02
	Mean	*7869*	*53*	*2.37*	*1.85*	*1.30*	*1.11*	*0.44*	*1.50*	*1.86*
	Std Dev.	*16535*	*6*	*3.24*	*2.37*	*1.14*	*1.41*	*0.29*	*2.31*	*3.44*
	(Insufficient data for Liechtenstein)									
13	Australia–NZ									
	Australia	21688	31	2.56	2.96	0.34	0.45	0.30	0.19	0.10
	New Zealand	19243	44	6.51	0.38	0.43	0.58	0.29	0.59	0.34
	Mean	*21236*	*32*	*4.54*	*1.67*	*0.38*	*0.52*	*0.29*	*0.39*	*0.22*
	Std Dev.	*1729*	*9*	*2.80*	*1.82*	*0.06*	*0.09*	*0.01*	*0.28*	*0.17*
14	Transition Economies									
	Albania	1392	38	1.19	0.40	1.69	0.05	0.09	0.15	11.31
	Armenia	884	69	1.39	1.20	0.93	0.04	0.09	0.51	1.11
	Croatia	4751	70	1.83	0.93	0.37	0.91	0.76	0.80	3.21
	Georgia	729	38	4.23	2.35	2.68	0.59	0.34	0.03	0.22
	Kyrgyz Republic	305	68	2.06	1.15	0.05	0.12	0.19	0.73	0.85
	Moldova	370	112	7.08	0.26	0.45	0.12	0.14	0.60	5.01
	Mongolia	424	102	1.40	2.80	0.24	0.01	0.02	0.24	6.31
	Russian Federation[d]	2138	48	0.77	5.01	2.53	0.64	0.26	0.18	0.08
	Ukraine	812	112	1.49	1.44	13.9	0.80	0.37	0.39	0.80
	Mean	*1312*	*73*	*2.38*	*1.73*	*2.54*	*0.36*	*0.25*	*0.40*	*3.21*

(continued)

TABLE 4.1 (continued)

Country	GDP/ cap[b]	Trade/ gdp%	Ag	Fuel/ min	Iron/Stl	Chem	Mchn	Txtl	Clthg
					RCA calculations[c]				

Country	GDP/ cap[b]	Trade/ gdp%	Ag	Fuel/ min	Iron/Stl	Chem	Mchn	Txtl	Clthg
15 North Africa/Middle East									
Bahrain	N/A	..	0.11	6.61	0.05	0.28	0.06	0.52	1.04
Egypt	1622	21	1.72	3.63	2.54	0.71	0.02	2.01	1.26
Morocco	1278	52	2.60	0.76	0.20	1.05	0.38	0.66	10.83
Oman	..	..	0.54	5.31	0.29	0.10	0.21	0.35	0.32
Std Dev.	*474*	*28*	*0.99*	*2.65*	*1.06*	*0.40*	*0.18*	*0.71*	*5.60*
			(Insufficient data for: Jordan, Kuwait, Qatar,						
			United Arab Emirates)						
16 South Asia									
Bangladesh	395	32	0.75	0.04	0.05	0.02	0.01	3.22	20.67
India	511	21	1.56	0.88	2.09	1.22	0.28	5.34	3.88
Maldives	2548	82	5.63	0.02	0.00	0.00	0.00	0.00	7.94
Pakistan	546	30	1.38	0.20	0.08	0.22	0.03	21.70	7.59
Sri Lanka	921	65	2.51	0.09	0.01	0.07	0.14	1.79	17.49
Mean	*510*	*24*	*2.37*	*0.24*	*0.45*	*0.31*	*0.09*	*6.41*	*11.51*
Std Dev.	*896*	*26*	*1.93*	*0.36*	*0.92*	*0.52*	*0.12*	*8.77*	*7.18*
			(Insufficient data for: Myanmar, Nepal)						
17 Mercosur									
Argentina	7165	33	5.25	1.63	1.70	0.73	0.27	0.33	0.07
Brazil	3510	25	3.71	1.08	2.84	0.57	0.61	0.68	0.14
Paraguay	1407	56	9.61	0.03	0.31	0.30	0.01	0.47	0.37
Uruguay	5235	39	7.14	0.17	0.31	0.53	0.07	1.06	0.91
Mean	*4080*	*28*	*6.43*	*0.73*	*1.29*	*0.53*	*0.24*	*0.64*	*0.37*
Std Dev.	*2454*	*13*	*2.55*	*0.76*	*1.22*	*0.18*	*0.27*	*0.32*	*0.38*
18 Andean Community									
Bolivia	1017	41	3.71	3.95	0.01	0.12	0.11	0.20	0.91
Chile	5196	56	3.97	3.24	0.19	0.61	0.05	0.18	0.05
Colombia	2017	34	2.65	3.10	1.70	0.91	0.09	0.80	1.68
Ecuador	1368	46	5.19	3.41	0.07	0.18	0.08	0.31	0.16
Peru	2131	29	2.51	2.94	0.16	0.25	0.02	0.59	2.43
Venezuela	4009	39	0.14	6.30	1.80	0.31	0.07	0.03	0.01
Mean	*2663*	*40*	*3.03*	*3.82*	*0.66*	*0.40*	*0.07*	*0.35*	*0.87*
Std Dev.	*1631*	*10*	*1.72*	*1.26*	*0.85*	*0.30*	*0.03*	*0.29*	*1.00*
19 Africa 1									
Kenya	341	43	6.00	1.75	1.02	0.46	0.08	0.54	0.10
Malawi	157	68	9.82	0.01	0.01	0.09	0.02	0.19	2.49
Namibia	1845	76	5.58	0.65	0.25	0.09	0.23	0.25	0.06
Tanzania	309	33	5.07	0.57	0.24	0.12	0.04	0.74	0.14
Uganda	277	29	2.78	0.01	0.20	0.06	0.02	0.03	0.05
Mean	*319*	*42*	*5.85*	*0.60*	*0.35*	*0.16*	*0.08*	*0.35*	*0.57*
Std Dev.	*707*	*21*	*2.54*	*0.71*	*0.39*	*0.17*	*0.09*	*0.29*	*1.07*
			(Insufficient data for: Angola, Botswana, Burundi, Gambia,						
			Lesotho, Mozambique, Nigeria, Sierra Leone,						
			Swaziland, Zambia, Zimbabwe)						

20 Africa 2									
Cameroon	634	37	4.42	4.21	0.05	0.08	0.03	0.05	0.00
Centr. African Rep.	229	20	1.61	1.53	0.00	0.01	0.00	0.08	0.00
Côte d'Ivoire	597	75	6.82	0.96	0.17	0.36	0.24	0.30	0.05
Madagascar	233	34	5.93	0.13	0.00	0.09	0.01	0.53	9.21
Mauritius	4161	83	2.83	0.02	0.07	0.16	0.11	1.77	17.02
Niger	178	33	2.42	2.70	0.00	0.02	0.02	1.54	0.00
Rwanda	260	18	5.85	2.07	0.01	0.04	0.15	0.42	0.01
Senegal	485	57	3.93	1.60	0.40	1.86	0.09	0.28	0.02
Togo	292	57	2.71	0.53	1.90	0.15	0.47	0.37	0.03
Mean	*432*	*53*	*4.06*	*1.53*	*0.29*	*0.31*	*0.13*	*0.59*	*2.93*
Std Dev.	*1277*	*23*	*1.82*	*1.34*	*0.62*	*0.59*	*0.15*	*0.62*	*6.10*

(Insufficient data for: Benin, Burkina Faso, Cape Verde, Chad, Congo, Democratic Rep. of Congo, Djibouti, Gabon, Ghana, Guinea, Guinea Bissau, Mali, Mauritania)

21 CACM/Caricom									
Barbados	9256	51	3.64	1.09	0.06	1.45	0.36	0.36	0.17
Belize	3635	77	3.86	0.00	0.00	0.00	0.00	0.00	0.00
Costa Rica	4410	79	3.53	0.09	0.29	0.65	0.84	0.25	1.65
Dominica	3447	64	4.01	0.34	0.00	5.60	0.03	0.00	0.01
El Salvador	2129	60	1.55	0.26	0.87	0.53	0.04	1.03	20.92
Grenada	3861	64	6.05	0.02	0.76	0.23	0.76	0.05	0.49
Guatemala	1675	38	6.05	0.71	1.45	1.66	0.11	0.94	1.39
Guyana	942	147	5.46	0.37	0.03	0.13	0.09	0.05	0.77
Honduras	927	66	4.98	0.37	0.50	0.42	0.05	0.43	12.78
Nicaragua	767	61	8.61	0.15	0.38	0.33	0.03	0.09	0.03
Panama	4167	30	8.89	0.19	0.02	0.75	0.00	0.00	0.43
Saint Lucia	N/A		8.08	1.24	0.01	0.22	0.90	1.18	2.06
St. Vincent &Grenadines	N/A		8.25	0.01	1.19	0.05	0.35	0.22	0.42
Trinidad &Tobago	7520	78	0.64	4.15	3.15	1.39	0.06	0.23	0.08
Mean	*2148*	*57*	*5.26*	*0.64*	*0.62*	*0.92*	*0.26*	*0.35*	*2.94*
Std Dev.	*2637*	*29*	*2.59*	*1.08*	*0.87*	*1.45*	*0.33*	*0.41*	*6.14*

(Insufficient data for: Antigua/Barbuda, Dominican Republic, Haiti, Jamaica, St. Kitts/Nevis, Suriname)

[a] All WTO members are included in the available groupings, with the exception of Cuba (see text) and the two most recent members, Tonga (which could join ASEAN-Plus, for example) and Saudi Arabia, which would fall in the North Africa/Middle East group). Russia, currently negotiating WTO accession, is also included (note d).

[b] Constant 2000 US$

[c] RCA = ratio of a country's share of exports of a product in its overall exports to the share of world exports of the product in overall world exports. An index measure greater than unity therefore shows that the country exports the product in a greater proportion than the product's world share of exports.

[d] Currently negotiating WTO accession

Note: Means are weighted by population share for GDP/cap and by GDP share for Trade/GDP; means are simple averages for RCA calculations

Sources: GDP/cap: World Bank, WDI. RCA calculations: WTO on-line database.

arrangement, with deeper economic and institutional integration internally, has made possible joint representation of disparate countries. Economic theory in fact suggests that the optimal partners in a customs union will have either contrasting comparative advantage patterns or otherwise complementary trading patterns with each other, so that the agreement maximizes the net gains from trade. Note that this sort of partnership does not necessarily imply that these same countries, without a customs union agreement, would have common external trade interests as they typically arise in WTO negotiations. None of the other regional groupings represents a complete customs union (Caricom is a partial customs union, and some groups are, or contain, free trade areas), and joint representation becomes difficult if the regional partners do not share social identity and exchange trust.

Some of the regional groups show a coherent alignment of export interests in terms of certain groups of products, such as the African countries, Australia and New Zealand, CACM/Caricom, and Mercosur in agriculture, South Asia in terms of clothing, and the Andean Community in fuels and minerals. Yet in goods trade, table 4.1 indicates that the RCA pattern of comparative advantage can vary significantly within the regional groups. Even when there is a broad consistency in trade interests regarding, for example, agriculture in Africa 1 and Africa 2, trade negotiating "flash points" may occur at narrower levels for a subset of the group, such as cotton, which was the focus of controversy in the Cancún Ministerial.[32] A wide dispersion of RCA values is also likely to indicate differences in negotiating trade-offs among regional group members, making it difficult to forge a common position on specific sectoral negotiating issues.

Table 4.2 presents information on trade restrictions among selected countries in the groups shown in table 4.1, which is another important dimension of trade negotiations. The first column shows an indicator of the use of non-tariff measures, and the remaining columns show average bound and applied tariffs for agricultural and manufactured imports, along with measures of internal dispersion of the applied rates by country and the margin of difference between the bound and applied tariff rates. There is also a calculation of the mean and standard deviation for the grouped countries' agriculture and manufactures tariffs and of the margin between bound and applied rates. The data is limited for many of the groups, but some general observations can be made regarding the alignment of negotiating positions.

In many of the groups, the use of non-tariff barriers to trade varies widely. Based on the available information, only the Andean countries and

TABLE 4.2 Nontariff and tariff information, selected countries, 1995–98

	Core nontariff measures (%)[a]		HS2	Bound	Applied	SD	CV	Margin
				Tariff rates, by sector (%)				
AFRICA 1 Group								
Kenya	N/A		Agriculture	98	40	7.1	0.2	59
			Manufactures	84	35	7.7	0.2	49
Nigeria*	11.5		Agriculture	150	N/A	N/A	N/A	N/A
			Manufactures	46	N/A	N/A	N/A	N/A
Uganda	3.1		Agriculture	61	23	5.6	0.2	38
			Manufactures	63	15	1.4	0.3	48
Zambia	1.0		Agriculture	118	18	4.0	0.2	100
			Manufactures	80	15	4.0	0.3	64
Zimbabwe	N/A		Agriculture	134	15	6.4	0.4	119
			Manufactures	106	18	6.4	0.4	88
		Mean	Agriculture	112.2	24.0			79.0
		SD	Agriculture	34.5	11.2			37.1
		Mean	Manufactures	75.8	20.8			62.3
		SD	Manufactures	22.6	9.6			18.7
AFRICA 2 Group								
Benin*	1.0		Agriculture	79	N/A	N/A	N/A	N/A
			Manufactures	119	N/A	N/A	N/A	N/A
Cameroon	N/A		Agriculture	80	23	4.9	0.2	57
			Manufactures	79	20	4.6	0.2	59
Cote d'Ivoire	30.9		Agriculture	15	17	0.2	0.0	−2
			Manufactures	13	22	0.3	0.0	−9
Ghana	N/A		Agriculture	87	20	3.9	0.2	67
			Manufactures	67	16	4.0	0.3	52
Mauritius*	16.7		Agriculture	119	18	N/A	N/A	101
			Manufactures	65	30	N/A	N/A	35
Senegal**	N/A		Agriculture	30	0	0.0	0.0	30
			Manufactures	12	13	N/A	N/A	0
		Mean	Agriculture	68.3	15.6			50.6
		SD	Agriculture	38.7	9.0			38.9
		Mean	Manufactures	59.2	20.2			27.4
		SD	Manufactures	41.0	6.5			30.6
ANDEAN COUNTRIES								
Bolivia	N/A		Agriculture	40	10	0.0	0.0	30
			Manufactures	40	10	0.1	0.0	30
Chile	5.2		Agriculture	32	11	0.0	0.0	21
			Manufactures	25	11	0.2	0.0	14
Colombia	1.3		Agriculture	85	14	3.0	0.2	71
			Manufactures	40	12	3.5	0.3	28
Peru	N/A		Agriculture	38	18	2.5	0.1	20
			Manufactures	30	19	2.2	0.1	11

(continued)

TABLE 4.2 (continued)

	Core nontariff measures (%)[a]		Tariff rates, by sector (%)				
			HS2	Bound	Applied	SD	CV	Margin
Venezuela	17.7		Agriculture	50	15	2.7	0.2	35
			Manufactures	35	14	2.7	0.2	22
		Mean	Manufactures	34.0	13.2			21.0
		SD	Manufactures	6.5	3.6			8.4
ASEAN–PLUS								
Fiji*	2.5		Agriculture	41	12	N/A	N/A	29
			Manufactures	40	13	N/A	N/A	27
Indonesia*	31.3		Agriculture	47	9	24.3	2.8	39
			Manufactures	37	10	15.7	1.6	27
Malaysia	19.6		Agriculture	17	5	8.3	1.7	12
			Manufactures	20	9	14.9	1.6	10
Philippines	N/A		Agriculture	35	35	12.6	0.4	0
			Manufactures	26	29	9.2	0.3	−3
Singapore	2.1		Agriculture	10	0	0.0	0.0	10
			Manufactures	8	0	0.0	0.0	8
Thailand	17.5		Agriculture	34	38	8.0	0.2	−4
			Manufactures	27	21	9.1	0.4	6
		Mean	Agriculture	30.7	16.5			14.3
		SD	Agriculture	14.3	16.0			16.7
		Mean	Manufactures	26.3	13.7			12.5
		SD	Manufactures	11.6	10.1			12.1
CACM								
Costa Rica	6.2		Agriculture	44	17	9.9	0.6	27
			Manufactures	45	11	4.1	0.4	34
Dominican Republic	6.2		Agriculture	40	21	4.8	0.2	19
			Manufactures	40	20	5.1	0.3	20
El Salvador	5.2		Agriculture	47	14	6.0	0.4	33
			Manufactures	37	9	4.9	0.5	27
		Mean	Agriculture	43.7	17.3			26.3
		SD	Agriculture	3.5	3.5			7.0
		Mean	Manufactures	40.7	13.3			27.0
		SD	Manufactures	4.0	5.9			7.0
MERCOSUR								
Argentina	2.1		Agriculture	23	9	1.4	0.2	14
			Manufactures	31	14	2.4	0.2	18
Brazil	21.6		Agriculture	36	11	2.4	0.2	30
			Manufactures	32	13	3.0	0.2	26
Paraguay	0.0		Agriculture	0	10	2.6	0.3	−10
			Manufactures	0	11	3.7	0.3	−11
Uruguay	0.0		Agriculture	35	13	7.3	0.6	22
			Manufactures	30	12	5.4	0.4	18
		Mean	Agriculture	23.5	10.8			14.0

Country								
		SD	Agriculture	16.7	1.7			17.3
		Mean	Manufactures	23.3	12.5			12.8
		SD	Manufactures	15.5	1.3			16.3
NORTH AFRICA–MIDDLE EAST								
Egypt	N/A		Agriculture	92	34	24.6	0.7	58
			Manufactures	42	24	12.9	0.5	18
Tunisia	N/A		Agriculture	115	35	7.4	0.2	80
			Manufactures	49	30	7.5	0.3	19
		Mean	Agriculture	83.7	32.7			51.3
		SD	Agriculture	36.2	3.2			32.5
		Mean	Manufactures	41.3	28.3			12.7
		SD	Manufactures	8.0	3.8			10.1
SOUTHEAST ASIA								
Bangladesh	N/A		Agriculture	84	30	14.5	0.5	54
			Manufactures	84	27	14.9	0.6	56
India*	93.8		Agriculture	112	N/A	N/A	N/A	N/A
			Manufactures	44	N/A	N/A	N/A	N/A
Pakistan	N/A		Agriculture	101	71	16.6	0.2	30
			Manufactures	51	67	16.2	0.2	-16
Sri Lanka	22.7		Agriculture	50	35	10.6	0.3	15
			Manufactures	50	20	7.2	0.4	30
		Mean	Agriculture	86.8	45.3			33.0
		SD	Agriculture	27.1	22.4			19.7
		Mean	Manufactures	57.3	38.0			23.3
		SD	Manufactures	18.1	25.4			36.5
Turkey	19.8		Agriculture	53	18	10.1	0.6	35
			Manufactures	21	8	3.1	0.4	12
Average			Agriculture	59	21	12.2	0.6	34
			Manufactures	42	17	6.3	0.4	23

[a] Frequency ratio (%) relative to 97 product categories at the Harmonized Standard- (HS-) 2 level.
N/A = not available; SD = standard deviation; CV – coefficient of variation = SD/Mean of bound tariffs.
Agriculture products: HS 1–24; manufactured products: HS25 97.
* WTO, TPRs. **Import weighted

Sources: WTO, IDB, TPRs (1995–99); Finger et al. (1996); Based on Michalopoulos (2001), tables 4.2, 4.5, and 4.7.

CACM have reasonably consistent records of non-tariff measures, which are at low levels as measured by their use in HS-2 categories. They would therefore be more likely to start at similar negotiating positions in multilateral trade talks (data on tariff and non-tariff barriers applied by the Caricom customs union, as part of the CACM/Caricom group, were not available). Regarding tariffs, the two general issues are tariff levels and the difference between applied and bound tariffs. Based on table 4.2, most groups of developing countries have high bound tariffs, but with considerable dispersion around the mean within the group, except for CACM. Since applied tariffs are almost always much lower, the margin between bound and applied tariffs is also large, a potentially important trade bargaining issue. Again, the dispersion of margins within the groups tends to be large, suggesting that a common negotiating position on tariff cutting and harmonization within the groups would be difficult to achieve in most cases.

The information in tables 4.1 and 4.2 suggests that regionally based representation in the WTO, especially among developing countries, is possible, but limited in scope. This conclusion may be overly pessimistic to the extent that there are many regional negotiating areas on which finding common ground on important issues is possible, for example in terms of setting negotiating agendas on the Singapore issues, TRIPS, special and differential treatment, and anti-dumping reform. Typically, negotiating rounds begin with a broad agreement on the scope of issues and then proceed toward progressively more detailed and often divisive specifics, where common negotiating positions among countries may require much more extensive cooperation and trust. Based on the history of the GATT/WTO system, regional groupings have had some success in effective joint representation. Blackhurst et al. (2000) note that successful cooperation among the Nordic Group (Denmark, Finland, Iceland, Norway, and Sweden) in the Kennedy and Uruguay Rounds appears to have been based on geographic proximity, history of political and cultural affinity, and a tradition of cooperation in the region, which together created the necessary social identity and exchange trust. They ceased joint activities after Denmark (1973) and Sweden and Finland (1995) joined the EU. More recently, Mercosur and groups of African countries have each worked jointly on agenda-setting issues for the Doha Round (Schott and Watal, 2000). Narlikar (2003) lists seven regional groupings that have played a role in multilateral trade negotiations: ASEAN, the Latin American Group (with a fluid membership), Mercosur, the group of African countries mentioned above, Caricom, the Paradisus Group,[33] and the African, Caribbean, and Pacific Group.[34] In most of these cases, the scope for cooperation was either very broad, in terms of setting agenda items, or very narrow, in terms of specific negotiating goals. An important caveat appears to be that cooperation within successful coalitions may include an agreement to support a common position, but not necessarily to speak on each other's behalf. Narlikar (2003, chap. 7) and Blackhurst et al. (2000) note that even the relatively successful ASEAN coalition has pursued only a limited agenda in the WTO, with no presumption of joint representation in negotiations. In these, as well as

in all other coalitions, a successful coordination of activities and/or negotiating positions among the partners has generally been limited in terms
of longevity and the importance of the issues. One general observation
emerges from most of the accounts of coalition strategies in the GATT/
WTO system: geographical proximity does not necessarily imply an alignment of trade interests. This factor suggests the difficulties of establishing
formalized regional representation.

New Developments and a Proposal: Coalitions, Issue Platforms and Proxies

After the Seattle debacle, D-Gs became sensitive to the criticisms regarding
Green Room participation, and tried to make such meetings as inclusive as
possible. In the meantime, even though the WTO countries remained far
apart on the major negotiating issues, most observers and trade diplomats
from the developed countries felt that the Green Room was not responsible
for the stalemate. At the other extreme, NGOs speaking on behalf of developing countries that are typically outside the Green Room system have
called for its complete removal as a part of WTO decision making (Sharma
2003, Jawara and Kwa 2004), to be replaced with a more "democratic"
model. Presumably, what would be left to take its place is debate within
the plenary WTO General Council, with some form of ad hoc behind-the-
scenes caucusing and coalition building. As long as the consensus rule
prevails, however, it is unlikely that multilateral negotiations will be able to
reach closure in such a fragmented forum. The Green Room has played an
important role in achieving consensus in multilateral trade negotiations,
and if it were officially suppressed, informal negotiations among the largest and most influential countries—both developed and developing—would
probably replicate themselves and bring their small-group agreements to
the plenary meetings. There is, in any case, little that other WTO member
countries can do to prevent countries from meeting and negotiating among
themselves, even if the imprimatur of a DG-led Green Room is removed.
Proposals to establish a parliamentary-style, one-country-one-vote WTO,
with majority or supermajority decision making, would clearly allow developing countries to dominate, but would just as clearly lead to a withdrawal
of the rich countries from the system.[35]

In addition, any top-down approach to reform, such as a formal consultative board based on regional groupings, runs the risk of reducing
the Green Room's ability to facilitate consensus. In this connection, it is
noteworthy that WTO negotiations themselves have begun to adapt to the

representation problem. The most significant change is the increasing incidence of coalition building in the WTO, as noted by Diego-Fernandez (2008). Narlikar (2003) has documented the formation of coalitions in the Uruguay Round, concluding that they had occasionally been effective, but were vulnerable to internal dissent and weak commitment among members. However, the emergence of large developing countries such as India, Brazil, and China in trade negotiations, combined with the increasing engagement and experience of developing countries in general with trade issues and negotiations, has created strong incentives to pursue coalition strategies in the Doha Round. Narlikar and Tussie (2004) observe that the learning process led to successful coalition building and internal discipline by developing countries at the Cancún Ministerial, as shown in chapter 2. In addition, many trade issues cut across North-South lines, so that coalitions among developed and developing countries are common. In most cases the coalitions form around specific negotiating issues rather than along lines of ideology, region, or income. This development is important for the future of the process of reaching consensus. Coalitions benefit their participants by enhancing their bargaining power, allowing the pooling of negotiating resources, and facilitating each participant's representation in a Green Room meeting. At the same time they benefit the negotiating process by reducing the number of negotiating positions and encouraging compromise within the group, thereby reducing the disruption of extreme positions. The effective formation of coalitions has the potential to reduce the complexity of the WTO bargaining process by introducing subordinate negotiations among coalition partners. The adaptation of WTO countries to the challenges of consensus building through broader coalition tactics is an encouraging sign, signaling the evolution of decision-making processes to match the evolution of the institution as a whole. Wilkinson (2006) has observed that the GATT/WTO system has often displayed this adaptive ability under conditions of crisis and stress.

Building on this development, a new "platform" proposal may be able to address the problem of representation. It would refocus Green Room representation, and in fact representation within the WTO system generally, toward the development and voting presence of discrete platforms, whereby countries not present at the meetings themselves would give their voting proxies to a country or countries representing the specific platform. Such a system could be combined with guaranteed seats for the strong countries and for regions as appropriate to the issue under discussion, but the important difference is that *issue platforms* would be represented formally in the Green Room. The recent trend toward the formation of coalitions among countries on specific issues would be instrumental in this regard. Such representation has occurred in the Cairns Group (agricultural exporting countries, both developed and developing), the Like Minded Group (developing countries with more protectionist policies), and Friends of the Round (developed and developing countries with liberal trade policies; see Michalopoulos 2001, p. 165). New coalitions might emerge along various dimensions, such as transition economies with similar state subsidies policies, countries importing patented medicines, and poorer countries with limited trade policy capacity.

Under a platform-and-proxy Green Room process, it would be necessary to promote the coalescing of trade interests into coherent and consistent negotiating positions. At the same time, individual countries could belong to different platforms on different issues. Clearly, there would need to be a way of limiting the proliferation of platforms on a specific issue, given the limited number of available seats—otherwise there could be 153 platforms on each issue. Some weighting system based on countries' world trade shares, combined with the number of sponsoring countries, might provide the basis for identifying the most important platforms. Alliance building and cross-issue compromises within a given platform group could, for example, expand the platform's constituents, and hence its political weight in the Green Room deliberation. Indeed, formal recognition of platforms in the Green Room would provide a strong incentive for countries to form coalitions on important issues, and thereby move the negotiating process forward toward consensus. While it would be best to have a designated representative for each of the recognized platforms in the Green Room, improved information sharing and communication could allow bargaining positions to be actively updated. On crucial negotiating points, platform groups would have to stage internal caucus meetings, but this need not require all interested parties to be present in the Green Room. A representative platform would in this regard have the salutary effect of presenting a position on the issue for *all* countries identified with it, and thereby expand the Green Room's reach. In addition, such a system would provide a credible forum for accurately identifying the negotiating trade-offs and bargaining chips that would play a role in forging a consensus among the entire group.

Such a system would also require increased transparency in Green Room deliberations, which may be a major hurdle in any efforts at reform, in view of the long-standing tradition of secrecy and direct country-to-country bargaining in trade negotiations.[36] Yet a robust system of representation along these lines could allow member countries to recognize more clearly the relevant trade-offs in negotiations and thereby hasten progress toward consensus. The bargaining power of the United States and EU would be likely to remain strong under such a system, but the influence of leading representatives of developing countries, such as India and Brazil, would probably increase in line with the trend observed in the Doha Round. At the same time, countries with weaker bargaining power individually could more efficiently form alliances, based on articulated platform positions, and thereby improve their joint bargaining position.

The platform approach, reinforced by the trend toward forming coalitions, would, in effect, set out to change the structure of Green Room deliberations from bilateral country-focused bargaining to broader issue-based (and perhaps multi-issue-based) bargaining, in which smaller individual countries would face limited negotiating flexibility at the Green Room meeting itself. For this reason, some smaller OECD and developing country participants in the Green Room might object to the reforms, as platform representation gained at the expense of country representation. However, these are also likely to be countries that would take leadership roles in constructing issue platforms. Even so, it may still be necessary for the United States and EU in particular (and perhaps Brazil and India as well) to provide assurances or compensating arrangements to countries that lose Green Room representation—for example, offers to champion platform issues of special interest to those countries. Otherwise, countries without a seat at the Green Room would have a strong incentive to seek out or form coalitions to represent their interests on their own, which might add to the number of platforms and delay the formation of consensus.

In many ways, the success of platform- or issue-based representation in the Green Room would in fact depend on the development of a more effective framework for building coalitions within the WTO. One can argue that more effective coalitions representing weaker countries would assure increased bargaining power for those countries even in the absence of any Green Room reforms. Yet achieving a more effective system of coalitional representation in the WTO is a tall order. Narlikar (2003) documents the checkered performance of coalitions among weaker countries in the GATT/WTO system, noting that negotiating success is dependent on a combination of inner coherence and discipline of coalition members, effective strategy, and the presence of favorable external factors beyond the control of the coalition. Some recent successes indicate the possibilities of an effectively managed coalition, however, as in the cases of TRIPS reform and the G20 strategy at the Cancún ministerial, as described in chapter 2.[37]

An additional problem may lie in the dangers, as some countries perceive them, of giving formal recognition to platforms or coalitions within the otherwise informal Green Room process. On the one hand, it may be argued that the Green Room already incorporates platform representation through existing coalitions, but with the understanding that countries are present only to represent themselves. The danger of allowing platforms to receive formal representation is that an individual country representative may not be a trustworthy broker for the other platform constituents' interests. In general, countries are typically loath to allow another country to represent their interests in a forum traditionally based on national representation and interests. Most smaller WTO member countries know firsthand the risk of placing too much trust in a coalition partner, making the joint position vulnerable to selective U.S. or EU offers of attractive side payments or other inducements to break the coalition. A more viable solution for the weaker countries, according to this view, would lie in strengthening the coalition's influence and leveraging it through plenary meetings and negotiating committees, using the Green Room to represent the coalition's views through individual members, but without official platform status. A major challenge is certainly that there is no easy way to get a stable consensus within coalitions through compensation or internal trade-offs, as is the case for example in the EU's trade policy formation (no easy task even then). Achieving stability in a WTO system of coalitions may therefore require further economic and perhaps political integration among its members.

Outlook

Informal decision-making channels seem to have served the interests of the United States, the EU, and other large trading countries in the WTO, and to the extent that the system has generated multilateral trade liberalization, the rest of the world has benefited from this process as well. The large trading countries are unlikely to give up this system, even if it appears to be excruciatingly slow and prone to crisis. It is largely through these informal processes that large country interests are protected in a consensus-based organization, and they appear to be willing to wait out the long negotiations that tend to result. However, the membership of the WTO has become so diverse, and the menu of trade-related topics has become so large, that informal decision making within the organization shows signs of losing its ability to move negotiations forward, and it must therefore adapt to its more complicated environment if progress is to occur in current and future multilateral negotiations. In particular, it has become increasingly difficult in many cases for the D-G to organize a Green Room meeting that will effectively represent the variety of positions that can serve as the basis for a consensus among all members. Reform in the informal decision-making process is likely to be difficult, because any changes will upset the traditional negotiating processes that allow current Green Room participants to protect their bargaining interests. The Green Room problem itself is one of representation, and a wider scope of participation through issue platforms and proxies could address the structural requirements of reform. However, it is necessary to add that an opening up of the negotiating process may also require the scope of negotiating issues for large Green Room countries to broaden into uncomfortable areas that had previously remained protected by the politics of preemptive, power-based bargaining. In this regard, progress in complicated multilateral negotiations may increasingly require a more active market in side payments (foreign aid or other non-trade-related items) in order to avoid "hold-up" problems and facilitate a broad-based consensus. Even this strategy is unlikely to break a serious logjam if several countries stand in the way of an agreement, however, and formal compensation is not possible in a WTO agreement, an issue that will be addressed in chapter 6.

At the same time, it is extremely unlikely that the institution of consensus-based decision making at the WTO can be replaced with anything along the lines of a formal executive board empowered to act on behalf of the entire membership. A fragmented "democratic" process of voting or spontaneous consensus is equally unlikely to solve the problem. For this reason, WTO negotiations will continue to require, as they always have, leadership in setting trade agendas and initiatives as well as cooperation and compromise among all members to conclude a mutually welfare-enhancing agreement. The United States and the EU have held the leadership role in the past, and India and Brazil have emerged as representatives of a large bloc of developing countries in the Doha Round. There seems to be no substitute for large country leadership and compromise in the WTO. If the platform approach to Green Room reform develops into a more effective process of forming alliances and coalitions among WTO members (which in itself requires compromise), the outlook for broader agreements and movement toward consensus may be correspondingly more positive. In any case, the Green Room itself appears destined to continue as a decision-making institution, and the weak states will find it increasingly important to form effective alliances—to influence decision making both inside and outside the Green Room—in order to make progress on their trade agendas.

5

Developing Country Representation in Dispute Settlement

I N 1995, THE NEWLY FORMED WTO INTRODUCED A REVISED DISPUTE
settlement understanding (DSU), replacing the GATT system's procedures. Many observers regarded the new DSU as a major accomplishment
of the Uruguay Round, promising to bring order and legal precision to the
settlement of disputes among WTO members. Many developing countries,
in particular, appeared hopeful that the legalization of trade disputes under
the new agreement would more effectively protect their interests than the
GATT system had. The DSU established an independent panel to examine allegations that a WTO member has violated its obligations, and to
determine what, if any, actions that member must undertake to remedy
the violation. A major change was that the panel report or any supersed-
ing appellate report must be accepted unless vetoed by the collective WTO
membership, which meant that DSU decisions would have real power. In
this manner WTO rules and provisions would in principle be upheld systematically and transparently and disputes adjudicated through objective
legal principles evenhandedly, for large and small, rich and poor member
countries alike. An important purpose of the new DSU was, in this sense,
to improve the *representation* of developing countries in the WTO system,
even when many of these countries were too small to have a significant
impact in multilateral trade negotiations.

In the years since the introduction of the WTO and its new dispute
settlement system, however, disappointment has spread in many quarters
over the alleged failure of the DSU to create a truly level playing field and
to serve the interests of developing countries. Of the 128 countries that

were charter members of the WTO in 1995 and the 25 that have joined since then, only 46 have taken part in a DSU case as complainant, respondent, or third-party participant. Some criticism of the lack of developing country participation has come from developing countries themselves and from critics of globalization and the WTO, which generally regard the DSU as part of an unbalanced WTO system dominated by rich countries.[1] Yet many economists and political scientists have also noted that developing countries appear not to be benefiting from the system as much as they could. The title of one article refers provocatively to the "missing developing country cases" (Bown and Hoekman 2004).

This chapter sets out to examine the concept of country representation in the dispute settlement process as part of the broader WTO system, and to explore the possible ways that effective representation does (or can) take place in resolving disputes. The definition of representation itself requires clarification, and the following discussion will consider various dimensions of the concept, including participation, "free-riding" (through Most-Favored Nation effects), and systemic benefits of WTO membership. There will also be a review of the evidence of representation along these lines from the existing literature and from additional statistical evidence. Possible solutions to the problem of inadequate representation will be explored.

DSU Procedures

Under the earlier GATT system, dispute settlement relied formally on consensus among the complainant and respondent parties.[2] GATT dispute panels of trade experts would render a judgment as to whether the respondent party had violated a GATT rule, or had otherwise "nullified or impaired" benefits entitled to the complainant through the GATT. However, the procedures for correcting the violation were weak, and while retaliation to enforce compliance was theoretically possible, the respondent country had the right to block any retaliation that the panel might approve. This was because the dispute panel's decision had to be adopted unanimously by the GATT General Council, which included all members. Since the respondent thereby ultimately had veto power over the decision, GATT dispute settlement decisions had no real teeth. The system did, however, offer the legitimacy of a legal review and a framework for political negotiations, since there was a strong desire among GATT Contracting Parties to maintain the integrity of their relationship established through GATT rules. Reputational and systemic factors therefore encouraged signatories to the GATT to place long-term relationship value on the agreement.

In the language of transaction cost economics, participants in the contractual agreement faced a situation of *bounded rationality*, in which the contingency of future disputes required agreement on a third-party mechanism of resolution.[3] This factor will be important to keep in mind in evaluating the effectiveness of WTO dispute resolution under the revised DSU. Hudec (2002, p. 82) indicates that, despite the lack of formal enforcement, most violation rulings by GATT panels were adopted, and most of these led to successful resolutions. Developing countries, initially few in number,[4] were somewhat less successful in achieving corrections of alleged violations, but still appeared to do reasonably well under the system. They filed 28 complaints under the GATT, 17 of which led to legal rulings, and of these, 11 indicated a violation, with 10 culminating in a successful correction of the violation (ibid.). Their rates of achieving successful resolution of the disputes was only slightly less than those for the GATT as a whole.[5]

The motivation for reforming the dispute settlement process appeared to have been the trend among GATT members beginning in the 1980s to bring increasingly contentious issues to dispute panels when they could not be resolved so easily on the political track. A comprehensive system of dispute settlement that included more politically sensitive cases, it was thought, would require a more legalistic procedure. The DSU therefore introduced two important new features: the elimination of veto power by individual countries and the establishment of appellate review of panel decisions. The first of these provisions required adoption of the panel report unless all WTO member countries vetoed it, while the second new provision built in an instance of appellate review. In general, these measures increased the formal legal weight of DSU panel and Appellate Body decisions and tilted the dispute settlement mechanism toward judicial methods.

The process of bringing a case under the DSU involves the following steps (see Petersmann 1997, p. 184):

1. The complainant country requests preliminary consultations with the respondent country;
2. If there is no resolution of the issue, the Dispute Settlement Body (DSB) establishes a panel to investigate the allegation, while "third-party" countries with an interest in the dispute are afforded a limited role in the proceedings (and a larger role if there is an appeal);
3. The panel examines the evidence, drafts its report and submits it to the DSB;

4. The DSB either rejects the report unanimously or adopts the report within 60 days unless appealed to the Appellate Body (AB);
5. If there is an appeal, the AB reviews the case and issues its report within 60–90 days, after which the DSB either unanimously rejects the report or adopts the report within another 30 days;
6. The DSB monitors compliance, and if there is noncompliance after a "reasonable amount of time" the parties are required to negotiate compensation or resolution;
7. If noncompliance cannot be resolved and compensation cannot be agreed upon, the DSB can authorize the complainant to impose proportionate retaliatory measures against the respondent.

In moving away from the consensus approach of GATT dispute settlement, the DSU set out to establish a level playing field for all WTO members. The impetus for the change came, however, mainly from *developed* countries, particularly the United States, supported by a number of smaller developed countries such as Australia, Canada, Hong Kong, and New Zealand (Smith 2004, p. 547). As part of the larger Uruguay Round bargain, the official "spin" on the dispute settlement process emphasized the leveling effect it would have on all countries. In order to strengthen this point with regard to developing countries, there were explicit provisions in DSU Article 27 (2) to provide technical assistance to developing countries in bringing cases. Another important boost to developing country support came with the establishment of the Advisory Centre on WTO Law (ACWL) in 2001, which has provided legal advice at subsidized rates to developing countries on DSU matters. Decisions by the AB in subsequent cases have also given poor countries the right to use private counsel from other countries to appear on behalf of their client governments in DSU cases (see Smith 2004, pp. 565–567). These steps have been designed to improve the access of developing countries to the DSU process, but they have been only partially successful so far.

The legalization of dispute settlement under the DSU has created a distinctive incentive structure for participants in a case. Because of the effort and expense to see a case through, a country will generally begin a case only if it is reasonably sure that a violation can be demonstrated. Based on a sample of 181 disputes from 1995–2002 (Davey 2005, pp. 45–49), only about 6% of those that reached the stage of a panel report resulted in the finding of nonviolation. In other words, in the cases in the sample that proceeded to a decision, the defendant was usually found "guilty" in some aspect of the complaint. Approximately 27% of cases led to an outright victory for the complainant, 35% were settled at some point before the panel report, and 21% of the cases were dropped, whether because the respondent removed the challenged trade practice, because the complainant country's commercial interest in pursuing the case changed, or for other reasons. Many respondent countries seek to settle out of court once a complaint is filed against them, especially if the case appears to be particularly strong. Busch and Reinhardt (2003) contend that the key to benefiting from the DSU lies in extracting concessions from the respondent early in the process, and that developing countries have found this difficult because of their lack of legal capacity.

The Representation Issue in the Context of Dispute Settlement

Representation is a concept that takes on various meanings, depending on the context. In normal usage it is associated with political enfranchisement, such as the right to vote or actively participate in a political decision. This is also the sense in which it was discussed in chapter 4, in which the focus was participation in the deliberative process. In the context of the WTO, all member countries achieve political representation in the formal negotiations and agreements through the consensus rule: no agreement can be reached on binding rules and negotiated outcomes in the WTO unless all members provide their formal consent. In this sense, consensus need not require active agreement; the absence of objection can provide implicit consent. Years of experience with the GATT/WTO system show that the concept of representation, in the sense of participation in decision making, has certainly not been democratic in these organizations. The Quad countries (United States, EU, Japan, Canada) and other developed countries dominated the GATT/WTO trading system until recently, since they could block consensus on important trade issues. More recently, Brazil and India have exerted strong influence within the WTO, so that they, too, can block consensus. It can be said in this sense that politically powerful countries enjoy strong representation in the WTO, in that they have a strong influence on the outcome of negotiations.

Yet it is very useful to consider also the purely economic dimension of representation in the WTO, since its purpose is to enhance all members' economic welfare through trade. Political representation may indeed contribute to a member country's ability to benefit from trade, but in the end the gains from trade accrue to *all* members that participate in trade liberalization. These gains come not only from trade-opening measures, leading to both static and dynamic welfare gains, but also from the rules and principles that reinforce them and back them up, such as the MFN clause, reciprocal tariff concessions, and dispute settlement. In order to focus on the economic benefits, this analysis will therefore apply a working definition of representation in the WTO as the *ability of a member country to use the organization's institutional facilities to enhance its economic welfare*. This concept is useful in comparing the varying degrees of representation among WTO members themselves, and also in comparing a WTO member's representation in the world trading system to that of a country that is not a WTO member.

The most direct measure of WTO representation as it pertains to the DSU is that of active participation in filing cases. It is important to consider first, however, the pattern of overall case filings since the system began in 1995. Table 5.1 shows the pattern of annual DSU case filings by complainant countries and by respondent countries from 1995 to 2008, highlighting the role of the most active countries in the process and by designation of developed and developing status.[6] The overall pattern is that the number of new case filings by respondent country increased significantly from 25 in 1995 to 50 in 1997, and since then has gradually declined, averaging 16.4 cases per year from 2005–08.[7] It is unlikely that the number of disputable issues among WTO members has declined during this time period, so alternative explanations must be considered. One major consideration is that WTO members have become increasingly involved with other trade issues, including the Doha Round trade negotiations, as well as preferential trade agreements, leaving less time for their trade officials to spend on DSU cases (Leitner and Lester 2005, p. 232). In addition, multilateral

TABLE 5.1A Annual filing of dispute settlement cases by complainant country, 1995–2008

	'95	'96	'97	'98	'99	'00	'01	'02	'03	'04	'05	'06	'07	'08	Total
United States	6	17	17	10	10	8	1	4	3	4	1	3	4	3	91
European communities	2	7	16	16	6	8	1	4	3	5	2	5	0	3	78
Canada	5	3	1	4	2	1	3	4	1	2	0	1	2	2	31
Brazil	1	0	4	1	0	7	4	5	0	0	0	0	1	1	24
India	1	4	0	3	1	2	2	2	0	1	0	1	0	1	18
Other developed	1	5	8	3	6	5	0	7	4	3	1	1	1	1	46
Other developing	12	15	4	4	9	11	13	11	15	4	7	9	5	8	127
Total DSU cases filed	28	51	50	41	34	42	24	37	26	19	11	20	13	19	415

TABLE 5.1B Annual dispute settlement cases by respondent country, 1995–2008

	'95	'96	'97	'98	'99	'00	'01	'02	'03	'04	'05	'06	'07	'08	Total
United States	4	8	10	6	11	11	6	19	6	7	2	5	3	6	104
European communities	8	4	4	9	3	2	3	6	8	4	2	3	3	4	63
Japan	4	4	3	1	0	0	0	1	0	1	0	1	0	0	15
India	0	1	7	4	1	0	0	1	1	2	0	1	1	1	20
Canada	0	1	5	3	1	0	1	1	0	1	0	2	0	0	15
Brazil	1	4	2	1	1	2	1	0	0	0	1	1	0	0	14
Other developed	5	4	10	8	1	1	0	3	1	1	0	2	1	0	40
Other developing	3	13	9	9	9	18	12	6	10	3	6	5	5	8	116
Total cases filed against	25	39	50	41	30	34	23	37	26	19	11	20	13	19	387

TABLE 5.1C Adversarial patterns among developed and developing countries in DSU cases, 1995–2008

	'95	'96	'97	'98	'99	'00	'01	'02	'03	'04	'05	'06	'07	'08	Total
Developed vs. developed	11	13	20	23	15	8	5	15	5	9	1	6	3	3	137
Developed vs. developing	3	16	20	10	8	9	0	3	3	3	3	4	4	6	92
Developing vs. developed	8	5	9	4	1	7	6	14	10	4	3	6	4	7	88
Developing vs. developing	4	6	1	4	6	11	13	5	8	3	4	4	2	3	74
Total complainant filings	26	40	50	41	30	35	24	37	26	19	11	20	13	19	391

Source: Leitner and Lester (2008) and updates from WTO Web site, http://www.wto.org/english/tratop_e/dispu_e/dispu_status_e.htm.

or bilateral negotiations may be seen as providing alternative forums for attempting to resolve disputes. In this regard, the DSU should be considered one of multiple channels within the WTO to provide representation for its members. Unlike a traditional court system in sovereign countries, the DSU may be but one way of achieving a member country's trade goals within the WTO.

Table 5.1A and 5.1B also show the pattern of case filings by complainant and respondent countries. Overall, the United States and the EU together have dominated both categories, representing 41% of all complainants and being named as respondents in 43% of all DSU cases. Furthermore, 48 of the 387 cases (12%) have been over disputes between the United States and EU. Developed countries, defined as those in the upper quartile of per capita income levels, as a whole have represented 59% of all complainants in DSU cases and 61% of respondents. These same developed countries represent just 29% of WTO members and approximately 20% of the population of all WTO countries, but it should be noted that exports and imports of the developed countries represent approximately 70% of world trade. Based on the shares of trade and diversity of trading partners, statistical studies have shown that the developed world is not overrepresented in usage of the DSU system (Horn, Mavroidis, and Nordstrom, 1999).

It is therefore noteworthy that *developing* countries have been filing more DSU cases in recent years. Based on table 5.1, they represented 52% of complainants as a proportion of total cases from 2000 to 2008. The larger trading countries in this group have been most active: Brazil, Chile, India, Republic of Korea, and Mexico. Table 5.1C tabulates the cases according to "rich" (developed) and "poor" (developing) countries' filings against countries in and outside their group. Developed versus developed country cases have been trending downward, from 44% of the total in the 1995–99 period to 27% in the 2000–08 period, while developing versus developing cases have risen from 11% to 26%. Using these same time periods, developed versus developing cases fell from 30% to 17%, while developing versus developed cases rose from 14% to 30% of the total.

The basic statistics on DSU case filings show that developed countries, and a relatively small subset of developing countries, have used the system most intensively, and presumably to their benefit. Filing a case appears to carry a high probability of reforms that increase the complainant's access to the import market in question. As a measure of representation, as defined by the use of the WTO system to enhance a member's economic welfare, active participation in filing cases therefore appears to be a valuable component of this calculation. Even if a country is a respondent—and is therefore likely to lose the case or modify its import policies in response to it—economic welfare considerations suggest that this country also gains from the process, although it is unlikely to regard the outcome in this light. A DSU case against a country, like the WTO system in general, provides an external anchor for liberal trade policies and practices, empowering the country's internal trade-liberalizing political forces in their confrontation with domestic protectionist interests.[8] This political economy consideration reveals one of the great ironies in representation: consumer interests in the importing country are often tied closely with the "mercantilist" interests of foreign exporters. If a respondent opens its market as a consequence of a

DSU case, its economic welfare will almost certainly rise. The gains for *both* sides of a dispute that results in additional trade liberalization form part of the core benefits of WTO system of rules and obligations to the world economy. If the goal of introducing a more legalized dispute settlement process was to enhance the participation of poorer countries in active case filings, however, the results remain unsatisfactory. Based on case-filing patterns, only 25 DSU complaints out of a total of 415 have been from countries in the lowest quartile income bracket, and only 23 out of 387 respondents were from countries in this group (Leitner and Lester 2008). In only one instance, Bangladesh versus India regarding AD duties on batteries (2004), has an LDC filed a DSU case.

Economic analysis suggests that filing a case is based essentially on a cost-benefit consideration by the country's government. If the expected value of bringing a case—achieving additional market access with net proceeds to the economy—is greater than the cost of litigating the case, then the decision would be to file a DSU complaint. However, for small and poor economies the calculus of this decision is particularly harsh. First of all, complaints typically emanate from private companies that experience market closure abroad, and in small developing economies, firms are often too small and scattered to organize effectively to pursue their collective interests at the national level, and often cannot afford the expense of gathering information and preparing a case.[9] In addition, the legal and support cost alone of bringing a case may be prohibitive for the domestic firm, industry, or government in a developing country. Bown and Hoekman (2005) estimate that such costs range from approximately $200,000 to $500,000 or more, depending on the complexity of the case. Nordstrom and Shaffer (2008) identify three general stages of a case (consultations, panel, and appeal) and distinguish among cases of low, medium, and high complexity to form a cost matrix, based on estimated costs of $500 per hour. Their total cost estimates per case range from the very simplest, at around $54,000, to the lengthiest and most complex, at $882,500. These cost estimates do not include the technical expertise and overhead cost necessary to support a preliminary investigation on the issue, or the public relations and lobbying cost that may be required to pursue compliance, assuming the case is successful.

In addition, small and poor countries may not be able to compel a richer respondent country to comply with a ruling. A number of econometric studies of DSU case filings have concluded that the potential ability of the complainant country to retaliate against the respondent country through a withdrawal of trade concessions is an important determinant of filing a case in the first place (Bown 2005a). Jawara and Kwa (2004, p. 7) report an anonymous interview with a trade official from a developing country:

My country has not yet been involved in a dispute, because it is a very long and expensive system to get engaged in. Although we do now have the independent ACWL to assist us, it is still much more practical for us to settle out of court. The [EU], for instance, banned all fish exports coming from my country...saying the fish was infected with the cholera bacteria...The WTO formally objected to this notion because there was no scientific proof that our fish were infected. Yet we could not afford to go through the dispute settlement process...We eventually settled the matter bilaterally with the EU after suffering huge losses in fish exports. Really, the power of enforcement of the rulings...is based on your capacity to retaliate against a country that has bent the rules. As a small country, however, the impact of retaliating against a big country is virtually nil, though some developing countries have been able to do this with some amount of success.

Other sources of rich country leverage that could discourage poor country DSU filings against them would include development assistance and other forms of foreign aid, military and regional trade relationships, and political pressures in other international organizations (Bown 2004a). It should be noted, however, that a rich country's repudiation of a successfully prosecuted DSU case brought by a poor country—or any country—would tend to impose reputational costs on the rich country, along with the systemic cost of devaluing the dispute settlement agreement in general. Yet the poor country's lack of resources and the perceived risk associated with the outcome may leave it vulnerable to rich country intimidation. In addition, rich countries have shown that they can effectively delay implementing rulings that go against them through partial or incomplete compliance, which would typically require further expensive DSU litigation to challenge. The United States and EU have done this repeatedly in the banana and beef hormone cases, for example (see Tehrani 2008).

The asymmetry in power relationships among WTO members poses potential difficulties to the WTO as an institution to the extent that such situations may deprive poorer countries of market access and opportunities for economic growth. The presumption of this contention is that a disputable case of, for example, blocked imports from India to the EU would typically lead to India filing a DSU case, whereas a similar instance of blocked imports from Lesotho to the EU would not be filed. While we observe the India filing and do not observe a Lesotho filing, the pattern suggests that Lesotho (or another poor country) often has a valid case. Not only do such missed opportunities for trade liberalization diminish the value of the institution for some of its members, they also diminish its credibility as a forum for trade negotiations in general, as they may reduce poor country members' willingness to offer market opening of their own due to the lack of access to effective third-party review of disputes.[10] Bown and Hoekman (2008) suggest that the lack of willingness of both developed and developing countries to bargain reciprocally may be the result of the fact that both sides have anticipated the lack of DSU enforcement with regard to developing country trade, especially with small countries. Furthermore, developing countries will suffer welfare losses because potentially efficient domestic industries will not be able to count on their governments to avail themselves of DSU remedies.

If the DSU has fallen short of being the great equalizer of access to WTO "justice," some of the disappointment may stem from the inflated expectations of a legal system without an independent enforcement mechanism. Unlike legal systems in sovereign countries, the WTO has no police force and no jail to capture and punish governments found to be in violation of their WTO obligations. Political power continues to play an important role in WTO negotiations and in the bilateral trade relations among its members. It would be folly to expect a DSU proceeding to supersede political factors completely, even if the members have jointly accepted responsibility for supporting the system as the basis for containing trade disputes and seeking peaceful resolutions to them.

Alternative Sources of Representation in the DSU and the WTO

While recognizing the shortcomings of the DSU in terms of equal access among all countries, it is also important to acknowledge the indirect benefits that all WTO members derive from the system. The hidden benefits generally come from Most-Favored Nation (MFN) treatment of liberalizing measures, through market access opening and trade policy reforms, and from the incentive structures of the WTO system itself.

MFN Dividend

The most important of these benefits is the "MFN dividend," or gains from free riding. The former term is more accurate, since the term "free riding" implies that the country has received benefits at no cost. MFN treatment, on the other hand, is a contractual benefit of WTO membership, "purchased" with the member country's accession agreement and commitment to adhere to WTO rules. In some (not all) DSU cases, the MFN effect would come to exporters not participating in the case, as the market opening by the respondent country allows more imports not only from the complainant country but also from all other WTO member countries supplying the market and thereby guaranteed MFN access. This would typically occur in goods and other market access cases, where nondiscriminatory treatment is expected.[11]

Controlling Unfair Trade Protection

Other sources of beneficial representation in the DSU are more difficult to measure directly, but come as the straightforward application of the MFN application of broader trade reforms and constraints on trade restrictions. Most significant of these benefits may be the ability of dispute settlement cases to limit the usage of anti-dumping (AD), and to a lesser extent, countervailing duty investigations. Such trade laws are subject to bureaucratic and domestic protectionist interest capture, and tend to target imports from developing countries in particular. Table 5.2A shows the year-to-year trend in anti-dumping case initiations reported to the WTO from 1995 until mid-2008. A total of 3,305 such cases were initiated during this period, 1,919 (58%) against developing country imports. It is important to note that developing countries themselves have been initiating more antidumping cases (59% of the total) than the developed countries since the WTO was founded (see table 5.2B). Among developing countries, India, Argentina, South Africa, China, Brazil, and Turkey have filed the most cases, mostly against other developing countries.[12] This fact is also borne out in the filing pattern of the 75 AD-related DSU cases through 2008 (table 5.3). Forty-nine of these DSU cases (65%) have been filed by developing countries, a little more than half of which have targeted developed country AD policies and practices, the rest targeting other developing countries' practices.[13] This

TABLE 5.2A Antidumping cases initiated against imports from developing and developed countries

	'95	'96	'97	'98	'99	'00	'01	'02	'03	'04	'05	'06	'07	'08*	Total
Developing countries	82	129	107	126	194	169	212	195	121	123	140	142	111	68	1,919
Developed countries	75	96	136	131	162	123	154	117	111	91	60	60	53	17	1,386
Totals	157	225	243	257	356	292	366	312	232	214	200	202	164	85	3,305

TABLE 5.2B Antidumping cases initiated by developing and developed countries

	'95	'96	'97	'98	'99	'00	'01	'02	'03	'04	'05	'06	'07	'08*	Total
Developing Countries	75	132	108	161	187	161	200	225	138	129	147	129	99	53	1,944
Developed Countries	82	93	135	96	169	131	166	87	94	85	53	73	65	32	1,361
Totals	157	225	243	257	356	292	366	312	232	214	200	202	164	85	3,305

*Antidumping initiations reported in 2008 include only those from January–June.

Source: http://www.wto.org/english/tratop_e/adp_e/adp_e.htm, Statistics heading.

TABLE 5.3 Adversarial patterns in antidumping-related DSU cases, 1995–2008

	'95	'96	'97	'98	'99	'00	'01	'02	'03	'04	'05	'06	'07	'08	Total
Developing vs. developed	0	1	2	2	1	3	2	2	3	1	1	3	1	4	26
Developing vs. developing	1	1	0	1	4	6	2	1	1	3	1	1	0	1	23
Developed vs. developed	0	1	0	2	2	1	3	5	1	1	0	3	0	0	19
Developed vs. developing	0	0	1	1	1	2	0	0	2	0	0	0	0	0	7
Total AD-related DSU cases	1	3	3	6	8	12	7	8	7	5	2	7	1	5	75

Source: http://www.wto.org/english/tratop_e/dispu_e/dispu_e.htm.

trend is the unfortunate result of developing countries following the demonstration effect of the rich countries, which had previously dominated the use of AD investigations. Now the developing countries face the need to bring this form of protection under control from all sources, making dispute settlement, as well as general WTO reform of AD practices, all the more important.

The ability of WTO members to dispute AD laws is limited by the terms of the Uruguay Round agreement, and most DSU cases can only challenge details of the laws, such as how anti-dumping margins are calculated. Yet the pernicious effects of such laws on trade work through the bureaucratic details of their administration, and DSU-induced corrections can have a significant impact on market access. Products most likely to be the subject of an AD investigation are intermediate industrial goods such as steel, cement, and chemicals; basic manufactures such as batteries and paper; and agricultural goods. Developing country exports consist of many such products. Fighting an AD order requires expensive legal and technical support services, which implies that any additional discipline that can be imposed upon AD laws will tend to benefit developing countries especially. It should be clear, in this regard, that reducing the number of AD cases will tend to increase welfare in both the initiating and in the target countries. Representation, if not participation, in the WTO's dispute settlement system therefore carries at least the potential benefit of reducing the frequency or severity of AD restrictions on market access for all countries that are vulnerable to them, while also reducing the cost of protection in the importing countries.[14]

Systemic Benefits

At the most basic level, WTO membership and the potential for participation in its DSU system may provide even the poorest nonparticipating members with benefits in the form of the existence of a legal venue for grievances. Davis (2006) compared the situations of Vietnam, before it became a WTO member, in its dispute with the United States over catfish AD duties, to that of Peru, a WTO member, in its DSU case with the EU over food labeling. Peru had the clear advantage over Vietnam in prosecuting its case, since it could force the respondent country to face it in a formal proceeding, with recourse to multilateral (as opposed to merely bilateral) rules that a third party would use to review the case. While the fact remains that not all WTO member countries have been able to take full advantage of the DSU, there is still an advantage in being "inside the house" rather than outside it. Even if a country does not file a DSU complaint, other countries must take into account the possibility that it could. Furthermore, in Peru's case against the EU, Canada and Chile joined as third-party observers, adding weight to Peru's case. DSU rules also allow joint filings and (as just noted) third-party participation, so that a poor country could become part of a larger case that includes more powerful complainant countries. The possibility of future NGO help, pro bono legal help, or other external assistance in bringing cases (see next section), or of future DSU reforms to enable poor country filings, all increase the potential value of DSU representation, even in the absence of current participation.

Improving Developing Country Representation

Bown and Hoekman (2005) present a country's choice on whether to file a DSU complaint in terms of a cost-benefit calculation. If the country's discounted stream of future profits with the disputed trade barrier removed, net of litigation costs, is greater than the comparable stream of future profits assuming the trade barrier remains in place, then the country should proceed with the case. This approach assumes an ability to make the relevant calculations, an adequate business-government interface, and coordination to support the internal political process of bringing a case, as noted earlier. According to the authors' logic, measures that can reduce the litigation cost to developing countries can thereby contribute to an increase in cases brought to DSU litigation. Legal services are offered by the WTO-sponsored ACWL,[15] endowed voluntarily by a small number of WTO members, which provides subsidized legal services regarding DSU cases on a sliding scale according to a country's income level. This service is limited to general legal services, not advice or support on presenting or defending against specific cases. In this sense, the subsidy has the advantage that it does not bias the selection of cases for which the beneficiary countries may use the legal services. At the same time, the ACWL is unlikely ever to be in a position to contribute critical legal support in specific cases, given its need to remain neutral as a WTO agency and its reliance on financial support from wealthier WTO countries that may be the target of DSU cases that receive ACWL support. In any case, ACWL resources are limited to a small legal and administrative staff, with access to some external legal counsel. Funding has remained limited in terms of total contributions and the number of donor countries.[16] As a mechanism for providing legal expertise, it is a start, but it would need to expand in order to provide adequate support services for the 100 or more WTO developing country members that have limited legal resources of their own.

Other legal support could come directly from pro bono work offered by international law firms, from NGOs and other issue-oriented groups, or from foreign legal counsel representing commercial interests aligned with those of the developing country. There is apparently nothing preventing such legal support from being offered under current DSU rules. While support from well-meaning and charitable groups could be a valuable source of additional legal resources for developing countries, the most obvious danger is that such groups have their own axes to grind, and may not have the best interests of the country at heart. They could therefore bias the selection of DSU cases that a particular country would pursue toward those that serve the goals and interests of the giver of the aid.

A broader and more systematic objection to the appeal to private sector contributions to developed country DSU activity is that the subsidies they represent may distort the country's allocation of trade policy–related resources. In this regard, the cost-benefit equation presented at the beginning of this section needs to be broadened to cover the entire scope of trade policy activities of the country, if not indeed all governmental activities that could contribute to economic growth. Money spent on DSU cases is money not spent on the country's WTO staffing, for example, or on other important trade delegations in critical countries. Blackhurst et al. (2000) have argued that developing countries should give priority to establishing or expanding their WTO delegation presence in Geneva, which would also contribute also toward their ability to weigh more accurately the costs and benefits of bringing a DSU case. In this view, the emphasis should be placed more on broader WTO representation rather than a more narrowly defined DSU representation, since countries may be able to follow diplomatic channels during ongoing WTO negotiations or even everyday operations as part of a strategy to resolve disputes. From this perspective, filing a DSU case may be less cost-effective than other alternatives. Economically, broad "program" subsidies to support trade policy infrastructure would be superior to specific subsidies to DSU case support, although probably less attractive to potential donors.

Nevertheless, subsidized legal and technical support from private and NGO sources may still be able to play a constructive role in enhancing representation in the WTO for the poorest countries, given the meager resources available to these countries in general. Proponents of such support should recognize, however, that the legalization of dispute settlement has created a shaky political balance in the system, now that panel and AB decisions have teeth. Large and influential countries in the WTO might respond with a political backlash, leading to a possible weakening of the DSU's legitimacy, if they became convinced that DSU cases were being brought by "client" poor countries at the behest of NGOs with their own ideological or political agendas. The proliferation of subsidized DSU cases would also have a negative systemic impact if it led to an overload of the DSB agenda (the DSB budget was strapped during the heaviest case-filing years). This consideration would argue for the advantages of an arm's-length structure of third-party trade policy, negotiating, and trade law support for developing countries, such as through think tanks, legal aid centers, and research facilities that could provide information and services to developing country clients upon request, funded perhaps through foundations or broad-based sources of support. Developing countries would benefit, along with the WTO as a whole, by maintaining autonomy over their DSU filing decisions.

Private sources of support can be particularly helpful in creating balance in the issue of amicus briefs in dispute settlement cases. The AB has admitted such "friend of the court" briefs in its deliberations on a case-by-case basis (see Smith 2004, pp. 561–565). The fear, especially among developing countries, is that admitting amicus briefs may tilt the balance in a dispute in favor of countries that can afford expensive legal support. In this context, NGO and other groups could legitimately play advocacy roles for their causes (or simply as a matter of pro bono support) through the filing of briefs on behalf of developing countries. In order to avoid an imbalance in the system, opening up more DSU cases to the submission of amicus briefs would presume the general proliferation of such activity on *all* sides of the issues, that is, without the ability of one side merely to outspend its opponents in order to gain an advantage. DSU procedures could establish reasonable rules for this practice.

Other reform possibilities include the designation of a DSU special prosecutor to take up cases on behalf of poorer countries. This approach to improving representation would probably lead to more cases filed and more WTO rule infractions brought into public view, but it could also result in explosive political repercussions. Again, in a system currently in a delicate political balance, an impartial process would be difficult to establish. Any decision by a special prosecutor to pursue a case would have to be selective, so how would the process work without some countries feeling victimized and others shortchanged? It is important to note that WTO rule violations and nonviolation cases[1] do not occur only among rich countries, so it would be possible for a special prosecutor to tilt investigations toward poorer countries (on behalf of other poor countries, for example), depending on the prosecutor's mandate and priorities. Despite its good intentions, the special prosecutor idea would be extremely difficult to implement effectively, and it would be better for countries to internalize the process of deciding to initiate DSU cases rather than having someone else do it for them. Other means need to be found to put poor country trade complaints on the table.

Nordstrom and Shaffer (2008) have proposed a "small-claims court" arrangement within the DSU. This idea is appealing in terms of directly addressing the cost issue of small exporters that have legitimate claims but lack the resources to justify the legal and associated costs of a normal case. The idea would be to limit the use of this facility to countries claiming damages below an agreed-upon threshold, with simplified and less resource-intensive procedures. A small-claims procedure could contribute to leveling the playing field for LDCs and small countries, but its design would have to avoid potentially serious political problems. Access to the procedure would probably need to be limited to the group of smaller countries; otherwise larger countries could flood the system with hundreds of small claims of their own. If access to the procedure is limited in this way, problems could arise if successful cases are brought against the larger countries. For example, if the small-claims settlement were subject to MFN implementation, the stakes for the large defendant country could be considerably larger than those of the plaintiff country, inviting either a large-scale appeal or a refusal to comply.[18] A provision limiting small-claims procedures to the smaller countries on both sides of the dispute would remove this problem, but it would also reduce the leveling effect that the procedure set out to establish. While this is an idea worth further investigation, it appears to be difficult to transfer the small-claims concept from a national or even regional context to the institutional peculiarities of an international organization, in which sovereign governments alone have legal standing.

A slower and more methodical approach to improving developing country participation in the DSU (and WTO in general) is possible, but will not lead to dramatic improvements quickly. For example, in the first 11 years of the DSU, a mere handful of cases have been filed jointly. Developing countries may not have fully benefited from filing joint DSU cases, a strategy that would require more coordination but would allow cost sharing and would add political weight and legitimacy to their cases. Countries may also be able to benefit more from the system by finding larger and wealthier "patron" countries to file cases in which their interests are aligned. An example of this approach is the *Upland Cotton* case against the United States (DS 267), filed by Brazil, with third-party participation by Argentina, Benin, Chad, China, India, Pakistan, Paraguay, and Venezuela, along with developed countries such as the EU, Canada, Australia, Chinese Taipei, and New Zealand. A particularly beneficial way for developing countries to take advantage of external private and charitable subsidies on legal and technical support may therefore be to use it to seek out important issues for which a coalition of countries and coordinated efforts by countries can lead to the filing of DSU cases with a high probability of success.

Another way in which surrogate countries could file cases would occur if large direct investments by multinational companies were affected by the disputed trade practice. This was evident in the banana case, in which the United States, which has no significant banana production of its own, filed a case on behalf of its multinational fruit companies with interests in dollar zone banana-producing countries. Ecuador, Panama, Mexico, Honduras, and Guatemala joined the United States as complainants in various stages of this long-lived dispute. While this phenomenon depends on specific trade and direct investment patterns and does not present a systematic solution to the general problem of small country participation in the DSU, it does show that the interests of small countries tend to find a potentially strong channel of influence in DSU cases in the presence of multinational investments.

At the WTO level, developing country representation can only be enhanced by an increased commitment of resources to active participation in WTO operations and negotiations. Since this is expensive, discussions of "aid for trade," multilateral support through the World Bank, IMF, and UN, national foreign aid programs, pro-development programs of NGOs and charitable foundations, and private benefits and contributions could benefit from recognizing the advantages of an expanded presence of developing country delegates in the WTO and other trade venues, given the links between trade liberalization, development, and economic growth. Chapter 6 will pursue this subject in greater detail. The advantages of increased participation for developing countries in the WTO would be further enhanced by an increased commitment on their part to multilateral trade liberalization, which would create new commitments of market opening by their trading partners that can be supported by the dispute settlement system. In general, the greater the degree of negotiated market opening, the more the cost-benefit calculation of filing a case would encourage DSU filings and increase the benefits of a successful case outcome.

Conclusion

The WTO's dispute settlement system cannot dispense justice in the way that a national court system can, and it is unreasonable to expect it to do away with power trade politics completely and give all members equal benefits from the process. Large and wealthy countries tend to pursue their interests aggressively through DSU case filings. In this regard, smaller and poorer developing countries in particular have weaker representation in the WTO—defined as the ability to use the organization to increase economic welfare—than do larger and richer country members. This is because the WTO has no independent authority or enforcement capabilities, and the ability to take advantage of the WTO system depends on a country's bargaining and potential retaliatory power. In the DSU, small and poor countries are further disadvantaged by the financial cost and infrastructure burden of bringing cases. However, even small developing countries enjoy WTO representation through MFN and systemic effects, even if they do not initiate DSU cases. Thus, developing countries (and all other member countries) in the WTO have enhanced representation in the world trading system compared to countries that are not members of the WTO. This is a major reason why none of the 153 WTO members have seriously considered quitting the organization, and why nearly all remaining nonmembers are so eager to join the WTO.

Yet there is a strong case for enhancing the representation of weaker countries in the WTO, not only to reinforce its institutional integrity (which is increasingly under attack) and its incentive structure to promote trade liberalization but also because the increased ability of weak countries to benefit from the system also implies increasing trade gains for all member countries. As trade enhances the development process and economic growth, the benefits of improved standards of living also imply internal stability and reduced conflict among countries, bringing additional benefits to the world economy and the world community as a whole.

Measures to improve the situation appear to require a combination of subsidies, alliance strategy, and systemic commitment by the developing countries themselves, along with some possible reforms in the DSU itself. Regarding subsidies, there is a tantalizing possibility of harnessing legal aid and support from private parties and NGOs to fill the gap between the heavy cost of litigating a DSU case and the modest benefits that would come to small countries with small market shares. The danger of this approach lies in the possible misalignment of interests and incentives between donor groups and recipient countries, which could distort decision making by developing country governments and undermine the integrity of the system. General, untied subsidies would better serve the interests of the developing countries, which could use them to enhance their WTO representation more broadly and effectively, but the incentive of donors would probably diminish as a result. A judicious acceptance of targeted legal aid for specific cases represents a possible compromise that could at least improve the situation. Of the many DSU reforms proposed for enhancing the ability of developing countries to file dispute cases, most involve potentially damaging political and systemic confrontations, although some sort of small-claims procedure may be able to provide opportunities for small countries to overcome the heavy cost constraint built into the current system.

Within the WTO system, more aggressive and effective alliance strategies by developing countries to file DSU cases jointly, or to find strong cases that larger countries could pursue on their behalf, would partially overcome the power imbalance within the organization. The same principle applies in negotiating forums: effective coalition building among weaker countries can enhance their bargaining power and hence their representation in the consensus-based WTO decision-making process. Beyond these political strategies, representation for developing countries will increase as their economic growth and participation in the trading system increases, including the hosting of multinational investment. This last point argues strongly for the increased engagement of developing countries in trade negotiations, with the goal of continuing multilateral trade liberalization, thus amplifying the gains from representation. This process, if sustained, will lead to more trade, more developed domestic institutions, increased resources for legal infrastructure, greater relative bargaining power, and an enhanced ability to benefit from the dispute settlement system and the WTO system in general.

6

Institutional Efficiency and Coherence in the Global Trading System

THE LACK OF TRADE AND TRADE POLICY INFRASTRUCTURE IN many developing countries has raised concerns about their ability to comply with new trade liberalizing measures, particularly those that seek to reduce "behind the border" protection. As a result, increasing attention is being paid to coherence in WTO-led trade liberalization. "Coherence" in this sense refers to support from outside the WTO for efforts to improve the functioning of the trading system, particularly with regard to "aid for trade" programs and capacity-building efforts in developing countries. Support can also come from other global and regional organizations and agencies, national governments providing aid, and the private efforts of groups and individuals. The study identifies three basic areas where such support is needed: 1) in preparing new members for accession to the WTO; 2) in the effective representation of WTO members in legal matters and trade negotiations; and 3) in the ability of WTO members to comply with new rules in terms of governmental regulatory and technical capacity.

This chapter sets out to apply the concept of comparative advantage to international institutions with regard to coherence issues.[1] In evaluating coherence among international institutions in pursuing the goals of the WTO, the analysis will extend the idea of comparative advantage to consider an optimal allocation of international aid resources to improve the effectiveness of the trading system. Activities in support of the trading system include the promotion of trade liberalization, the management of project aid, and the provision of trade-related information, expertise, and legal advice. At the same time, economic considerations require that the pursuit of these goals be consonant with the interests of the member countries in maximizing the effectiveness of their representation in international organizations and in pursuing their own domestic economic goals. The legitimacy of the institution in performing specific tasks or providing specific services is also an important dimension of effectiveness. In this context, aid supplied externally must exhibit not only an efficient delivery of services, but also an efficient alignment of interests or "agency" in supporting both systemic and individual country goals.

The chapter will first consider the meaning of "efficiency" in terms of institutional performance, and what this means in terms of the WTO's goals. The analysis then turns to the role of members' trade capacity regarding their accession, representation, and negotiating activities in the WTO system, and how this factor affects overall WTO institutional efficiency. The resulting set of problems serves as the basis for a discussion of coherence among international economic institutions within the framework of "institutional comparative advantage." There follows a discussion of systemic issues, using the trade facilitation negotiations as an example. The chapter concludes with a set of proposals for a comprehensive approach to institutional coherence based on comparative advantage.

Criteria for Institutional Efficiency and Coherence

The study of international institutions lacks a theory of coherence, a systematic explanation of how best to allocate global institutional resources to multidimensional tasks and problems.[2] The lack of such a theory derives in part from the gap between the process of creating international institutions and the complex and crosscutting nature of the issues they face. Typically, countries and other international actors create an international institution along a single, primary dimension or concept around which they can all establish fundamental agreement. The GATT/WTO system, as described in chapter 1, was founded on the goal of member countries to increase gains from trade, based on the idea that an organized effort to provide a forum for trade negotiations, rules for trade policy, and facilities for trade dispute settlement would benefit all participants. In recent years, however, many challenging problems have emerged in the global trading system that go beyond the WTO's mandate, including the provision of aid in building domestic capacity and infrastructure to make gains from trade possible in developing countries. Economic considerations suggest that efforts to achieve these goals should come from specialized institutions that are particularly adept at specific activities regarding development aid, legal and political advice, technical assistance and training, and other elements of internal transformation that will allow a country to participate effectively in the WTO and gain from trade. No single institution exists with a mandate to pursue this goal. A theory of coherence is therefore required in order to analyze not only the allocation of, but also the possibility of coordinating, institutional efforts to pursue serious problems that overlap or go beyond the mandates of individual organizations. In this regard it is helpful to keep in mind the literal definition of coherence as "a logical and orderly relationship of parts." This view implies an efficient allocation of activities, as one would expect from the concept of comparative advantage, but not necessarily a centralized, coordinated effort, which may involve significant organizational transaction costs.

A preliminary approach to the issue of coherence can be framed in terms of the ultimate ability of an institution like the WTO to achieve its mandate on its own. Frey and Gygi (1990), for example, proposed a test of individual institutions' economic efficiency. In evaluating international organizations, they concluded that it is generally impossible to measure their economic efficiency because it is difficult to determine empirically measurable output for them. Theoretically, the main difficulty lies in the heterogeneity of preferences among the member countries, which prevents establishing a measurable output function reflecting an aggregate preference of all members. In this regard, attaching value to the various activities and outputs of the WTO would indeed be difficult, but it is nonetheless tempting to focus on the value of increased trade resulting from WTO agreements as a possible criterion of efficiency. The WTO is closely associated with the goal of trade liberalization, and therefore of increasing gains from trade. Is it not reasonable to measure its efficiency in terms of the additional economic welfare it generates through trade liberalization?

The recent debate over the influence of the WTO on trade volumes (see Rose 2004 and Tomz, Goldstein, and Rivers 2007) highlights the difficulties in measuring the "output" of trade liberalization. Unfortunately, it is difficult to link increments in international trade at a global level to the specific influence of the WTO, as opposed to other influences. In view of the pervasive influence of a global trading system on many aspects of commercial activity, one would have to create a counterfactual based on the absence of the WTO and calculate the volume of trade under alternative institutional scenarios. Even so, most economists would agree that a global trading system based on multilateral rules, negotiations, and dispute settlement does make possible an expansion of trade beyond, for example, the ability of unilateral measures or of bilateral, regional, or other preferential trade agreements. At the same time, such preferential agreements themselves may be the result of WTO influences, for example to establish a stronger bargaining position in multilateral negotiations. Tomz, Goldstein, and Rivers (2007), after allowing for country-specific effects and the extended participation features of the GATT system, as described in chapter 3, provided evidence that the GATT/WTO system did in fact increase trade among those participating in it.

In the end, the output of any given trade negotiation is subject to the reservation negotiating positions of the countries at the bargaining table, each of which wants to realize liberalization on its own terms, subject to its preferences and political constraints. The outcome is subject to the many factors that affect the reservation positions of the bargainers, perhaps including the availability of benefits from outside the WTO. The efficiency of the WTO as an institution cannot therefore be measured simply as the sum of measurable welfare gains from trade resulting from negotiations under its auspices, but rather on its contribution to the process, its ability to provide a framework and forum for bargaining to get those gains. This chapter considers the possible role of coherent policies and resources that may enhance the ability of the WTO to liberalize trade.

The stated mandate of the WTO includes the following items, as enumerated in Article III of the WTO Agreement:

1. Facilitate the implementation, administration and operation of both multilateral and plurilateral trade agreements;
2. Provide a forum for new trade negotiations;
3. Administer a system of dispute settlement;
4. Administer and publish trade policy reviews of member countries;
5. Cooperate with the International Monetary Fund and World Bank on global economic policy making.

Using the approach of Frey and Gygi (1990), WTO members evidently want the institution to promote and "operationalize" trade agreements, that is, to ensure that trade agreements actually lead to more trade according to the terms established in the agreements, to settle disputes among members, to provide information in the form of periodic trade reviews of member countries, and to "cooperate" with the IMF and World Bank. This last point is the least precise of the stated WTO functions, since it is difficult to measure the performance of cooperation, and since the associated concept of "coherence" in international economic policy is still evolving. However, as the following discussion will show, this factor may take on increasing importance in terms of future WTO performance, although one must take a close and critical view of the costs and benefits of cooperation. In particular, the role of the World Bank, IMF, and even other institutions (global, regional, national) may be instrumental in helping the WTO pursue its primary mandate to facilitate trade liberalization. There is a strong and evidently growing interest in monitoring "aid for trade" and other cooperative activities among these organizations (Auboin 2007, OECD 2008), and funding for these activities has become a concern in connection with further progress on the Doha trade negotiations.[3]

In general, evaluating the efficiency of the WTO therefore comes down to finding a set of criteria that reflect progress toward fulfilling its mandate. This chapter proposes a combination of elements, including the ability of the WTO to move toward universal membership, to maintain trade order through its system of rules and dispute settlement, and to provide a forum for bargaining for more trade liberalization. Each of these elements also involves the provision of aid and technical support to promote the achievement of the goal with regard to developing countries, and each involves trade capacity dimensions that suggest an institutional division of labor to help countries lacking in adequate resources. The justification for the funding aspects of these efforts emanates in part from equity considerations and progress in global economic development, but also from the significant systemic benefits of a more inclusive and better functioning global trading system (see Prowse 2006).

Institutional Comparative Advantage

As part of the basic theory of international trade, comparative advantage predicts the pattern of trade among countries based on their relative factor endowments and the relative factor intensity of producing various goods and services. Applying this concept to international institutions can shed some light on the coherence issue, but some important modifications are also required in order to speak of the "comparative advantage" of an institution. International institutions have resources, traditionally defined, in the form of funding to pursue particular activities and human capital specialized in specific tasks (trade analysis, project management, legal expertise, and so on), and a straightforward application of this theory can link an institution's relative resource endowment to a comparative advantage in "producing" a particular institutional service. However, institutions also have endowments of *status and legitimacy* that emanate from the mandates received from their members or constituents. This element of institutional comparative advantage comes from the "collective intentionality" that serves as the foundation of the institution's purpose, as described in chapter 1. Countries that join together to create an economic institution do so with a specific purpose in mind, and in order to pursue this goal, they impart status to the rules and agents of the institution, which in turn creates what Searle (2005) describes as "deontic powers," a system of obligations and rights for its members. The institution thus acquires legitimacy in pursuing specialized goals through this collective pooling of its members' sovereignty over policies and other governmental activities. In the case of the WTO, it is the pooled sovereignty of its members over their individual trade policies that allows an international institution to establish rules regarding trade relations (such as MFN and national treatment), reciprocal bargaining for market opening, and dispute resolution. The collective intentionality of the WTO also limits the scope of its comparative advantage by defining what its members accept, through the consensus rule in this case, as a legitimate negotiating mandate. Finally, the members' commitment of funds and delegation of functional status to the Secretariat and supporting staff determines the "resource endowment" of the institution, which can then provide specific services assigned to specific tasks.

As an institution promoting trade liberalization, the WTO has comparative advantage in providing its members a forum for multilateral trade bargaining, based on the principle of reciprocity. It also has comparative advantage in the resolution of trade disputes among its members. These specialized activities are based on the underlying benefits to all its members of a rules-based, consensus-driven organization of nearly global membership that establishes a forum for negotiations and third-party facilities for resolving disputes. Its comparative advantage therefore also derives in part from its status and legitimacy "endowment" as an institution, that is, from the powers collectively assigned to it by the membership and from the trust its members place in achieving their collective goals. The recognition of its status functions allows the WTO to reduce the political risk of market access for its members' importing and exporting firms, and the integrity of the system is strengthened by a system of enforcement. The WTO thus secures the gains from trade for its members with a system of rules and procedures. The implication is that those aspects of trade liberalization involving reciprocal bargaining over market access and rules are most efficiently managed through the activities of the WTO. At the same time, the limits of an institution's mandate suggest that the WTO has a comparative *disadvantage* in other aspects of trade-related activities when compared with other institutions, especially those that involve ancillary costs in rules compliance. For example, the WTO has only a limited budget to finance activities related to trade liberalization, mostly for trade policy training, limited legal support in dispute settlement cases, and related technical assistance. The WTO Secretariat is correspondingly small. The central activity of WTO negotiations focuses on reciprocal concessions, and does not include implementing budgets or the implementation process itself. Its comparative disadvantages can thus also be traced back to the limits of its status endowment, described earlier. WTO members are willing to imbue the institution with powers to conduct negotiations, make rules, and adjudicate disputes, but not to spend its members' money beyond a narrowly defined budget.

Finger and Wilson (2006, pp. 29–30) note that multilateral obligations under the WTO in many policy areas typically require local infrastructure and institution building, which will be country- and project-specific and are therefore the province of specialized aid organizations such as the World Bank. Similarly, the dispute settlement process provides only limited support for the legal representation of small, poor, and politically weak countries, putting many countries at a disadvantage in WTO legal proceedings. The advanced state of economic development, trade policy infrastructure, and representation in the rich countries provides the necessary support for taking advantage of WTO membership. The more advanced and especially the larger developing countries can also take advantage of their resources and political influence to benefit from the WTO trading system.

A theory of coherence in international institutions requires an evaluation of other organizations along the lines of resource, status, and legitimacy endowments as well. The World Bank, for example, is an institution based on lending out its capital, consisting of reserves and money paid in by its country shareholders, with the purpose of financing specific development goals subject to approval by its boards of directors. With its economic expertise, access to funds, and project experience in developing countries, the World Bank has institutional comparative advantage in project planning, design, and implementation that can be applied to many aspects of trade capacity building. Its supporting research activities imply a comparative advantage in country-based trade analysis and trade and development policy consulting. As in the case of the WTO, the World

Bank's comparative advantage thus also derives from its status endowment, which in this case specifically involves a collective agreement of its
members to allocate funds in pursuit of development goals. Its institutional framework has also contributed to an accumulation of experience
in project design and delivery, the development of specialized human
capital focused on project implementation, and economies of scale and
scope in the magnitude of projects it manages and the broad international nature of its operations.

Other international institutions may be identified for their comparative advantage in trade-related components of multidimensional issues.
The IMF has comparative institutional advantage in certain aspects of trade
policy design, such as those dealing with fiscal policy and tariff revenues,
the adequacy of social safety nets, and customs administration. These specialized areas of expertise derive from its surveillance of client country
macroeconomic performance and program support. UNCTAD, as a long-
standing advocacy organization for developing countries, has comparative
advantage in training trade negotiators, providing advice on trade policy
implementation issues and the WTO accession process. The UNDP has
comparative advantage in sector-specific trade policy advice and assistance,
particularly in agriculture, fisheries, tourism, and textiles. The comparative
advantage of the International Trade Center (ITC) lies in advising countries
on private-sector issues associated with trade policy, including training and
analysis. Other development banks, such as the Asian Development Bank
(ADB) and the Inter-American Development Bank (IDB), have comparative advantage in the delivery of specific projects related to trade institution
building in their specific regions.[4] In general, the comparative advantage of
the larger international or regional institutions in trade capacity building
tends to be based on the mandates created for them by their members, the
trust they earn through their activities, and the specialized nature of their
experience and expertise.

Numerous other international actors exhibit comparative advantage
in specific and more narrowly defined trade policy–related activities. Specialized development agencies such as the German Technical Cooperation
Group and the Japan International Cooperation Agency provide economic
policy advice to developing countries. Individual governments themselves
can offer valuable advice on specific trade-related issues in which they have
an experience base and strong expertise. Many NGOs also have expertise in
specific trade-related areas, in which they often take strong advocacy positions, such as Oxfam International, the East-West Center, Focus on the

Global South, and Friends of the Earth. Some of them favor trade liberalization and the goals of the WTO; others are committed to undermining
the WTO. The status and legitimacy endowments of these smaller-scale
regional, national, and private institutions derives in part from their underlying commitments to specific goals, but also from reputational factors and
interaction with those countries and groups that consume the services they
provide. In this context, the goals of the specific group or institution, or the
strings that might be attached to aid from it, form an important element
in the efficacy of the service it provides. In terms of institutional analysis,
this consideration is essentially a matter of "agency" and therefore the perceived legitimacy of the institution in pursuing an activity on behalf of a
particular client country. What interests are motivating the service provided
by an institution?

In cases where services are sought freely by countries, this is simply
a matter of "let the buyer beware." Seeking legal counsel on WTO accession issues from an openly anti-WTO organization would not make much
sense, for example. A more difficult issue arises, however, if aid or advice
with questionable motives is part of a package. For example, Shaffer (2005)
quotes a developing country representative criticizing the WTO Integrated
Framework plan, a multiagency effort to provide technical and capacity-
building support to the least developed countries: "Ultimately, the donors
will control how the money is used. For example, when technical assistance
is provided on WTO agricultural issues, the U.S. Department of Agriculture will send an expert who will tell you what your position should be
in the Doha round..."[5] Shaffer (ibid, p. 259) notes that a trade-capacity-
building project's success lies above all in the extent to which it empowers
the recipient country's policy makers to develop effective policies of their
own. This element of self-help tends to distinguish effective aid from aid
delivered for partisan or other ulterior purposes.

Table 6.1 summarizes some key dimensions of institutional comparative
advantage related to the global trading system. Differential elements include
the institution's mandate or "status" endowment, its resource endowment's
capacity to pursue particular activities, and the "legitimacy boundaries" of the
institution, which help to define limits on its ability to enhance a particular
country's welfare in a competent manner. The table includes several high-
profile institutions that deal with trade-related issues (WTO, IMF, World
Bank, UNCTAD, ITC, UNDP, OECD), and otherwise indicates categories
of institutions that also play a role, such as regional development banks,
national government ministries, NGOs, and think tanks.

TABLE 6.1 Global institutional comparative advantage profile: trade-related issues

Institution	Scope	Governance type	Mandate/status endowment	Resource endowment	Trade-related activities	Legitimacy boundaries
WTO	Global	Consensus, delegation of dispute settlement powers	Trade liberalization	Secretariat staff specialized in trade analysis, trade law; limited budget	Trade negotiations, dispute settlement, consulting and training activities (Secretariat)	Limited ability to support national trade interests in WTO matters
IMF	Global	Executive Board	Program aid for external financing	Staff specialized in macroeconomic policy, analysis; funding through member subscription	Country surveillance, program aid, technical assistance	Funding leverage may conflict with national sovereignty
World Bank	Global	Executive Board	Development aid	Staff specialized in development, trade analysis, project management;	Development project management, economic and policy analysis	Balance of interests in project choice, impact
UNCTAD	Subglobal (developing countries)	Deliberative, independent working parties	Advocacy for developing countries	Staff specialized in trade and development issues	Intergovernmental deliberations, trade-related technical assistance; negotiations training	Problematic unification of developing country interests
UN Development Program (UNDP)	Global	Executive Board	Advocacy for economic and social development	Staff specialized in development	Coordination of sector-specific trade assistance; technical assistance	Balance of interests of affected countries

Organization	Scope	Governance	Goal/Focus	Staff/Capacity	Activities	Bias/Interest
International Trade Centre (ITC)	Global	Jointly administered by WTO/UNCTAD	Enterprise aspects of trade and development	Staff specialized in business-related issues in trade and development	Technical assistance, support services and information, training	Business focus
OECD	Subglobal (developed countries)	Council	Promote growth in member countries	Staff specialized in country economic analysis	Economic analysis, country studies, forecasting	Rich country interest
Regional Development Banks	Regional	Executive Board	Regional Development Projects	Subscribed capital, capital market funds staff specialized in regional development	Development, infrastructure projects; technical assistance	Regional and technical competency
Government ministries	National	Executive branch of national government	Pursue trade and related strategies for national government	Expertise in national trade policy; supporting infrastructure	Institution building, consultation, technical assistance	National interest
NGOs	Issue focus	varies	Specific issue, goal; quality of technical expertise	Staff with specialized technical knowledge; funding varies	Advocacy, technical assistance, analysis, aid coordination and delivery	Special interest
Think tanks, research endowments	Issue, program focus	Governing board	Selected focus, quality of funded research	Funding, staff specialized in research evaluation	Focused research projects; development and issues advocacy	Research agenda, bias of individual researchers

Sources: Prowse (2002), www.wto.org; www.adb.org (Asian Development Bank); www.worldbank.org; www.undp.org; www.unctad.org; www.oecd.org; www.imf.org; www.intracen.org (International Trade Centre).

Systemic and Coordination Issues

Comparative advantage considerations also arise in the question of international coordination of institutional efforts. Beyond the comparative advantage of an organization in providing a specific service, the question here is whether an organization can also have comparative advantage in coordinating an effort that involves diverse agencies. This is an extremely difficult issue, in view of the fact that international institutions typically derive legitimacy from the "collective intentionality" of a narrowly focused goal, not from coordinating its activities with other institutions. On this point, the coherence issues runs up against the constraints of global governance. National governance systems, for example, address the problem of coordination in terms of constitutional allocations of power and responsibility, in which a central government can assign functions to agencies or combination of agencies with a specific chain of command. In the absence of a world government that can delegate responsibilities in this manner, the coordination problem becomes very difficult. Which organization will be in charge of a project that involves trade, capacity building, and administrative infrastructure? What will be the expected contribution of each part of the "coherent" team? How will the outcome be assessed, and what is the structure of accountability?

In some instances, there is an overlap in interests among institutions, and when the benefits and costs of the project can be easily internalized by its recipients and benefactors, a specific coordinating function becomes less important. This situation is akin to a traditional economic system that spontaneously allocates resources without the need for intervention. Finger and Wilson (2006), for example, have observed that the concept of institutional comparative advantage has appeared to work well in the negotiations over trade facilitation, without extensive coordination activities by the WTO. This example, which will be the subject of further discussion below, appears to show a successful application of coherence through comparative institutional advantage in discrete aid activities, without the need for an overarching coordinating effort. There are many other areas in which coherence can be achieved in trade-related issues and problems through independent actions by organizations or agencies. Basic development assistance, famine relief, disease eradication, and education projects, for example, will in principle ultimately improve a developing economy's ability to gain from trade, but the aid efforts themselves will not require extensive coordination activities with the WTO (although they may require coordination among the specialized agencies providing the aid itself). In addition, when it comes to closing gaps in information, technical advice, or other specialized services or skills, a developing country should be able to choose among alternatives in a marketplace of aid. In this case, the problem typically lies on the supply side: encouraging the international availability and development of pro bono services and specialized skills for developing countries. Development aid policy in general should strive to bring the recipient country to a position where it can pursue its national goals according to its own lights, so that the developing countries themselves are setting the priorities and making the choices. Coherence, in this regard, achieves "a logical and orderly relationship of parts" through autonomous actions by the various actors in the provision and receipt of assistance.

Situations of smooth internalization of costs and benefits may be the exception, however. A broader perspective on the issue must therefore address those situations in which a systematic and coordinated commitment for capacity building or other aid-for-trade support, recognized as a legitimate and competent activity, may be necessary to complete, for example, a multilateral trade or WTO accession negotiation. The issue of legitimacy in particular raises an important and difficult question. Is it possible to endow a multiagency coherence arrangement with sufficient status, legitimacy, and competence to accomplish the joint goals of its participants? Winters (2007) is skeptical that coordination and funding among various agencies can be successful when transaction costs are high and the ultimate benefit of the aid-and-trade liberalization package is not the central focus. Organizations trying to deal with such crosscutting issues that include elements outside their immediate purview typically attack the problem in a bureaucratic way: by meeting, talking, issuing studies, defining categories, locating funds, counting expenditures, and recording all of their efforts in periodic reports. The act of coordinating meetings has not been difficult in the pursuit of coherence; coordinating successful action on the ground, on the other hand, has been elusive. The institutional problem lies in the lack of constitutive rules and what Searle (2005) calls deontic powers for the participating organizations and the recipient of the aid, including mutually recognized rights, obligations, and certifications associated with the project's activities. In order to impart status and legitimacy to joint or coordinated action, it may therefore be necessary to endow such action itself with institutional status, as might occur, for example, in a consensus-based decision of a WTO trade agreement to include explicit terms and scope for funding implementation measures through the World Bank. Note that such an agreement would also require a corresponding agreement on the source of funding.

The foregoing discussion of institutional comparative advantage suggests that there is a logical way to address multidimensional trade issues and problems requiring resources outside the scope of the WTO. There are three broad areas in which coherence plays a role in WTO policy discussions to improve the operation of the trading system: 1) accessions and general capacity-building measures, 2) logistical support for country trade missions, negotiations, and dispute settlement, and 3) aid to cover ancillary costs in trade agreements. The following sections will discuss the implications of the concept of policy coherence for each of these areas.

Accession and Trade Infrastructure

In terms of institutional efficiency, the WTO has done well to set the negotiating table with a broad membership of countries representing most of the world's population and economy, as documented in chapter 3. However, the accession process itself has received mixed reviews, based on the lengthy accession time and the long and growing waiting period for the applicant countries. Many developing and transition countries have been required to build domestic trade regimes, institutions, and infrastructure from scratch in order to comply with WTO requirements regarding TRIPS, customs valuation, technical barriers to trade, and sanitary/phytosanitary measures. In other words, for many WTO applicants, trade capacity constraints are very likely to have delayed (or are continuing to delay) accession. Efficiency in moving toward universal WTO membership has thus increasingly involved coherence issues: how to help countries lacking trade policy infrastructure to negotiate accession successfully, and how to support the often unfunded mandate of capacity building that WTO membership now requires.[6] While there are efforts to coordinate help for some applicant countries through the WTO's Integrated Framework (IF), they are presently limited to the least developed countries (LDCs), and are apparently not coordinated closely with the WTO accession Working Party (WP), which controls the agenda and makes all critical decisions.

The IF is a joint project of the WTO, the World Bank, the IMF, the International Trade Centre, UNCTAD, and the United Nations Development Program (UNDP). It sets out to provide a harmonized program of trade assistance in the context of an overall development strategy, and is designed exclusively for the world's poorest countries, the LDCs, most of which have requested IF assistance. The IF provides diagnostic assessments of the country's needs, the centerpiece of which is a Poverty Reduction

Strategy Paper, some technical assistance, and a prioritized plan for building trade capacity, which can then be taken to potential donor agencies
for funding consideration (see Prowse 2006). The IF is not specifically
designed for WTO accession candidates, although several countries have
received IF support during the negotiations, notably Cambodia, Nepal, and
Cape Verde, which have completed their accessions. Afghanistan, Ethiopia,
Laos, Samoa, São Tomé and Príncipe, and Vanuatu, which are in various
stages of the accession negotiations, have also received IF support.

In accession negotiations, a country may need to spend years before it
can complete its own internal preparation of the trade policy memorandum
that officially begins its interaction with the WTO Working Party on accession. The lack of trade capacity remains a major barrier to WTO accession,
not only because of the dearth of infrastructure but also because of the
lack of information, trade policy analysis, and expertise. All WTO accession
candidates are developing or transition countries facing these problems.
The daunting process of developing domestic institutions, legislation, and
administrative processes that will satisfy WTO compliance requirements
is likely to be overwhelming, and these are areas in which IF support can
be instrumental in facilitating the accession process. Prowse (2002) documents the enormous IF-sponsored capacity-building efforts devoted to the
preparation of Cambodia for WTO accession, a process of technical support, domestic institution building, and trade policy advising that included
dozens of international institutions, agencies, and bilateral country aid.
Even so, Cambodia's application process spanned nearly ten years.

The IF is a particularly sophisticated attempt at setting up a coordinated
and coherent system of "aid for trade" for countries acceding to the WTO
as well as existing LDC members of the WTO that need to build their trade
infrastructure. Its approach has been to work closely with the country's
government in order to maximize involvement in evaluating and prioritiz-
ing its trade needs, and its impact in terms of mainstreaming trade into
development strategy and government policy has been salutary. However,
Winters (2007, pp. 469–474) has judged the IF in general as a disappointing
attempt at "mid-level" cooperation that has failed to achieve concrete results
in coordinating aid with trade liberalization on a country basis. In essence,
the complicated structure of the multi-organizational effort and of funding
the aid, combined with an overbureaucratization of the process, has diminished the IF's ability to forge an effective link between targeted aid policies
and trade policy infrastructure. One of the key problems standing in the
way of effective IF support for accession appears to be that it is not linked
with the terms of accession, as determined by the WP. Reforms to improve

this situation would need to focus on the operations of the WP, which are dominated by incumbent WTO members with strong bilateral interests in specific elements of the applicants' trade policies and practices. Another problem is that IF donors may have their own agendas and motives, which could diminish both the value of the contribution to the recipient and the credibility of the process. If aid must be coordinated with the objective of fulfilling a trade obligation, the process must be carefully managed to ensure that the recipient is fully engaged in the effort and that it promotes the independence and autonomy of its policy-making capacity. It must also operate on the principle of institutional comparative advantage.[7]

Laird (2007) notes that coherence efforts are typically judged differently from the perspective of international institutions themselves. Officials at many international economic organizations appear, for example, to regard the elaborate administrative structure of WTO-led IF projects—including the identification of matrices of goals, constraints, resources, priorities, and funding sources for each case—as the best model for policy coherence. Whatever admiration one may have for the administrative elegance of such efforts, both Laird (2007) and Winters (2007) emphasize the main problem: *IF projects have had very limited success in supporting and promoting trade liberalization itself.* In particular, for all the attention paid to aid for trade and other financing facilities for developing countries participating in the Doha Round, there is still nothing on the negotiating table that would incorporate funding to support implementation costs of new WTO agreements. In addition to these problems, IF assistance is still limited to LDCs and would not address the trade capacity needs of developing countries above the poorest category. In view of these shortcomings, coherence of a meaningful sort may be a bridge too far for the WTO to reach through such cooperative efforts.

Within the context of the Doha Round, the WTO, along with the OECD, has also established a Doha Development Agenda Trade Capacity Building Database, which documents the funding of projects and efforts by 30 international agencies and 28 country governments in support of developing country trade infrastructure. These initiatives indicate that significant funding and expertise have been made available for capacity building in general, and the WTO itself has provided support through its training programs and through the efforts of coordinated agencies under the IF. As noted earlier, however, the WTO is not an aid agency and does not have comparative advantage in the implementation of aid. What is lacking in these efforts is a systematic link between negotiated WTO obligations and the provision of resources needed to support compliance with them. This will be the subject of the discussion on coherence in trade negotiations.

Overall, the burdens placed on developing and transition countries due to the requirements of WTO accession and the costs of new WTO obligations, if they remain unaddressed, may have long-term systemic consequences. If the acceding country regards the process as unbalanced, unfairly expensive, time-consuming, and out of line with its development priorities, it is less likely to take "ownership" of its WTO membership and to develop a commitment to trade liberalization through the WTO. The small island nation of Vanuatu, for example, was apparently overwhelmed by the lengthy, complicated, and often acrimonious negotiation process, during which it did not receive IF support. It finally received final WTO Working Party (WP) approval of its accession package, only to withdraw its application, as Vanuatu negotiators reportedly had agreed to concessions that were not acceptable politically at home (see Gay 2005). In addition to resources for building trade infrastructure, administrative capacity, and government regulation of trade, many countries suffer from a severely limited ability to generate and evaluate trade information and data and for the government to properly weigh the costs and benefits of trade proposals. Vanuatu has, in the meantime, begun to receive IF aid, but ironically any such assistance after the final WP report is unlikely to change the terms of accession that caused it to suspend its application

General efforts to assist developing countries in building trade capacity have been well-meaning and often highly structured. The main problems are that they have been limited in scope and detached from the relevant negotiations. Aside from changing the way the WP operates in accession negotiations (see the reform proposal in chapter 3) or introducing funding guarantees for new WTO obligations (see below), institutional solutions will need to focus on modifying the WTO requirements for new members and for complying with new obligations. Longer phase-in times may allow for more flexibility in developing the needed trade capacity.

Logisitical Support in WTO Disputes and Negotiations

Michalopoulos (2001, pp. 156–160) reports that, as of 2000, only 72% of developing countries in the WTO maintained missions in Geneva, leaving 29 countries without direct representation there. Average staffing per developing country delegation was also significantly smaller than for their developed country counterparts, 4.1 per mission as opposed to 7.3. There is also typically a lack of supporting trade ministry expertise and coordination in the home capitals (see Blackhurst, Lyakurwa, and Oyejide 2000). Aside from a lack of an educated and trained trade and legal staff, there is generally a poor political and business infrastructure through which trade interests are channeled and represented at the national level. This resource gap is even more damaging to developing countries when one considers that the WTO has moved the trading system toward a more technical, legalized institutional framework. Rich countries typically have a large trade policy infrastructure, with specialists in economics and law who can effectively develop strategies and represent various interests at the national level. Shaffer (2003) has noted the importance of commercial interests and their lobbying efforts in WTO dispute settlement cases, for example. In an environment with a high premium on legal and technical expertise and on commercially driven lobbying power, poorer countries are at a distinct disadvantage.

This issue became apparent during the Uruguay Round, during which developing countries found themselves negotiating on issues with which they were unfamiliar. They finally agreed to a "Grand Bargain" (Ostry 2000) whose net costs and benefits were difficult to calculate.[8] The proper evaluation of proposals required technical expertise that most developing countries did not have, implying the need for support in the form of information and consulting services. In addition, the final agreement, as noted in chapter 2, combined dissimilar concessions on intellectual property (TRIPS) by developing countries with textile trade liberalization and the conversion of agricultural quotas into tariffs concessions by the developed countries, and led to disappointing outcomes for developing countries in particular.

In view of their Uruguay Round experience it is understandable that developing countries would be wary of any future "grand bargains" in the Doha Round, even as such a broad and sweeping agreement has become a practical requirement for concluding negotiations under the WTO's "single undertaking" principle. This situation may indeed have created a critical structural problem for trade negotiations. Finger (2005a) has observed that finding the trade-offs necessary to negotiate a successful conclusion to a multilateral trade round has become more and more elusive, since it is difficult to calculate costs and benefits across disparate policy areas in the face of so much uncertainty regarding outcomes. Assistance in the form of technical expertise, access to relevant data, and advice on negotiating strategy and analysis would provide some of the critical tools countries need to represent their economic interests effectively in a multilateral trade negotiation. Providing external aid to bridge the gap in representative capacity presents difficult questions, however, in terms of serving a country's interests efficiently and effectively.

For a particular country, finding a solution must begin with its determination of how best to deploy its scarce resource of competent national representatives in foreign economic affairs. This approach implies a possible redeployment of representatives to the WTO in Geneva, if in fact the additional economic benefit of that activity exceeds those of the country's expenditures elsewhere. It is possible that the WTO itself could facilitate better representation through teleconferencing facilities and the use of regional meetings closer to the home country. Another possibility is for WTO countries to form alliances or coalitions in which their interests would be jointly represented, as described in chapter 4. This solution would be applicable in cases where there is a clear alignment of trade interests. However, the nature of WTO trade negotiations often involves multidimensional and complex trade-offs that are not easily amenable to joint representation. This implies that a truly effective and sustainable coalition would require the partners to move toward "deep integration" along the lines of a customs union, or even total economic union (such as the European Union), in which central trade and political authorities can manage internal compensatory side payments in order to maintain unity.

In general, providing adequate representation for a country without an adequate resource base of experts and practitioners will have to begin with external support for training, information, and data availability, as well as policy analysis. Ideally, a country will then develop these resources internally and organically, which will also require a concomitant development of markets and commercial interests, a process that may take many years. In the meantime, the country is likely to confront the problem of having to evaluate trade policy advice that may or may not correspond to its long-run economic interests. Bad judgments may result from external political leverage and influences or from corruption. In order to promote more efficient WTO representation, the most promising prospect for interim support would be access to arm's-length, objective, economic, legal, and policy analysis based on the specific country's economic data. The country's own representatives would then be in a better position to devise trade strategies that support the country's best interests. The systematic development of trade policy strategy consulting services for developing countries could, for example, proceed within the existing World Bank staff, which has specialized experience and knowledge in this area, or through an independent agency or think tank, as determined by comparative advantage factors. Since it would be naïve to expect that any particular organization would offer trade policy advice acceptable to all countries, an open market of information may be the best solution, including many organizations offering the widest possible range of views on trade. A competition of ideas in such a marketplace would then allow countries to assess the value of the advice in trade negotiations.[9]

Another example in which the lack of adequate representation can be particularly damaging to a country's interests and to the integrity of a rules-based trading system lies in the case of dispute settlement, which is an integral part of the GATT/WTO trading system. Chapter 5 showed that the system works best for countries that have the legal and diplomatic resources to pursue cases. In practical terms, the complaining country must usually have a certain degree of diplomatic presence and infrastructure at WTO headquarters in Geneva, just to be familiar with the process of filing a case. As noted above, many developing countries do not have representation in Geneva, and many others have minimal or cross-agency staffing. Legal capacity and an effective domestic business lobby—the sign of advanced trade capacity—are often crucial in initiating and pursuing WTO litigation.[10] External sources of support for DSU cases may be able to overcome the potential for inner-WTO conflict, but there are nonetheless many pitfalls, as noted in chapter 5 and above in the case of general trade policy advice. Political biases are likely if NGOs take on advocacy roles for countries in DSU cases; the agenda is then driven by the interests of the NGO rather than those of the country. In a broader sense, it may therefore be best to keep the poor country's own interests and allocative decisions in mind when designing aid-based improvements in its legal representation. It may, for example, be better economically for the country to use available aid to enhance its representation in Geneva (or to pursue other goals with higher social returns), rather than to fight a particular dispute in the WTO.

Logistical support for the trade missions of developing countries could play an important role in leveling the playing field in multilateral trade negotiations and in benefiting from the dispute settlement system, by giving countries the resources and technical tools to evaluate negotiating and legal strategies and thereby have access to the trade-enhancing benefits of WTO membership. Since it deals with discrete resource-based problems in allocating resources strategically, logistical support typically requires coherency without extensive interagency coordination. The issue is therefore making the resources available, in the form of general development aid (which may or may not be used for specific trade policy logistics) and specialized consulting and information services for legal and economic analysis. The pro bono provision of such services by a wide range and variety of NGOs, foundations, and universities, in addition to programs offered by the World Bank and other larger institutions, could provide a "market" for such support.

The Changing Nature of Trade Agreements

The discussion so far suggests that there are two interrelated dimensions of the coherence problem. One involves the general link between trade and development, independent of WTO membership, and belongs on the agendas of specialized international development institutions. The development part of the equation must address the strategies of the individual country and its transformation of the social, legal, political, and economic environment. Trade and trade liberalizing policies, in themselves, cannot promote development any more than plugging a broken or nonfunctioning machine into the electrical current will make it run. Trade is a complementary force in economic development. Within a domestic system of incentives, property rights, and markets, trade provides opportunities for specialization that can boost, but in most cases not initiate, economic development and growth. Most economic evidence points to the importance of openness to international trade as a necessary, but not sufficient, element for sustained economic growth. Domestic policies, reinforced with foreign aid and technical assistance, must bring countries to the point where they can gain from trade. This element of coherence is outside the scope of WTO activities.

The other dimension of coherence involves integrating specific development aid and assistance into the WTO process of trade liberalization. While these two dimensions are related, they are institutionally distinct. Because of the WTO's limited mandate to focus on gains from trade, it is necessary to simplify the coherence issue in terms of its core activities. In addressing the problem of coherence, the WTO should therefore focus on the coordination of aid and support that will make it possible for countries to commit to and fulfill their WTO obligations. In this regard, the inability of WTO members to conclude the Doha round can be traced to the institutional friction that has resulted from their failure to adapt to a changing trade negotiating environment. As an institutional issue, trade negotiations have been complicated especially by trade capacity issues, a problem that arose in the Uruguay Round. The wider scope of issues included many "behind the border" regulatory regimes, which introduced a more

difficult set of trade-offs to make within the WTO's traditional mercantilist bargaining framework. Whereas earlier multilateral trade negotiations
focused on market access issues based on reciprocal tariff reductions, the
Uruguay Round negotiations required a balancing of trade barrier reductions with different varieties of concessions, including intellectual property
enforcement, technical barriers to trade, sanitary and phytosanitary standards (SPS), customs valuation, and import licensing procedures. Acceptance of an agreement on these new issues implied the need for significant
investments by such countries in infrastructure, training, and other forms
of capacity building. In addition to the cost of compliance itself, the new
issues imposed an excessive burden on developing countries in terms of
gathering information and evaluating the proposals.

Finger and Schuler (2000) documented the cost of developing country
compliance with the new rules, based on World Bank, UNCTAD, and EU
Phare project expenditures to support infrastructure building in customs
valuation, SPS systems, and intellectual property. They estimated that, for
these three agreements alone, a typical budget for a developing country
to comply with the WTO obligations would come to $130 million, a sum
that was greater than the annual development budget for many least developed countries (ibid., p. 25). During the negotiations, the cost issue was
not addressed and the development implications of the compliance requirements were not considered, reflecting the inability of WTO alone to address
the problems of development and capacity building associated with trade liberalization. As a result of the Uruguay Round experience, Hoekman (2002)
and others have acknowledged that the world trading system now requires
additional institutional support outside the WTO, but linked to the fulfill-
ment of WTO obligations, in order to facilitate the integration of developing
countries, especially the poorest among them, into global markets.

An aid-for-trade approach to this problem would be to internalize the
costs and funding of compliance into the negotiations, so that countries
are not forced to consider, for example, the heavy net financial burden of
capacity building as a prohibitive cost of trade liberalization. The negotiated agreement would therefore have to include commitments for funding
the necessary capacity building projects.[11] The concept could be extended
to offers of contingency compensation in cases where, for example, tariff
reductions may impose fiscal burdens on countries without alternative tax
collection systems, or where agricultural subsidy reductions impose higher
prices on poor food-importing countries. In this manner negotiations
would be more transparent, and bargaining issue by issue would be more
self-contained. The challenge to the WTO system is that it would require

the participation of additional organizations representing aid providers in the negotiations, and there is no institutional provision for including such terms in a multilateral trade agreement.

In the special case of trade facilitation, as noted earlier, coherence can emerge in a spontaneous manner. Trade facilitation, which encompasses a wide range of logistical and communications activities impacting the delivery of traded goods through ports, warehouses, and customs facilities, was one of the new areas of the Doha Round.[12] In the end, it was the only one of the Singapore issues that developing countries accepted for inclusion on the Doha negotiating agenda.[13] The WTO's Doha agenda did attempt to correct the neglect of implementation issues in the Uruguay Round, citing the urgent need for aid and technical assistance for developing countries, but without specifying systematic commitments and responsibilities for capacity-building project support.[14] Nonetheless, developing countries have received significant aid, assistance, and financial support for trade facilitation projects in the meantime. The World Bank alone, which has identified trade logistics as a priority in development aid, reports aid-for-trade project support of $3.1 billion per year in 2002–05 and $4.9 billion in 2007 (see World Bank 2008).

The interesting upshot of the trade facilitation negotiations is that developing countries, with international aid and support, have made progress in this trade negotiating area without the successful conclusion of the Doha Round itself. Wilson, Mann, and Otsuki (2005) calculate that the economic benefits of improvements in trade facilitation are particularly high. They estimate, for example, that bringing the poorest performers in this area halfway toward the global average they have benchmarked would increase trade by $377 billion annually. The rewards of investment in this area are evidently sufficiently high to justify the efforts by developing countries to obtain aid and financing even without a WTO agreement, although the role of the WTO in presenting the issue was probably instrumental in promoting the idea. Still, trade facilitation appears to be an issue in which widespread support in the international community can internalize and thereby solve the capacity-building problem of completing trade negotiations.

It is tempting to present trade facilitation as a model for WTO coherence, but unfortunately it appears to be an exceptional case. For other negotiated WTO obligations requiring significant compliance costs, a more formal method of coordination will be needed. Tsai (2005, p. 11), for example, proposes provisions in WTO agreements that include a specific coordinating role by the WTO, based on the need for aligning corollary aid with WTO compliance, with information sharing and broader efforts for long-term interorganization cooperation on capacity building. This proposal presumably does not include guaranteed funding of compliance costs. In trade matters, such an arrangement would in principle be easiest when the joint goal is clearly consistent with each institution's mandate and agenda, as well as the development strategies and priorities of all country participants. Taylor and Wilson (2008) have suggested, for example, that the WTO's Trade Policy Review Mechanism would serve as an efficient basis for planning aid-for-trade projects at the World Bank, but this arrangement would not necessarily imply a coordinating role by the WTO.

Coordination becomes more difficult when interests are not aligned, or when the transaction costs of implementing the aid are very high. A rich country trade proposal, for example, such as TRIPS compliance, may require costly domestic investments in poor countries for which they would not invest or seek aid in the absence of a reciprocal negotiated benefit and perhaps legally binding funding commitments. In such cases, the developing country's reforms may be of greater economic benefit to the rich countries proposing the measure than to the respondent developing countries themselves. In this case, closing a beneficial trade deal may imply the need for a "side payment" to the developing countries, thereby justifying a financial commitment on their part to make the investment and the deal happen. Furthermore, the successful conclusion of the entire negotiations could depend on such direct and legal commitments for capacity building.

How should the WTO negotiation be structured to deal with complementary objectives outside its mandate and outside its area of comparative advantage? The WTO itself in this case may find it difficult to coordinate a cross-institutional effort with binding WTO obligations and binding commitments on funding. Finger (2007) for example, has stated that it is impossible to make side payments legally binding in the WTO, at least under its current structure. The foregoing analysis suggests in fact that a competent institution such as the World Bank may be needed to play the coordinating and implementing role in such difficult cases, but such an arrangement would, under the current negotiating mandate, lie outside a formal WTO agreement. One possibility is that the World Bank could provide the needed channel for funding and project logistics through direct negotiation, with the rich countries sponsoring the proposal and the developing countries receiving the aid. The trade facilitation example shows that the World Bank already plays this role in an informal manner. Even this sort of arrangement may not be sufficient to complete the negotiation, however, since there would still be no formal link between negotiated WTO obligations and funding support. An agreement making this linkage, along with an agreement on financial burden-sharing and implementation, would presumably require a new type of binding instrument in the WTO. Finger's (2007) suggestion that funding commitments could be made under a plurilateral agreement may provide the means for such linkage, although it would be unprecedented. This type of accord in the GATT/WTO system has been reserved for partial agreements among a subset of WTO members, which is not binding on (but is open to accession by) the rest of the membership. In this proposal a plurilateral agreement, concluded as part of the WTO negotiations, could be used to bind specific countries to funding commitments to cover the costs of compliance by other countries, with implementation by other institutions. This issue brings the discussion of WTO institutions into uncharted waters, and it is not clear how such arrangements could be implemented. Yet the systemic demands of this coherence issue are likely, in one way or another, to require more formal and perhaps binding obligations from potential donor countries in the future, in order to overcome a trade capacity bottleneck in WTO negotiations.

Summary and Conclusion

As an issue in trade policy, "coherence" has come to signify the importance of cooperation among international institutions in those activities that can build countries' trade capacity and their ability to participate in the trading system. It is important, however, to consider the literal definition of coherence as "a logical and orderly relationship of parts," which does not necessarily imply the need or desirability for formal coordination among bureaucracies. In this context, the concept of comparative advantage provides a useful tool in understanding how a country's gains from trade may depend on a multidimensional, "logical and orderly" set of institutional assets and activities. For countries that do not already have the necessary institutional capacity to capture the gains from trade, the efficiency of the process of securing them improves if there is a rational allocation of aid and assistance, according to the specialized abilities of institutions. This chapter has suggested that the comparative advantage of institutions is based on both resource and "status" endowments, and that the WTO has comparative advantage in its capacity to sponsor trade liberalization negotiations and adjudicate disputes. Other institutions have comparative advantage in specific trade capacity building and trade support activities, including the World Bank, the IMF, development banks, various other UN and international agencies, national government ministries, and possibly even some NGOs. Improved coherence in the form of an allocation of complementary tasks according to comparative advantage among institutions therefore could make possible improved efficiency in WTO efforts to liberalize trade. Based on the activities of international organizations so far, however, cross-agency coordination in this sense tends not to contribute significantly to successful coherence.

There are three areas in which improved coherence can play a significant and positive role in the WTO: accession, supporting logistics, and negotiated multilateral trade obligations. WTO accession provides particularly challenging problems. A systematic program of aid for applicants in complying with all negotiated entrance obligations is needed, which will require extensive capacity-building efforts by aid providers. The accession Working Parties can help by simplifying and clarifying accessions standards and coordinating their agenda with the aid programs, such as the Integrated Framework. With regard to logistical support, the problem comes down to the availability of information and resources in order to deliberate and make informed decisions. General aid to support the presence of developing countries in Geneva would be helpful. Support for training in law, negotiations, and other trade-related activities, as well as access to multiple independent sources of information and advice, would also allow many WTO member countries to improve their capacity to negotiate effectively. In this instance, coordination is not generally at issue. The issue of coherence in trade negotiations presents a different set of challenges. In some cases, trade issues imposing capacity-building or other financial burdens on developing countries may be resolved without the need for any binding funding commitments, as in the case of trade facilitation. However, in this case successful spontaneous coherence appears to be the exception that proves the rule. Visible and compelling mutual gains tend to generate their own coherence, while top-down attempts to coordinate coherence, usually in the form of transfers, tend to run aground on the shoals of bureaucracy. This rule raises troubling questions for the outcome of future multilateral negotiations, which may depend on specific funding for compensation arrangements and therefore may require a broader scope and more formal role for aid providers. The WTO negotiations have conspicuously failed to propose any binding commitments for such aid. An aid-for-trade component may therefore have to emanate from outside the WTO, in the form of organized side payments spearheaded by the rich countries, brokered deals of support involving the World Bank and other institutions, or new WTO instruments, such as plurilateral agreements, that would bind donor countries to support other countries' compliance costs, in order to internalize an otherwise intractable ancillary financial obligation in trade liberalization.

A comprehensive treatment of the optimal allocation and coordination of institutional resources and activities must await the further development of a general theory of institutional coherence. In particular, more evidence needs to be gathered on international, interagency cooperative projects, including cost-benefit analysis. Improvements in coherence will require a framework of clear goal setting, decision making, agency, and accountability. In cases of successful execution of the project, a preliminary view suggests that it is important that the benefits be internalized, through "ownership" of the project, as in trade facilitation. The most difficult issue is the question of coordination on a trade issue when the underlying proposal is controversial and may require a negotiated side-payment. The World Bank or other major funding institutions, for example, may play an increasing role in trade negotiations when funding and implementation are critical to the conclusion of an agreement. Success in this endeavor will depend on a broader and more open system of eleemosynary support, based on institutional comparative advantage, and avoiding the pitfalls and transaction costs of bureaucratic interagency coordination.

7

Getting Over the Doha Blues

THE WTO PLAYS AN ESSENTIAL ROLE IN THE WORLD ECONOMY, providing the framework for negotiations on trade liberalization, rules for the trade policies of its members, and the peaceful settlement of disputes. By making it possible for its members to conclude agreements on these items, the WTO itself is a global public good: it overcomes the difficulties individual members would have on their own in achieving cooperation and the multilateral gains from trade. In pursuing these goals, the WTO represents the better part of our civilization's propensity to "truck and barter," through reciprocal, negotiated market opening among sovereign countries rather than through conquest and war. The history of trade diplomacy shows that the most efficient and effective way to maximize the global gains from trade is through a system of multilateral bargaining and rules based on institutions that can transmit the shared trading motivation into consensus on trade opening agreements. It requires a disciplined and patient process of agenda setting, bargaining, and compromise, with leadership among the larger trading partners and flexibility in finding new ways to reach consensus. The challenge for the WTO membership is to provide the political bargains at home, the institutional framework for meaningful participation by all members, and the ambition for a large global deal to open markets for goods and services that will benefit all countries. As a successful international economic institution, the GATT/WTO has been not only a machine for generating the gains from trade but also a system of peaceful and productive interaction among countries. It is worthy of all its members' support and efforts to nurture and strengthen it.

This system has in many ways been the victim of its own success. Multilateral trade liberalization efforts from 1947 to the end of the Uruguay Round in 1995 led to vast increases in world trade and welfare, fueling an expansion of its membership and an eagerness to expand the scope of trade negotiations. Thus we have a WTO with nearly universal membership that began the Doha Round with an ambitious negotiating agenda. These goals, however, have been difficult to pursue in the context of the changing structure of the global economy, the emerging problems of the global commons, and the expanded role of developing countries. Institutional features of the WTO that support the interaction of its members to achieve the gains from trade have not kept up with these new developments, creating an extremely difficult environment for the negotiations. The failure of the WTO countries to deliver a successful conclusion has been disappointing, and progress toward that goal continues to be elusive. Can the WTO overcome the Doha Blues?

World trade has faced crisis conditions in the past, and it is under such circumstances as we see today that adaptive institutional change is most likely to occur. At the same time, it is unlikely that a dramatic institutional breakthrough will occur quickly to save the Doha Round and make it a ringing success; a more modest outcome is therefore the appropriate goal. The roots of the WTO's institutional problems reach back into the Uruguay Round and have grown over the intervening years. While some adjustments within the WTO have begun to take place, such as the development of the Integrated Framework and more inclusive decision making, much work still needs to be done. The main issue comes back to the question of what it will take to complete a multilateral trade deal. Consensus remains the holy grail of WTO negotiations. How can WTO member countries find their way toward a consensus that will lead to a significant global trade deal—if not now, then in the future? This final chapter will present proposals in three general areas that, if successful, would strengthen the global trading system: domestic reforms among WTO members, WTO internal reforms, and policy coherence among international organizations. Because the WTO is an institution in delicate balance between the goal of creating gains from trade and allowing its members to maintain sovereignty over their trade policies, there are no quick and easy solutions. While it is important to consider strategies that will bring the WTO from the Doha Round to the next stage of trade negotiations, the essential issue is to build the institutions for a global trading system for the twenty-first century. The study concludes with observations on the challenge of keeping the WTO relevant in policy makers' minds, on the probable consequences of a decline in the WTO's role in trade relations, and on the outlook for the future.

Domestic Reforms

In its function as a machine for trade liberalization, the WTO depends on the ability of its members, particularly the large, important, and influential members, to find domestic political bargains to overcome the inevitable mercantilist and nationalist opposition to trade expansion at home. With this requirement in mind, the main proposals for domestic reform are to:

1. Expand adjustment programs, focusing particularly on worker retraining and transitional assistance, especially in slower-growth countries;
2. Promote new business growth through entrepreneurship;
3. Mobilize exporter interests in support of trade liberalization; and
4. Improve agricultural productivity, particularly in developing countries.

Heads of state in the important countries must take the initiative and in some cases must take political risks in order to expand their bargaining positions. A final multilateral trade agreement will in any case remain impossible in the absence of the requisite political leadership, compromise, and commitment that have been absent from the Doha negotiations in recent years.

Adjustment

Sustaining domestic support in favor of trade liberalization has become more difficult for many countries in recent years, for reasons outlined at the beginning of chapter 1. The world has become an uncertain place, not only regarding economic security but also in terms of terrorist threats and the uncertainties of global warming and environmental damage. Prospects of a brighter future through inexorable advances in technology and specialization, buoyed by global integration and growing world markets, have dimmed as crisis has piled upon global crisis. In addition, the perceived threat of rapidly growing countries such as China and India has caused the rich industrialized countries to become more and more preoccupied with protecting their traditional industries. The emerging-market countries themselves also lack safety nets for displaced workers, which may not be a problem as long as economic expansion and growth provide employment opportunities. As these countries continue their economic transformation, however, adjustment to higher wages, structural changes, and competition from other countries will inevitably cause disruption and political difficulties with trade liberalization. In general, governments must do a better job of managing the domestic challenges of structural economic change.

There are no provisions or guidelines in the WTO regarding adjustment policies for its members, whose political and economic systems vary widely, or for their supporting education, labor, and resource policies or incentives to adapt to changing markets. In general, the challenge of adjustment is how to achieve flexibility in a particular political environment. In rich countries, the policy debate turns on adjustment assistance for workers, and this issue often gets tangled up in the distinction between job displacement due to trade and displacement due to other causes, such as technology or market trends. Often there is a combination of factors that leads to job losses. The best approach would be to avoid making this distinction and to focus on a general employment adjustment program, one that focuses on protecting the worker, not the job.[1] The key to an effective adjustment program in advanced economies is to focus on retraining and education, with transitional benefits and incentives to move to a new job. Supporting policies are needed to maintain flexibility in labor and other resource markets, so that labor, capital, and other factors of production will be mobile enough to move to new jobs when old jobs become redundant. It is also important to provide education to the entire population from a young age in order to prepare future workers, both men and women, for flexibility in future employment. In the end, countries generally get the standard of living that they earn, based on investments, technological advancements, and education that contribute to increasing worker productivity.

Entrepreneurship

Much of the anxiety associated with globalization and trade is centered on jobs, but most job growth now comes from small and medium-sized businesses. A common problem in the adjustment process is the tendency of governments to protect "national champions" or other large companies from competition or adverse market conditions, which locks economic resources in activities that drag down economic growth. Such protectionist policies often discriminate against new business development and the innovations it produces. In a recent global survey of early-stage entrepreneurs, many small businesses show a strong reliance on export sales, especially those in smaller countries with market opportunities in nearby international markets.[2] Yet the contribution of entrepreneurship to trade liberalization stems not just from the association of new businesses and jobs with trade, but also as a channel of adjustment for displaced workers to find new jobs, for workers to gain job skills, and for new domestic markets to develop. In developing countries, necessity-driven entrepreneurship is particularly important in providing employment.

Exporter Interests

Exporters are the natural allies of trade liberalization. In rich countries they continue to be reliable supporters of WTO negotiations, but their voices have been muted in the Doha Round. In part this is because separate plurilateral agreements of interest to them, such as the WTO's financial and telecommunications accords, were concluded separately. More broadly, corporations now benefit increasingly from specialized market access arrangements with countries in which key supply chain operations are located. Thus host countries can offer targeted reductions in applied tariffs on intermediate goods to the corporation's home country in exchange for FDI and export platform operations, for example. Such preferential arrangements tend to create a welter of possibly discriminatory and trade-diverting market access arrangements, and also siphon exporters' advocacy away from broader trade liberalization efforts. On this issue, governments and exporting interests must forge a more systematic domestic strategy for trade liberalization that can bring the full weight of exporter interests to bear on the country's trade negotiating platform at the WTO.

In developing countries, the domestic political influence of exporters on trade policy is often weaker, especially if the exporting industry itself is in an early stage of development. Furthermore, trade policy itself may not always be "mainstreamed" in the government's economic strategy, and in the absence of a strong pro-trade voice, protectionist interests are more likely to prevail. For this reason, it is important that exporter and consumer interests have a political role to play in their countries' trade policy, especially now that developing countries are actively involved in the negotiations (see Shaffer 2005; Hoekman and Kostecki 2001, chaps 3–4). Much as labor union representatives have become active in promoting worker rights groups in developing countries (see Arnold 2001), there is an equally compelling case for international business organizations and NGOs to lend assistance to local exporters, importers, and consumers in developing countries in organizing and fostering political links with their political representatives. As smaller firms become more involved in export markets, this recommendation also applies to organized pro-trade lobbying activity in developed countries.

Agriculture

Among the top priorities in global trade policy is the reform of agricultural policies and improvements in agricultural productivity. These reforms must take place largely at the national level, although there will be a need for foreign aid as well. Agricultural trade presents the single biggest stumbling block facing multilateral trade negotiations, and the solutions lie largely outside the WTO's sphere of influence. No other subject in trade policy remotely approaches the level of passion seen in agricultural anti-trade sentiment. At the WTO's Cancún Ministerial Meeting, a Korean farmer committed suicide publicly as part of an anti-WTO protest. In India, there is an ongoing suicide watch for desperate, debt-ridden farmers, who take their lives at a rate of approximately 17,000 per year.[3] Farmers in poor countries like India typically represent the majority of the population, and their income rests precariously on food prices. In rich countries, where agriculture usually employs only a small percentage of the workforce, the farm lobbies vehemently protect their domestic markets from foreign competition. France has long held virtual veto power over EU trade liberalization in agriculture, while the United States clings stubbornly to agricultural tariffs and subsidies promoted by farming lobbies in Congress. The traditional approach to WTO trade liberalization has proven very difficult to apply to agriculture, as shown in chapter 2. Much of the problem must therefore be addressed from inside domestic markets.

After many decades of resistance to trade liberalization, a few key issues have emerged. In poor countries, farms are typically small, inefficient, deprived of adequate tools and farming methods, and financially vulnerable, with few economic opportunities for farm workers in other sectors. The goal should therefore be to improve agricultural productivity and to provide job opportunities for workers who are freed up from the agricultural sector as efficiency improves. Increasing productivity will require improved methods, tools, seeds, and irrigation, as well as market reforms and incentives, including access to credit. The other side of the equation is to provide alternatives to farmers, for example through openness to foreign direct investment, particularly with regard to labor-intensive manufactures, and policies conducive to local entrepreneurship. The task of reforming agriculture in poor countries tends to be difficult because for most of the population it is the only way of life they know, and the transformation of agriculture is typically a central element of the development process itself. However, the quality of economic policy makes a difference, and there have been some notable successes in improving agricultural productivity, notably in China (see OECD 2005). Foreign aid and external financing will be needed, a topic addressed later in this chapter. With sufficient internal measures to improve agricultural productivity in place, the discipline of external prices may then pave the way for a more open trade regime.

In the rich countries, most observers agree that agricultural support programs are wasteful and inefficient, and economic analysis shows that the main benefits of reducing farm subsidies and tariffs will accrue to the domestic countries themselves. These large subsidy programs and tariffs benefit a small portion of the population. What will probably be needed to dislodge these programs are sufficiently large trade opportunities in other areas in each of these countries, along with gradual phase-in periods for support reductions and trade liberalization. Domestic political support for new trade opportunities may then be able to overcome entrenched agricultural protectionism. It is becoming abundantly clear that agricultural support programs are blocking significant trade benefits at the bargaining table.

The Institutional Connection

The importance of domestic factors for institutional reform in the WTO is that multilateral negotiations follow the principle of mercantilism: import market access is a concession, and export market access is the goal. This mind-set defines the political economy of domestic trade policy. If concessions are too costly in domestic political terms, then the support of domestic exporters and other organized beneficiaries of trade liberalization may be insufficient to offset formidable protectionist opposition. The gains from trade, large as they are, still require effective domestic political support, and the predictable opposition to trade liberalization must typically be neutralized in some way. What most countries need is a more effective way of managing political opposition to trade, and this is why adjustment mechanisms and domestic economic flexibility are so important. With safety nets in place and new opportunities visible, job displacement becomes less of a rallying cry for trade barriers.

WTO Internal Reforms

When trade talks become subject to perpetual deadlock, WTO members must find ways to increase flexibility in the negotiations. The Doha Blues have come about as the result of frustration with the slow progress toward consensus on a single undertaking, combined with a sense of apprehension, suspicion, and resentment among many members regarding what they regard as an imbalance in the trade agenda and in the possible outcome. The evolving global trade environment and the increasing role of developing countries in the negotiations require the entire WTO membership to take a fresh look at the way it does business, including efforts to:

1. Provide more flexibility for new members to phase in WTO obligations;
2. Improve the system of WTO deliberations through formal "platform" representation in Green Rooms and mini-ministerials;
3. Introduce a "small claims" procedure in WTO dispute settlement; and
4. Increase the flexibility of the single undertaking.

Accession

Chapter 3 suggested that the lack of progress in multilateral trade negotiations may already have begun to affect accession negotiations. In the absence of new trade deals, incumbent members are more tempted than ever to assert their superior bargaining power to extract concessions from new WTO members, and accession negotiations have taken longer and longer to conclude. The asymmetry of bargaining power may also lead to an erosion of good will among new members that could haunt future WTO negotiations. While all WTO members should be expected to meet their obligations, many developing countries may need additional time to "ramp up" to these requirements. Special and differentiated treatment, including additional phase-in times, combined with expanded assistance through the Integrated Framework Program, should be allowed for these countries. In addition, Working Party procedures should not foist "WTO-plus" obligations upon new members.

Representation

Many of the internal stresses in the WTO have grown from two particular problems: representation and complexity in the scope of negotiations. With such a large membership, decision making is impossible without some form of Green Room. The tensions that have arisen over the exclusivity of Green Room deliberations have led to informal measures by the D-G to be as inclusive as possible when calling such meetings. In the context of focused deliberations, it is generally possible to identify in advance all countries that have a compelling interest to attend, and the scope of country representation is enhanced by the presence of organized coalitions on specific issues. These incremental measures demonstrate the ability of the WTO to adapt to the institutional requirements of an expanding membership. It is, however, more difficult to manage emergency Green Room meetings that the D-G may need to call on short notice to resolve broader issues that are critical to the negotiations. One way to assure inclusiveness is to encourage more coalition building across the spectrum of negotiating issues, and then to make sure that all significant coalitions regarding the relevant issues have a seat at the meeting. In the course of the Doha Round, for example, India and Brazil have often played leadership roles in representing developing countries' interests on issues such as the debate over the Singapore issues and rich country agricultural subsidies. Yet on other issues, countries within such coalitions may diverge, and adequate representation is not guaranteed. As suggested in chapter 4, the development of a well-organized system of platforms representing the main bargaining positions on specific aspects of the negotiations may allow more transparent communication and caucusing, while setting up points of convergence to facilitate more efficient and flexible bargaining that can lead to consensus.

Dispute Settlement

Small and poor countries are underrepresented in the WTO's dispute settlement system, mainly because of the high cost-to-benefit ratio of prosecuting a case. For political reasons, it would be difficult to rebalance the system to resolve this problem, since efforts to favor cases filed by developing countries (or any WTO member) could lead to a damaging backlash by other countries. With this constraint in mind, it would be best to pursue some form of "small-claims court" arrangement. In general, developing countries may also enhance their representation in dispute settlement by jointly filing cases. Foreign aid and pro bono help from external sources may also help to correct the resource gap in legal expertise and advice (see the section below on coherence), but it is important for such aid to come with no strings attached, in order to protect the integrity of the dispute settlement system.

The Single Undertaking

The single undertaking had the goal of unifying the WTO in terms of a common set of rights and obligations for its members, and this feature should not be abandoned recklessly. However, it has also created a strait-jacket in terms of consensus building, and the WTO members must find ways to increase the flexibility of the negotiating process. Many business groups and policy makers have become impatient with the strictures of the WTO's single undertaking rule (see Business Roundtable 2006, WTO 1998, and Schott 2008). One common complaint has been that the Doha negotiations are too complex to have any hope of a single comprehensive, unified agreement. Lawrence (2006, 2008) has proposed restructuring the WTO into a "club of clubs," allowing for a set of plurilateral agreements among subsets of WTO members. The WTO currently does include plurilateral agreements on government procurement and trade in civil aircraft, carried over from the GATT, plus GATS agreements on telecommunications and financial services that do not include all WTO members (Hoekman and Kostecki 2001, chaps 7 and 11). The "club of clubs" approach would build on this system, and the precedent for such agreements goes back to the "codes" approach of the GATT. However, it was precisely because the United States and other countries regarded the codes as a fragmenting influence that they proposed the single undertaking. Despite the deviations from this principle indicated above, WTO members have generally been reluctant to allow plurilateral agreements to proliferate, in fear of undermining the discipline of a universal negotiating agenda. In addition, a club of clubs would make WTO obligations more complicated, particularly with regard to the scope of dispute settlement concessions or retaliation.[4]

From the point of view of institutional efficiency, an assessment of the single undertaking must consider its practical usefulness in facilitating consensus in the WTO and delivering the gains from trade to WTO members, which would require discretion. In negotiating theory, the opportunity for bargaining trade-offs among disparate issues often increases the final welfare gains for all participating parties (see Levy 2006), especially when various members perceive strong gains from concessions that cut *across* the disparate issues, but not *within* the individual issues. On the other hand, including an issue in the negotiations on which no convergence toward a broader agreement is possible can only bog the negotiations down. The tension between these two stylized situations forms the basis of the debate over the single undertaking. The issue is made more complicated by the fact that the chances of a broad deal are often difficult to evaluate in advance. Gains from broad negotiations are typically larger if a breakthrough can occur with an agreement over disparate topics, as in the Uruguay Round's "Grand Bargain" balancing TRIPS and MFA liberalization. Yet, as noted in chapter 2, this "bargain" may have soured developing countries in particular on such wide-ranging deals in the Doha Round.

Ultimately, WTO members will probably have to modify the single undertaking in order for the WTO to capture some of the more difficult gains from trade. There are precedents for such deviations, based on special and differential treatment for developing countries, special rules for least developed countries, and existing plurilateral agreements. The GATS, for example, has not fit well with the traditional multilateral negotiating process, as shown by the disappointing results in the Uruguay Round and in the Doha Round so far. In fact, the limited degree of services trade liberalization has taken the form of sectoral agreements in financial services and telecommunications, as mentioned earlier. Many of the services sectors involve politically sensitive sectors, and it may be necessary for these countries to acquire the experience of smaller-scale integration—through preferential trade and investment agreements, for example—before they can develop the political tolerance for broader multilateral liberalization. East Asian countries, for example, have been particularly active in concluding PTAs that include services agreements. If one believes in the "building block" view of PTAs, this trend may eventually lead to more ambitious services market opening in the WTO (see Fink and Molinuevo 2008).

The multilateral negotiating agenda needs to reflect more strategic and flexible thinking among the major WTO members. In principle, areas in which there is a good prospect for consensus among the entire membership, such as trade facilitation, should be subject to an "early harvest." At the same time, areas in which the strong expectations of one group of countries meet with extreme reluctance from another group may benefit from a plurilateral approach, with agreements among a subgroup of WTO members. Trade in politically sensitive services with significant regulatory and investment implications may be ready for such a new approach. Following this principle of negotiating efficiency is certainly easier to observe in theory than in practice, especially since the prospects for agreement (or lack thereof) may not become clear until after much laborious bargaining. It is always tempting to remain optimistic that a breakthrough will lead to a larger cross-issue bargain. Yet on this point the developed countries should keep in mind the history of "Grand Bargains." Asking developing countries to break new ground and accept liberalization in regulated services areas in exchange for lower agricultural subsidies and tariffs in the United States and EU will cause many delegations to think back on the TRIPS-and-textiles Grand Bargain in the Uruguay Round, which they came to regard as a particularly bad deal. Once burned, twice shy. Some areas of services trade may therefore not yet be ripe for multilateral liberalization. In the meantime it would be best for WTO members to identify those modes of services trade with the best potential for cross-issue bargaining, since services commitments are likely to be necessary as part of a broader deal with agriculture and NAMA. It will then be possible to consider the prospects for more progress on separate sectoral services agreements.

Coherence

The discussion in chapter 6 observed that the evolution of the trading system has exposed development gaps among WTO members that have made progress in trade liberalization difficult. Specifically, these gaps have made consensus more difficult to achieve. Yet efforts to close the gaps fall outside the ambit of the basic WTO mission, as agreed by its members. The ultimate goal of coherence as it relates to the WTO is to establish a global institutional structure that will improve the performance of the trading system and enhance the gains from trade. Many important issues in trade negotiations now involve cost issues that cannot be covered in WTO agreements themselves, implying a role for other international organizations. The main proposals with regard to coherence are to:

1. Limit WTO participation in coherence activities to aid and assistance directly related to WTO accession and WTO obligations;
2. Secure funding to support WTO obligations coherence through binding plurilateral agreements among donor countries; and
3. Promote and encourage other trade- and development-oriented aid through a wide spectrum of specialized agencies.

Scope and Limits of WTO Responsibility

One huge mistake that has haunted the WTO throughout the Doha Round is the expectation created by its designation as the "development round." The WTO is not a development organization, because it has neither the resources nor the mandate to pursue the basic development goals that many of its members have. Despite the acknowledged role of trade in development in the WTO preamble, the WTO's toolkit does not include instruments for the fundamental transformation of less developed into more developed countries. At the same time, economic theory and empirical research indeed suggest an important role for trade in the development process, and this is the proper role of the WTO. Participation in a system of trade rules and negotiations will aid and abet development through commitments to external disciplines, improved resource allocation, and foreign market access.

Recognizing the important but complementary role of trade in the development process is the first step in addressing one of the great development challenges of our time: how to bring the poorest countries in the world out of poverty and into the global economic system, where they can benefit from international trade and investment. This is one of the central goals of coherence in the world economy. Institutions tend to be founded on narrow mandates, based on goals that are common among their members. Since the WTO's mandate focuses on the gains from trade, it makes no formal provisions for aid or financing as part of a trade deal that may impose costs on resource-poor members. While such deals are possible behind the scenes, the WTO rules cannot guarantee them, but improving the trading system and expanding the gains from trade depend more and more on building trade capacity and infrastructure in developing countries, a costly proposition.

A Division of Institutional Labor

A solution to the coherence conundrum must be based on some combination of better coordination among global institutions and developing new global institutions. The main problem with coordination is that it involves heavy transaction costs. Pursuing project goals at the WTO, the World Bank, the IMF, regional development banks, or NGOs generally involves internal bureaucratic decision making that is designed for self-directed execution, not cross-agency coordination. The typical result of a successful coordinated project is that agencies will meet and draw up plans, leading to an action plan, funding, and execution of the project. But the acid test is whether there are concrete and verifiable results on the ground, such as an increase in trade liberalizing measures, trade volumes, improved processing through customs, wider participation of businesses in trade, or a closer alignment of domestic with world price ratios. The outcome must then be set against the resource cost used to accomplish it.

With regard to building trade capacity, much of the external help should be subject to choices made by the recipient country. Gaps in trade capacity related to regular and ongoing WTO activities, for example, can be filled by specialized international agencies, foundations, universities, and NGOs that provide pro bono support or direct aid, without the need for cross-agency coordination. Examples include legal advice for dispute settlement cases, country-specific economic analysis of trade liberalization proposals, training for trade officials, and resources to support more effective participation in the negotiations. In filling these gaps, inter-agency coordination is not as important as the availability of an open and transparent system of consultancy, technical support, and aid providers that will deliver services in an efficient manner, based on the decisions of the recipients.

Some forms of coherence, however, will require broad international agreement and cooperation, and this will be difficult, since existing global institutions do not provide for it. For example, an agreement on compensation for tariff revenue shortfalls due to trade liberalization in poor countries would require the wealthier WTO members to establish parallel "side agreements" in the form of a plurilateral code committing them to a financing plan for that purpose. Similar agreements may be necessary to provide a structure for dealing with the WTO's other unfunded mandates. If external resources are required in order to carry out infrastructure and capacity-building projects linked with specific WTO negotiated commitments, then funding sources, project management responsibility, and clearly defined compliance criteria should be established. It is only when the formal provision of committed funds can be matched with the ancillary cost of WTO commitments that a coherent solution to this problem can be found.

Making the WTO More Relevant

The great global challenges of terrorism, environmental degradation, climate change, energy crises, widespread food shortages, and world poverty, not to mention the ravages of a major financial crisis in the world economy, have made the problems of the Doha Round pale in comparison. While trade negotiators fuss and fume over the details of special safeguard mechanism triggers and the percentage levels of tariff-cutting formulas, the world's attention has been drawn toward these compelling threats to the security and livelihood of the earth's population. In this regard, one of the most serious casualties of the Doha Round has been the diminishing sense that trade liberalization matters to the world economy. Global trade negotiations have become, it seems, half-hearted, small-minded, marginalized, even irrelevant.

Since each of the serious global problems mentioned above has a connection with trade, it is tempting to bring the WTO into the public discussion by adding them to the trade agenda. Yet these problems demand global institutions of their own in order to establish global cooperation, coordination, and support in working for solutions. The public debate has indeed led to proposals that trade policy, particularly punitive trade restrictions and other protectionist measures, be used to pursue or enforce national or global remedies, such as tariffs based on carbon content of trade, anti-dumping duties based on deficient environmental policies of exporting countries, food export restrictions, international capital and investment restrictions, and many other anti-globalization measures designed to prevent or roll back the integration of world markets. What role should the WTO play in such matters?

One basic principle worth emphasizing in any and all policy forums is that protectionism in the pursuit of national and global environmental, security, poverty reduction, and financial stability goals is almost certain to be disastrous. There is rarely a clear economic welfare benefit from restricting trade itself, and the use of trade restrictions as a weapon to enforce agreements is only a formula for international conflict and capture by domestic political lobbies. Making this simple point does not require a WTO negotiation or Ministerial Conference, it should rather be shouted from the rooftops at every meeting at which these issues are discussed. However, the WTO would indeed benefit from a formal statement, endorsed by all members in a plenary session, pledging abstention from new protectionist measures while these global crises are being addressed at the national and international levels. A resolute statement by the WTO denouncing protectionism would be especially welcome in times of global financial and economic crisis, when governments face political pressures to engage in self-defeating beggar-thy-neighbor trade, investment, and exchange rate policies (see Barfield 2009).

As part of a growing global system of cooperation, the WTO would also benefit from the development of global institutions to address these problems. Any agreement among sovereign nations on joint action will have to proceed on terms that are widely accepted by all participants, and are therefore likely to be based on cooperative, rather than punitive, measures. Most previous international agreements on environmental and labor rights, for example, have either avoided or openly renounced the use of trade restrictions as enforcement measures.[5] While there are always potential problems of how to deal with conflicts between treaty obligations, formal multilateral cooperation on global issues would almost certainly reduce political pressures to use trade sanctions that would undermine the WTO.

On certain pressing issues, the WTO does indeed play a potentially significant role in areas that are the proper subjects for trade negotiations.

Examples include food security, immigration and migrant workers, and market access for technology and investment to address environmental problems. These issues have trade connections through WTO regulations on export restrictions, services trade (mode 4: movement of people across borders), and trade and direct foreign investment restrictions, respectively. Their public profile in the Doha Round has been low, partly because of the slow progress in the negotiations in general and the limited scope of the agenda, and partly because agreements in any sector are subject to a single undertaking package, which prevents them from emerging as dramatic stand-alone agreements. Thus the WTO certainly has relevance in addressing these questions, but they remain captive to the constraints of WTO negotiations as a whole.

In other areas, the WTO's role is not as clear, and entanglements should probably be avoided. The most serious problems in global energy trade, for example, center on supply restrictions by OPEC and natural gas suppliers such as Russia. It is highly unlikely that WTO-sponsored trade liberalization can address these problems, in which cartel policies and price controls are protected from formal international legal action by the doctrine of foreign sovereign compulsion. Another important conflict is alleged exchange rate manipulation, especially by China. This is a long-standing issue in trade relations, but the WTO is ill equipped to deal with it, and any WTO enforcement measures could potentially lead to a flood of dispute cases over changes in exchange rates.[6] A new institutional method of engaging countries in cooperative agreements to prevent disruptive currency, perhaps through the IMF, would be the best way to proceed.

For business interests, the WTO would become more relevant if it took up the issue of foreign direct investment policies more directly, as noted earlier in the discussion of exporter interests. Trade and investment are closely intertwined, and international business strategy has focused increasingly on the efficiency and logistics of supply chains. In the absence of more detailed WTO agreements on investment measures, multinational corporations and their home country governments have resorted to bilateral investment treaties, which are often ad hoc and discriminatory in nature. An aggressive effort to multilateralize the liberalization of foreign investment is needed in order to engage and energize business lobbies in promoting WTO negotiations.[7]

The WTO's relevance will also depend on its ability to adapt to a negotiating environment that will continue to shift bargaining power to the developing world. The trend toward the increasing importance and role of developing countries in world trade that accompanied the Uruguay and

Doha rounds will continue and intensify in the coming decades. Quite simply, the locus of global growth has shifted, and continues to shift, toward the emerging markets of the developing world. GDP growth rates among low- and middle-income countries since the turn of the millennium are already more than twice those of the high-income countries.[8] Long-range projections of economic growth, while based on many critical assumptions, tend nevertheless to show sustained growth rates in emerging markets that far outstrip those of the high-income countries. Table 7.1, for example, shows projected annual growth rates through 2050 in real per capita GDP in Brazil, China, and India that are two to more than four times as high as in the G6 countries (United States, Germany, Japan, France, UK, and Italy). At these rates of compound growth, the size of emerging markets will approach, and possibly even surpass, the size of the U.S. economy by 2050 (see table 7.2), although their per capita income will still be smaller. With long and sustained growth comes not only greater export capacity but also strong import growth, particularly with the development and expansion of the middle class to great numbers that will exceed those of the current developed world, and it is in their potentially massive import markets that the emerging markets will gain bargaining power in world trade. This potential is already evident in the growing role these countries are playing in the WTO. Through trade and investment, these rapidly growing countries would contribute directly or indirectly to the reduction of poverty for hundreds of millions and play a critical role in economic growth in OECD and least developed countries. Still, these beneficial effects would depend upon good policies in the emerging economies and a robust global trading system. In order to bring about such a monumental increase in global welfare, it will be necessary for WTO members to maintain a commitment to trade liberalization and flexibility in trade negotiations. It will require an increased engagement among the United States, EU, and other OECD countries and the developing world in matters of economic governance, a process which so far has advanced in fits and starts. The first meeting of the new G-20 countries to discuss the global financial crisis in November 2008 was a promising, if ineffectual, effort to promote global cooperation in economic policy.[9] Broader and deeper efforts to integrate economic policy making and to provide aid and technical assistance will be necessary in order to forge the sort of economic partnership among these diverse countries that can lead to progress in further trade liberalization.

In the end, the best way to make the WTO more relevant is to broaden and deepen its agenda for trade liberalization. There are in fact significant gains from trade that are still untapped, and it is up to the WTO members

TABLE 7.1 Projected annual per capita real growth rates (%), 2010–50

	Brazil	China	India	G6
2010–20	6.3	8.4	7.3	1.8
2020–30	4.5	7.0	7.9	1.8
2030–40	5.2	6.4	8.9	2.1
2040–50	5.0	5.6	7.9	2.1

Note: G6 consists of United States, Germany, Japan, UK, France, Italy

Source: Goldman Sachs (2003).

TABLE 7.2 Projected real GDP ($billion), 2020–50

	Brazil	China	India	U.S.
2020	1,333	7,070	2,104	16,415
2030	2,189	14,312	4,935	20,833
2040	3,740	26,439	12,367	27,229
2050	6,074	44,453	27,803	35,165

Note: In 2003 dollars.

Source: Goldman Sachs (2003).

to find ways to put them on the negotiating table. Policies to support adjustment, economic expansion, and productivity at home; an open and accommodating negotiating process of representation and reciprocity; and ancillary aid and funding commitments to finance the necessary trade capacity for poorer members: these are the building blocks of economic and negotiating confidence, and thereby political will. Countries gain from trade; governments need to agree on taking actions that will make multilateral trade liberalization possible. If there is a lack of confidence, then governments must act to restore confidence; if the gains from trade lie in new sectors, or those previously untouched by foreign competition and trade, then governments need to develop new methods and new political bargains to make liberalization possible.

Consequences of a Declining WTO

The alternative to WTO-sponsored trade opening is not necessarily wholesale protectionism, although that danger lurks especially in times of recession and economic structural change. As the global financial crisis pushed the world economy into a deep recession in 2008, the volume of world trade plummeted and calls for more protection of national markets proliferated, threatening to turn trade institutions toward a new low point in Jan Tumlir's cycle of learning and unlearning. Under these conditions, multilateral trade liberalization could freeze for many years, and the WTO would be likely to retreat to a position of rules-keeper, but with diminishing influence on the course of its members' trade relations. As noted earlier, the problem of being relegated to a rules caretaker is that simmering trade disputes can no longer be channeled into active multilateral trade bargaining.

In the absence of WTO leadership in trade liberalization, the ongoing search for gains from trade would also lead to a further proliferation of regional and other preferential trade agreements (PTAs). As the Doha Round has faltered, the United States, the European Union, Japan, Korea, ASEAN countries, and many others have intensified their efforts to conclude PTAs. From the point of view of economic theory, such agreements are almost always inferior to multilateral trade liberalization, and they violate the WTO principle of nondiscrimination. However, they are allowed under WTO rules, and they are better than no trade liberalization at all if the trade expansion effect ("trade creation") exceeds the cost of inefficient sourcing ("trade diversion"). In addition, PTAs may actually help WTO negotiations by encouraging those outside a PTA to push for broader trade liberalization in order to maintain market access parity with its participants. PTAs may also serve to break the ice on issues that are politically sensitive and require a smaller-scale regional agreement in order to provide an example and a framework for subsequent multilateral agreements; this is perhaps the case in services trade, as noted earlier. One may therefore judge the value of PTAs for global trade liberalization by determining whether they are building blocks for further and broader trade opening or stumbling blocks meant to create exclusive protected trading zones.

On the negative side of the trade negotiations ledger, these negotiations draw resources away from WTO negotiations. Large trading entities like the United States and EU protest that this is not true, given their large and diversified trade bureaucracies. However, the real resource cost often comes in securing legislative approval, where extended political battles are possible: examples include CAFTA and the Columbian, Peruvian, and South Korean FTA ratification fights in the U.S. Congress. The opportunity cost may also be of a more subtle variety. In view of the typically complicated and mentally exhausting nature of a broader WTO negotiation, smaller PTAs are bound to be a distraction. Another problem is that smaller and developing countries are unlikely to have as much bargaining power in a PTA as they would have in a WTO-sponsored global trade agreement. Not only does the MFN principle require general market access terms to apply to all WTO members equally, but the less powerful countries can work together in the WTO to avoid being isolated by the more powerful countries. It is surely more attractive for the major trading countries to negotiate PTAs, where they can maximize their bargaining leverage and where special interests in the large countries can assert themselves more forcefully. If developing countries are interested in getting a more balanced deal on meaningful trade liberalization, the WTO is the place to do it.

It is important to keep in mind that trade negotiations are conducted by people, not by machines, and the interaction of negotiators is crucial to the process. Consensus represents not only the acknowledgment of common economic interests and mutual gains from trade but also the more subjective recognition that the deal was satisfactory and honorable. Trade officials pursue them with a knowledge of their historical context, conscious of rules that reflect the political balance of power. In this context, institutions have consequences, in that they affect confidence in the assessment of proposals, trust in the process of bargaining, and the legitimacy of the negotiated outcome. There are still gains from trade to bargain for, but finding the holy grail of WTO consensus has changed. Achieving consensus still depends on the mutual recognition of economic interests in trade liberalization; this remains the bedrock of any multilateral trade agreement. Yet the process of agenda setting and decision making must be regarded as fair, and representation of the various countries' interests must be inclusive. For countries in which adjustment is a critical political issue, there must be confidence that the gains from trade will be widely shared and that job displacement will be met with new opportunities. Domestic flexibility is needed in order to open up new markets for trade, so that the agenda is broad and global gains are large and spread widely across countries. Countries, especially those with fewer negotiating resources and trade infrastructure, must be able to bargain with the confidence that the deals are significant, transparent, and without undue financial burdens of compliance.

The Doha Round, in the meantime, has become a rather dismal affair, like a meager potluck dinner party with only small portions to choose from. The disgruntled and dyspeptic guests hold themselves back from the festivities, wary of taking anything from the table for fear of what they may be required to offer in return. Then again, the other courses on offer appear small and hardly filling, and no one seems ready to offer anything interesting or new. And must they all wait until everyone agrees on what a "balanced" plate must look like before they can sit down to dinner? Yet, despite the melancholy mood, the guests continue to linger, even if they are dissatisfied. They still want the party to continue, so that they can go back home to brag of how popular their exported cooking was with the foreign guests. How then can this glum affair be saved? To continue the metaphor, the cure for the Doha Blues is to expand the menu so that everyone brings bigger and more varied dishes, so that there is a bigger and more exciting banquet to attend. Then it is important to encourage the guests, and to make it easier for them to fill their plates, by removing the constraints and inhibitions in their bargaining activities. And perhaps some of the eating can begin early, without consensus among all the guests on what every-one's final portion will be.

For practical purposes, a modest Doha Round agreement is still possi-ble, perhaps with additional time and patience, and a collective understand-ing that more is at stake than the humble gains from a smaller deal. As this study has shown, the Doha Blues have been a long time in the making, and many of the proposed reforms would require time and considerable effort to accomplish. Adapting to the new trading environment is a long-term project, but a short-term, stopgap remedy for the blues may be the best way to move forward. Many WTO officials and negotiators acknowledge the underlying problems, but most agree that ambitious reforms should wait until after the Doha Round is completed. There is a certain weariness in this statement that reflects the practical, if somber, view that plans for a grand and glorious agreement, based on the initial hopes and enthusiasm for the Doha Round, will indeed have to wait until the next round. In the meantime, sustaining the WTO's role in trade relations may require the conclusion of a small Doha Round bargain, tying up the little strings of tariff bindings, modest agricultural reforms, limited services market open-ing, and various rules. To be sure, even this modest effort would require additional compromise among all the WTO members, as well as a sense of what is at stake for the global trading system in general. It would not be a great agreement, but it could represent the beginning of bigger and better things to come—after the institutional adjustments are made. The optimist might say that it is time, not for a coffee break, as D-G Lamy had called the earlier collapse of the talks, but for a pause between courses of the meal. Make the Doha Round the appetizer, and get to work to prepare the main course in the next round.

Notes

1. The proliferation of literature on the Doha Round has generally followed lines of specialization according to sectoral negotiating topics (agriculture, services, and so on), developing country issues, legal and governance issues, analyses of episodes and ministerial meetings during the Round, and political economy aspects of trade liberalization. For WTO resource guides and bibliographies, see the WTO website's list of links: http://www.wto.org/english/res_e/reser_e/links_e.htm.

2. See Martin and Messerlin (2007) and Schott (2008) for similar reviews of the Doha Round's problems.

3. Specialization and trade based on relative factor abundance is based on comparative advantage theory, which continues to explain a large amount of trade to this day. More recent additions to trade theory have emphasized production technologies, differentiated tastes, market structure, and location. See *Handbook of International Economics*, Vol. 1, 3 (1984, 1995) for an overview, especially chapters 1, 7 (Vol. 1); 24, and 25 (Vol. 3).

4. Based on the earlier discussion of institutions, legitimacy may be defined as the acknowledged right of the institution to create specific status relationships and to pursue collective goals. See Lawrence (2008) for a more politically based discussion of this issue with regard to the WTO. Trust as an institutional attribute may be defined as the confidence that status functions regarding process (especially in decision making) will meet expectations.

5. Watson (2005, Introduction) links the origins of primitive barter trade with the development of human language and communication.

6. Countries facing less than perfectly elastic import supply schedules can theoretically improve their welfare with "optimum tariffs." As Bagwell and Staiger (2002) have pointed out, however, even these countries can gain from multilateral

trade liberalization, insofar as reciprocal tariff cuts raise each country's welfare as compared with the Nash equilibrium tariff regime.

CHAPTER 2

1. See Dam (1970), Curzon (1965), and Irwin (1996, chap. 1). In ancient times, tariffs were levied essentially for revenue purposes. Bargaining over tariffs began early in the nineteenth century.

2. The agreements were in principle to apply on an MFN basis to all countries, although MFN exemptions were allowed, which 9 of the 69 telecommunications signatories filed.

3. The first Director-General was Sir William Wyndham White (UK), followed by Olivier Long and Alfred Dunkel (Switzerland) and Peter Sutherland (Ireland), who was also the founding D-G of the WTO, followed by Renato Ruggiero (Italy).

4. See Jawara and Kwa (2004) for a discussion. The official proposal is found in WTO Document no. WT/CG/W/471/24 April 2001.

5. Narlikar and Odell (2006) refer to it as a "strict distributive strategy," in which one party in a negotiation attempts to garner benefits without making any concessions on its own. It is very difficult for any set of weaker countries in a negotiation, even in a coalition, to succeed in such a strategy if their counterparts have superior "best alternatives to negotiated agreements" (BATNA).

6. The coalition eventually had over 60 members, including Brazil, India, and other Asian, Latin American, and Caribbean countries (Odell and Sell 2006, p. 99).

7. Unexpected circumstances that occur following "normal" trade liberalization measures are in principle covered by the GATT "escape clause," which was incorporated into the WTO rules. Yet this could only apply in the familiar cases of surges in imports, which could under certain criteria justify the use of emergency safeguard trade restrictions.

8. See http://www.wto.org/english/tratop_e/serv_e/gatsqa_e.htm.

9. Mattoo and Subramanian (2008), however, note that Doha formulas for tariff bindings would still leave most developing countries with so much "water" in their bound tariffs (i.e., the difference between bound and applied rates) that they would subsequently still be able to raise applied tariffs substantially without violating WTO bindings.

10. All countries implicitly claim the need for "policy space" with regard to politically sensitive industries they want to exempt from trade liberalization. The concept becomes a major problem in negotiations, however, when countries extend it to cover all or most of their import markets.

11. Effective tariffs are tariff rates as a percentage of value added. Typically, tariff structures escalate along the supply chain, so that more heavily processed goods, further along the supply chain, will have higher nominal tariff rates than those on basic or commodity level goods. Even small nominal tariffs on processed goods will therefore often have high effective tariff rates, which discourages many

exporting countries from downstream processing of labor-intensive products. See Michalopoulos (2001, p. 108) for a brief explanation.

12. The G20 group at the 2003 Cancún Ministerial consisted of Argentina, Bolivia, Brazil, Chile, China, Colombia, Costa Rica, Cuba, Ecuador, El Salvador, Guatemala, India, Mexico, Pakistan, Paraguay, Peru, Philippines, South Africa, Thailand, and Venezuela. Egypt and Kenya would later join this group, renamed the G22. See Narkilar and Tussie (2004). A new and much different "G20" formed during the 2008 global financial crisis; see chapter 7.

13. The four Singapore issues included government procurement, trade facilitation (customs issues), trade and investment, and trade and competition. See Narlikar and Tussie (2004). The protest against the Singapore issues at Cancún began with the so-called Core Group of developing countries, and was eventually joined by many other countries.

14. See *Bridges Weekly Trade News Digest*, vol. 12, no. 27, August 7, 2008. Technical negotiations at lower levels over the previous months had raised the status of the July 2008 meeting to that of a culminating summit, creating hopes of a breakthrough.

15. As reported in *Bridges* (August 7, 2008), cotton subsidies and TRIPS issues represented other potential stumbling blocks. An agreement on NAMA modalities and exclusions, tied with the terms of agricultural trade liberalization, was apparently within reach. Services offers were also contingent on an agricultural agreement.

16. Standard WTO parlance refers to the negotiations as the "Doha Development Round," with a "Doha Development Agenda." Despite these efforts by WTO members to create a development focus for the round, this study will continue to refer simply to the "Doha Round," in order to avoid repeating the unfortunate irony of these terms.

CHAPTER 3

1. D-G Renato Ruggiero declared in 1997 the priority for the WTO "to continue momentum towards universal membership" (WTO 1997). All other D-Gs since then have continued to refer to universal membership as a goal. See for example Pascal Lamy's reference to it in WTO (2007).

2. The chapter will not focus on the details of individual accession cases, many of which have been the subject of separate studies. Among the growing literature on accessions, see Ostry, Alexandroff, and Gomez (2005) regarding China. For Russia's unfinished accession case, see Tarr and Navaretti (2005) and Jones (2004a). Several transition economy cases are discussed in Langhammer and Lücke (1999). The case of the Kyrgyz Republic is treated in Mogilevskii (2004). Broude (1998) discusses the accession negotiations of Jordan and Saudi Arabia. Adhikari and Dahal (2003) discuss Nepal and Cambodia, and Gay (2005) discusses the strange case of Vanuatu (see also note 22 below and chapter 6 of this volume).

3. Of the 23 founding members, China, Czechoslovakia, Syria, and Lebanon would later withdraw from the GATT. Czechoslovakia's successor states, the Czech Republic and Slovak Republic, rejoined using an Article 33 protocol in 1993. China and Taiwan (known as Chinese Taipei in the WTO) joined the WTO in 2001 and 2002, respectively. Lebanon has applied for WTO membership and Syria has not, as of February 2009. Other countries that joined the GATT and later withdrew include Liberia, which has not joined the WTO, and Yugoslavia, whose successor states following its dissolution in 1991 either joined the GATT (Slovenia, thus becoming a founding WTO member) or the WTO (Croatia) or have applied for WTO membership (Serbia, Montenegro, and Bosnia-Herzegovina).

4. Rose (2004) has challenged the received economic wisdom that WTO membership, in itself, increases trade, and thus the gains from trade. Tomz, Goldstein, and Rivers (2007) offer a response that strengthens the WTO-trade link.

5. Protracted multilateral trade negotiations tend to increase the transaction cost of trade liberalization compared to a shorter negotiation, and some countries may turn to speedier bilateral negotiations as a result. Still, the broader participation and scope of WTO negotiations make possible, in principle, more efficient and far-reaching trade liberalization.

6. Under the GATT, new Contracting Parties were required to implement fully parts I, III, and (after 1964) IV of the GATT, but part II only to the extent that its provisions were consistent with the country's existing legislation. Parts I and III contained the essential MFN clause, tariff obligations, and procedures; part IV included provisions for developing countries. Part II (articles 3–23) contained rules regarding national treatment, customs procedures, antidumping, quotas, subsidies, state trading, emergency protection, and exceptions, among other topics. Grandfather clauses and exemptions under the Protocol of Provisional Application allowed countries to modify their obligations under GATT part II. See Lanoszka (2001) for additional discussion.

7. GATT accession protocols for Poland (1967) and Romania (1971) included mainly quantitative targets for increased imports from other GATT members, since they did not have market-oriented, price-based tariff systems in place. Both of these countries renegotiated their GATT accession terms during the Uruguay Round, after replacing their Communist economic structures with market-based trade regimes. Hungary's 1967 protocol, in contrast, did contain traditional tariff schedules, even though Hungary was a nonmarket economy. The 1965 protocol for Yugoslavia was more consistent with the GATT norm of market-based tariffs and trade measures, but it still reflected the circumstances of a mixed economy. Yugoslavia's successor states have had to negotiate separately for GATT and WTO access (see note 3). See also Dam (1971), pp. 328–329; Lanoszka (2001), pp. 580–582; and Jones (1981).

8. See Constantine Michalopoulos (2002), pp. 61–70. Kavass (2007) also provides a detailed description of the accession process. The WTO secretariat (WTO 2008) has compiled a comprehensive training handbook for negotiators.

9. The Doha Declaration is available at http://www.wto.org/english/thewto_e/minist_e/min01_e/mindecl_e.htm.

10. Even smaller incumbent WTO member countries can exert considerable bargaining power in an accession negotiation. See Lacey (2007).

11. See Milgrom and Roberts (1992, chap. 5) for a general discussion. Yarbrough and Yarbrough (1992, chaps 2 and 6) discuss bounded rationality in the context of WTO issues.

12. WTO accession WPs may have many members, and their composition is determined largely by the interests of countries most affected by trade with the applicant country. However, the United States, EU, Japan, Switzerland, and Australia tend to sit on most of them and may be the source of most of the bargaining power "learning." It is also likely that the learning from earlier accession cases is shared directly or indirectly with members of WPs in subsequent cases.

13. See "Russia and the WTO," *The Economist*, July 6, 2006. In August 2008, in the context of the crisis over Russia's military action in territories in Georgia, Russian government officials declared their willingness to walk away from WTO accession negotiations in the face of threatened blockage in the WP by the United States and other countries. See the *Financial Times*, August 27, 2008.

14. Charnovitz (2007) discusses the legal aspects of WTO-plus provisions in protocols of accession, including the issue of whether such obligations are subject to adjudication under the WTO Dispute Settlement Understanding. Kennett (2005) discusses the types of rule commitments and the difficulty in categorizing them.

15. Accession terms that specifically exempt a new member from a WTO benefit or protection, such as nondiscriminatory treatment in safeguard actions, are often referred to as "WTO-minus" provisions. Charnovitz (2007), however, argues that any measures that impose greater discipline on an acceding member should be regarded as WTO-plus provisions.

16. More details on WTO commitments contained in the protocols of accession are found in WTO (2004), Annex 3.

17. In the (2003a) Secretariat, the WTO has classified these commitments as: 1) statements of fact; 2) obligations to abide by existing WTO rules, sometimes specifying national measures to be amended to bring them into conformity with WTO provisions on the subject in question, sometimes elaborating on the WTO provisions on the subject in question; 3) obligations to abide by rules created by the commitment paragraph and not contained in WTO Multilateral Agreements (WTO-plus commitments); 4) obligations not to have recourse to specific WTO provisions (WTO-minus rights); 5) specific identification of transitional periods that may be used; and 6) authorizations to depart temporarily from WTO rules or from commitments in the Schedules.

18. Cape Verde's WP report was completed earlier than Ukraine's, but the Cape Verde government ratified its WTO membership later; hence Ukraine is the 24th new member to join officially, Cape Verde the 25th.

19. The WTO App variable identified six acceding countries (Kyrgyz Republic, Georgia, Oman, Vietnam, Tonga, and Cape Verde) that applied for WTO membership after the organization was launched. The statistical results must be regarded with care, since these countries may have had common elements reducing the length of their accession that were unrelated to the timing of their applications.

20. The application of WTO rules regarding anti-dumping (AD) investigations, combined with access to dispute settlement review, is a significant benefit of WTO membership for countries facing AD cases, and may encourage harder bargaining among WTO incumbent members in accession negotiations.

21. The correlation coefficients for all of these variables with each other ranged from 0.87 to 0.99.

22. However, with this caveat, a case study of Vanuatu, which was on the verge of WTO membership when it withdrew from the process in 2001, documents the problems faced by a small, poor country with limited resources and the lack of a robust political strategy for joining the trading system. See Gay (2005).

23. In their study of WTO accession impacts on countries' economic performance, Tang and Wei (2008) use World Bank index measures of "regulatory burden" and "rule of law" as indicators of government quality. Their results support the hypothesis that countries with weaker governance gain more from WTO policy commitments in terms of improved economic performance.

24. See Kaufmann, Kraay, and Mastruzzi (2007, p. 3): *Government Effectiveness*, measuring the quality of public services, the quality of the civil service and the degree of its independence from political pressures, the quality of policy formulation and implementation, and the credibility of the government's commitment to such policies.

25. The World Bank index of political stability did not show any statistically significant impact on elapsed time-to-accession for the 25 new WTO entrants. However, compared with the sample of acceded WTO members, the group of 26 applicants exhibited a lower mean index of stability, with a higher standard deviation. In view of the pattern of increasingly lengthy accession negotiations, the ability of the less stable applicants to maintain a continuous negotiating mandate, and to carry through on WTO compliance measures, was doubtful.

26. Iran first submitted a request to initiate WTO accession negotiations in 1996. The United States blocked official receipt of this request by the WTO General Council 21 times but finally refrained from impeding its submission, which occurred in May 2005. See Evenett and Primo Braga (2005), footnote 4.

27. See Stoler (2003) for a discussion of the practical problem of applying the single undertaking principle with regard to developing countries. Levy (2006) provides a broader discussion of cross-sector negotiations and the alternative of "variable geometry."

28. The General Council decision (WTO 2002) also includes the following provisions: 1) WTO members shall exercise restraint in seeking concessions on trade in goods and services from acceding LDCs, benchmarked against existing WTO LDC members; 2) Special and Differential Treatment shall be applicable to all acceding LDCs; 3) transitional periods and arrangements foreseen under specific WTO Agreements shall be granted in accession negotiations taking into account individual development, financial, and trade needs; 4) commitments to accede to any of the Plurilateral Trade Agreements shall not be a precondition for accession to the WTO; and 5) efforts shall continue to be made to streamline accession procedures for LDCs to make them more effective and efficient and less onerous. The

WTO Council decision therefore sets out to curb WTO-plus requirements on LDCs, and otherwise to soften the terms of accession.

29. The General Council decision (WTO 2002) does indeed provide for implementation, but without deadlines or specificity in defining S&D treatment. Informal measures without specific commitments appear to be setting the boundaries on implementation of the Council decision.

30. Participants in Integrated Framework, founded in 1997, include the WTO, the International Monetary Fund, the United Nations Development Program, the United Nations Conference on Trade and Development (UNCTAD), the International Trade Centre (run jointly by the WTO and UNCTAD), and the World Bank. See chapter 6 for a further discussion.

31. See Susan Prowse (2002), pp. 1235–1261, for an account of the Integrated Framework efforts to help Cambodia in its preparation to join the WTO.

32. For a strident developing-country perspective on the lopsided power relationships in the WTO, see Jawara and Kwa (2004). Most smaller countries, rich and poor, tend to complain that the United States and EU use their political leverage in the WTO. In accession negotiations, however, even smaller incumbent WTO members can exert political pressure on applicant countries. See Adhikari and Dahal (2003) for a description of the pressure placed on Vanuatu during its WTO accession negotiations by New Zealand and Australia regarding agricultural goods.

CHAPTER 4

1. M'Bow (1978) describes the operation of consensus in the U.N. General Assembly, as well as the process and conditions for reaching consensus in a large organization.

2. See the websites www.imf.org/external/about.htm and www.worldbank.org.

3. Multilateral trade negotiating rounds under the GATT and WTO have included: Geneva I (1947); Annecy, France (1949); Torquay, UK (1950–51); Geneva II (1955–56); Dillon, named after U.S. Treasury Secretary C. Douglas Dillon (1960–61); Kennedy, named after U.S. President John F. Kennedy (1963–67); Tokyo (1973–79); Uruguay (1986–94); and the current Doha Round (2001–).

4. As of February 2009; see chapter 3. There are also 26 countries with observer status in the WTO, usually a precursor to an application for membership. Among countries still outside the WTO, the Russian Federation is the largest in terms of trade and population, and it is in the late stages of negotiating a protocol of accession.

5. See Hoekman and Kostecki (2001, pp. 126–128) for an overview of WTO negotiating procedures.

6. Another type of informal meeting, outside the official negotiating framework, is the "mini-ministerial." See Wolfe (2005, pp. 640–641) for a discussion of the distinction between mini-ministerial and Green Room meetings.

7. The Green Room meetings that led to the agreement to restart the Doha negotiations in July 2004 were chaired by the chairman of the General Council,

Ambassador Tadamori Oshima, since the deliberations were part of an extended General Council meeting attended by several representatives at the ministerial level (correspondence with WTO official). Most Green Room meetings are held either in Geneva or at the locations of ministerial meetings and are chaired by the D-G.

8. Odell (2000, p. 27) discusses the importance of this concept in economic negotiations among countries, and notes that the term originated with Fisher and Ury (1981).

9. In the GATT/WTO system, the United States and EU especially have at times used preferential trade agreements (PTAs) with selected trading partners as a device to wring additional concessions from other countries in multilateral negotiations. The EU itself was formed as a PTA, and increased its trade bargaining power as a result. PTAs are in principle discouraged in the GATT/WTO system, but are allowed under the conditions of GATT article 24. It is important to add that most other PTAs, especially among smaller developing countries, have had little impact on multilateral bargaining power. For a general discussion see De Melo and Panagariya (1993).

10. OECD members include Australia, Austria, Belgium, Canada, Denmark, Finland, France, Germany, Greece, Iceland, Ireland, Italy, Japan, Luxembourg, the Netherlands, New Zealand, Portugal, Spain, Sweden, Switzerland, Turkey, and the United States. Members of the EU are represented together at the WTO. Cohn (2002, p. 5) presents a world trade governance pyramid with the United States and EU at the top, followed by the G7/G8 (United States, Canada, UK, France, Germany, Italy, and Japan, plus Russia), Quad, and OECD. The WTO system is subordinate to these countries in world trade governance, according to Cohn's paradigm. At the bottom is the G77 (developing countries group) and United Nations Conference on Trade and Development (UNCTAD).

11. See Bagwell and Staiger (2002, pp. 36–39 and 68–70). Their approach is, however, to treat the GATT/WTO rules system as a method of minimizing power-based bargaining by dominant countries. Odell (2000, chap. 2) emphasizes the "resistance points" that set the boundaries of the "zone of agreement," especially in bilateral negotiations.

12. Robert Zoellick, U.S. trade representative during the early years of the Doha Round, made plain the alternative U.S. strategy of concluding preferential trade agreements in attempting to motivate recalcitrant WTO trading partners to continue multilateral trade negotiations. See Zoellick (2003).

13. See Bagwell and Staiger (2002, pp. 18–41). It is important to remember that political considerations are central to the GATT/WTO mercantilist approach of reciprocity in trade negotiations, in which tariff reductions are regarded as trade concessions. This aspect of the rules contradicts the traditional neoclassical analysis of the gains from trade. In a perfect world with no political constraints or price-making power, and with equal players and no market externalities, the optimum tariffs would theoretically always be zero.

14. These views are based on correspondence with a former Quad trade official and with a former WTO official.

15. Martin Khor (2005) documents the following set of 27 Green Room participants at a pre–Hong Kong Ministerial session: the EU, United States, India, Brazil, Japan, Canada, Switzerland, Hong Kong, Zambia, New Zealand, Australia, Korea, South Africa, Malaysia, Lesotho, Benin, Chad, Thailand, Argentina, Mexico, Costa Rica, Jamaica, Egypt, Kenya, Pakistan, and China.

16. The first four negotiations used a line-by-line tariff approach, which became increasingly burdensome and was replaced by an across-the-board tariff-cutting approach in the Kennedy Round (see footnote 3). For a discussion of early GATT negotiating history, see Curzon (1965) and Dam (1970).

17. See Schott and Buurman (1994) for a review of the Uruguay Round results, and Hoekman and Kostecki (2001) for an analysis of the WTO system.

18. The first five GATT trade rounds took two years or less to complete; the Kennedy Round took four years, the Tokyo Rounds six, and the Uruguay Round eight. The Doha Round, started in 2001, entered its eighth year in November 2008, with no final agreement on the horizon.

19. See Hoekman, Michalopoulos, and Winters (2004) for a critique of special and differential treatment (STD) in trade negotiations with regard to the interests of developing countries. Indirectly, special and differential treatment may have contributed to the marginalization of developing countries in the Green Room process, since they were partially detached from the give-and-take of reciprocal trade concessions.

20. Correspondence with a formal trade official from a Quad country indicates that there were in fact several representatives from poor and other developing countries at the crisis-laden Seattle Green Room meeting. Thus, even a system of proportional representation would not necessarily satisfy countries left out of critical decision-making forums.

21. Members included Argentina, Bolivia, Brazil, Chile, China, Colombia, Costa Rica, Cuba, Ecuador, Egypt, Guatemala, India, Indonesia, Mexico, Nigeria, Pakistan, Paraguay, Peru, Philippines, South Africa, Thailand, and Venezuela. See "The WTO Under Fire," *Economist*, Sept. 18, 2003, and Narlikar and Tussie (2004).

22. Although the main impact of the G20 coalition of developing countries at the Cancún Ministerial was to block progress on the negotiations, the group had worked out a detailed platform, particularly on agricultural issues. See the discussion of the Cancún meeting in chapter 2, and Narlikar and Tussie (2004).

23. The mercantilist nature of WTO bargaining typically means that countries seek to maximize exports subject to an allowable political "price" of increased imports. Bagwell and Staiger (2003) model WTO bargaining equilibrium on the concept of balanced concessions in terms of the value of increased exports and imports for each country.

24. See Tussie (1993). Narlikar (2003, chap. 6) evaluates the effectiveness of the Cairns group and concludes that it has had mixed results, with success at times depending on favorable external and bargaining circumstances.

25. See Simon (1957, p. xxiv), and Williamson (1985, pp. 30–32 and 44–47). Yarbrough and Yarbrough (1992) apply the concept to various aspects of trade relations and the GATT system.

26. As Chen (2004) notes, the EU is a coalition operating in the WTO based on the Treaty of Rome, but it does not fit the negotiating model of power transformation (see Selten 1987) as described above, since the member countries did not bargain with each other specifically to form a WTO-based coalition. Even so, the enhanced trade bargaining power of the EU, as compared with what influence the 27 individual members would have separately, is certainly an enticement for potential coalition partners, whose bargaining incentives are shaped by the power transformation scenario.

27. See Krueger (1999) for a discussion of the debate over preferential trading agreements.

28. See Panitchpakti (2001), former WTO D-G, and Delcros (2004), a representative from the European Commission.

29. Schott and Watal (2001) have a seat for the Central European Free Trade Area, all of whose members joined the EU in 2004. Table 1 thus places those countries with the EU and uses the CEFTA seat for other transition economies.

30. The GDP/cap and Trade/GDP means are weighted by population and GDP shares, respectively. Means for the RCA calculations are simple averages.

31. The Like Minded Group, founded in 1996, includes Cuba, Egypt, India, Indonesia, Malaysia, Pakistan, Tanzania, and Uganda. See Narlikar (2003, chap. 8) and the discussion of their activities in the Doha Round in chapter 2.

32. The group of African cotton exporters—Mali, Burkina Faso, Benin, and Chad—form a subgroup of Africa-2 as shown in table 1. They pushed for the elimination of U.S. and other export subsidies on cotton, which played a role in the final collapse of the Cancún talks. Their principal ally on this issue has been Brazil, another cotton exporter.

33. Members included the Dominican Republic, El Salvador, Guatemala, Honduras, Nicaragua, and Panama; they focused on procedural issues of WTO institutional reform during the early Doha round negotiations. See Narlikar (2003, chap. 8).

34. This group included a large number of former EU colonies that banded together to press for an MFN waiver on the Cotonou Agreement on preferential access to EU markets. See Narlikar (2003, chap. 8).

35. See Jawara and Kwa (2004) for a critique of WTO governance from a developing country perspective. Steinberg's (2002) examination of the history of U.S. and EU deliberations over the governance structure for the GATT/WTO system is revealing. The Quad countries agreed that a consensus-based approach was best, with a nominal voting system (one country, one vote) that would rarely, if ever, be used in practice. Power-based bargaining would then allow the Quad to assert its interests, based on consensus among the Quad countries. In past instances of supposed threats to this arrangement through legal means by developing countries, counterproposals by the Quad for a separate GATT-plus or other exclusive arrangement have arisen. Thus, any attempt to "democratize" WTO decision making would likely lead to its marginalization in Quad trade relations.

36. See Cot (1972) for a general review of the role of secrecy in negotiations. Ullrich (2000) offers a specific proposal for increased openness in WTO negotiations.

37. See Odell and Sell (2003) and Narlikar and Tussie (2004).

CHAPTER 5

1. For particularly scathing accounts of the WTO and the DSU, see Wallich and Woodall (2004) and Jawara and Kwa (2004).

2. The General Agreement on Tariffs and Trade (GATT) was established in 1947 and was absorbed and superseded by the WTO in 1995. Petersmann (1997) provides a comprehensive analysis of the GATT and WTO dispute settlement systems. Hoekman and Kostecki (2001) provide a useful summary of the main issues and the structure of the DSU.

3. See Yarbrough and Yarbrough (1992, chap. 2) for a transaction cost approach to trade institutions and third-party review provisions.

4. Of the original 23 GATT Contracting Parties in 1947, only 10 were developing countries. Increasing numbers of developing countries joined over the years, however, and by 1986 nearly two-thirds of the 103 Contracting Parties were developing countries. Their proportion as the largest group of WTO members has continued to grow.

5. Hudec (2002, p. 82) notes that overall, 81% of GATT disputes based on confirmed violations in the contentious 1980s reached a satisfactory resolution, while the rate for developing countries complainants was 73%.

6. The designation of development status in this study is based on the World Bank ranking of country per capita income. See the World Bank website page http://www.worldbank.org/data/countryclass/countryclass.html. Here, countries in the lower three quartiles, with income less than $10,065 per capita, are considered "developing countries." A subcategory of 32 "least developed countries" receives special consideration in the WTO. See the WTO webpage http://www.wto.org/english/thewto_e/whatis_e/tif_e/org7_e.htm. This list corresponds roughly, but not completely, with the World Bank lowest income quartile countries that are WTO members.

7. Leitner (2008) also calculates the number of discrete issues associated with DSU cases, noting that a number of cases may in fact be associated with one particular policy. This calculation reduces the numbers shown in table 5.1, but does not alter the general trend or the inferences that can be drawn from it.

8. A prominent example of this phenomenon became apparent in the author's discussions with U.S. trade officials of the highly protectionist Byrd amendment to U.S. unfair trade law, which was challenged in a DSU case, leading to a panel and AB determination of a WTO rule violation and eventual repeal in the November 2005. Many U.S. trade officials would not speak publicly in favor of the DSU decision, but appeared nonetheless satisfied with the outcome. U.S. consumers certainly benefited from this U.S. "defeat."

9. See Hoekman and Kostecki (2001, pp. 92–93) and Bown and Hoekman (2005). Shaffer (2003) describes the public-private partnerships that exist in the United States and the EU regarding the filing of DSU cases, a situation that appears to put developing countries and their weaker business-to-government links at a disadvantage in bringing DSU cases.

10. See Yarbrough and Yarbrough (1992) and footnote 2 above. In the context of bounded rationality, the expected benefits of a trade agreement are reduced by the absence of a reliable and impartial mechanism to address unforeseen future disagreements, an analog to enforceable contract law in a domestic economy's legal system (but without direct enforcement provisions).

11. In contrast, a successful DSU challenge to anti-dumping provisions would presumably not lead to improved market access on an MFN basis, since the original AD measure discriminated against the complainant and may in fact have created trade benefits for other suppliers to the protected market. See Bown (2004b) for an econometric examination of various aspects of third-country export effects linked with dispute settlement outcomes.

12. See the WTO webpage for antidumping, statistics, at http://www.wto.org/english/tratop_e/adp_e/adp_e.htm.

13. Bown and Hoekman (2008) note that the statistics show developing countries themselves to be less likely targets of DSU investigations regarding AD, which compounds the problem, discussed above, that the beneficial discipline of DSU filings against WTO inconsistent practices has probably not been extended to developing countries.

14. Safeguards (also called escape clause measures) allow importing countries to impose temporary trade restrictions under certain conditions. Thus safeguards and AD measures may be substitutes for each other. Safeguards have been successfully challenged in the DSU, and it is possible that the number of AD initiations may have risen as a result. Securing improved market access conditions for WTO members, especially developing countries, must take into consideration the "nexus" of contingency protection devices and how WTO agreements and rules can promote adjustment to import competition, with the goal of reducing the demand for protection. See, for example, Alan Sykes (2003) and the response by Jones (2004b).

15. The ACWL website URL is www.acwl.ch.

16. The ACWL's 2007 Report of Operations lists a staff of ten, including eight lawyers, with funding of SFr 715,000 coming from just five donors: Sweden, Ireland, Canada, Denmark, and Norway. See ACWL (2008).

17. Nonviolation complaints arise when a WTO member's policies, while not in violation of WTO rules, may nonetheless result in a "nullification or impairment" of benefits claimed by a complaining country. See Petersmann (1997, chap. 4).

18. Even if the total trade impact for the large country were small, it could create a political backlash if politically influential firms in the large country objected to the small-claims decision. Additional troubles might arise if small-claims decisions were to establish precedents applicable to larger cases. Nordstrom and Shaffer (2008) discuss this and other potential objections to the small-claims proposal in detail.

CHAPTER 6

1. The concept of comparative advantage in this context appears to have first appeared in a communication from Japan to the WTO regarding the issue of trade facilitation (see WTO 2003b), as reported by Finger and Wilson (2006), who also apply it to that issue in their analysis.

2. See Suwa-Eisenmann and Verdier 2007 for a survey of the available literature on coherence.

3. See, for example, documents from the WTO symposium "Identifying Indicators in Monitoring Aid for Trade," September 2008, http://www.wto.org/english/tratop_e/devel_e/a4t_e/symp_sept08_presentations_c.htm, indicating a heightened interest in the classification, magnitude, and origin of aid-for-trade funding. See also Laird (2007) for a discussion of the political economy of aid-for-trade as a component of multilateral trade negotiations.

4. Prowse (2002) discusses the activities of these international organizations with regard to trade capacity building.

5. Shaffer (2005, p. 270). Shaffer conducted interviews with 26 officials from the WTO, various country trade delegations, international development agencies, and development-oriented NGOs.

6. Drabek and Bacchetta (2004) note that accession requirements also play a positive political role in establishing an external anchor for domestic reform. This benefit strengthens the argument for external assistance to fulfill WTO obligations.

7. See http://www.wto.org/english/tratop_e/devel_e/teccop_e/if_e.htm and Shaffer (2005).

8. See the review of the Uruguay Round in chapter 2. The term "Grand Bargain" was coined by Ostry (2000). Because of the disappointing outcomes in these areas for developing countries, Ostry (2007) later came to refer to the agreement as a "Bum Deal."

9. For those favoring more trade liberalization, the availability of more pro-trade advice from new sources, especially in the developing world, would be welcome. In the meantime, many poorer developing countries may be uncritically taking free advice from anti-globalization NGOs that leave trade liberalization options insufficiently explored.

10. These capacity considerations do not address other problems that may detract from the effectiveness of WTO dispute settlement for smaller developing countries, such as the asymmetry in retaliatory capacity between rich and large countries versus small and poor countries and non-trade leverage by large countries in terms of aid and political support. See the discussions in chapter 5 and in Bown and Hoekman (2005).

11. Including the World Bank, development banks, or other aid providers in the negotiations would be necessary if the recipient countries would not otherwise seek and receive the aid based on its own economic merits. See the discussion above in the section "Systemic and Coordination Issues."

12. Bagai and Wilson (2006) provide a detailed description. Anderson and Wincoop (2004) discuss trade cost implications. Tsai (2005) discusses coordination issues and incentives for developing countries.

13. See the discussion of the collapse of the Cancún Ministerial Meeting in chapter 2, and Finger and Wilson (2006).

14. See paragraph 12 of the WTO Doha Declaration, "Implementation-related Issues and Concerns," available at: http://www.wto.org/english/thewto_e/minist_e/min01_e/mindecl_e.htm#implementation.

CHAPTER 7

1. See Lori Kletzer and Robert Litan (2001), "A Prescription to Relieve Worker Anxiety (Washington, D.C.: Institute for International Economics); and Olivier Blanchard (2006), "European Unemployment: The Evolution of Facts and Ideas," *Economic Policy* 21: 5–59. The expression "protecting the worker, not the job" apparently originated in Dornbusch and Wolf (1994, p. 171).

2. See Bosma et al. (2008, pp. 39–49). Survey data are from the Global Entrepreneurship Monitor (GEM) Adult Population Survey, 2007, available at www.gemconsortium.org/about.aspx?page=re_adult_population_survey.

3. See "On India's Farms, A Plague of Suicides," *New York Times,* September 19, 2006.

4. Lawrence (2006) would limit the scope of retaliation or concessions to those items covered by the plurilateral "club."

5. See, for example, the Rio Declaration (UNCED 1992), principle 12, and the International Labor Organization's Declaration on Fundamental Principles and Rights at Work (ILO 1998), paragraph 5.

6. See Mattoo and Subramanian (2008), who also consider sovereign wealth funds, global financial regulation, and climate change as possible areas for WTO involvement. While all of these issues will require multilateral cooperation, it is not clear from an institutional perspective that the WTO is the appropriate body for negotiations.

7. WTO members may be gun-shy on the issue of international investment agreements because of an NGO-fueled backlash against the ill-fated Multilateral Investment Agreement, which was being negotiated among OECD members. See Graham (2000, chaps 1–3).

8. See chapter 2, table 2.1. The World Bank's 2008 *World Development Report* shows 2000–06 average annual GDP growth in low- and middle-income countries of 5.7%, as compared with 2.3% for high-income countries.

9. The G-20 countries include Argentina, Australia, Brazil, Canada, China, France, Germany, India, Indonesia, Italy, Japan, Mexico, Russia, Saudi Arabia, South Africa, South Korea, Turkey, the United Kingdom, the United States, and a special representative for the Eurozone. The apparent solidarity on trade raised hopes that a final deal on the Doha Round could be struck, but it soon became clear that governments were unwilling to introduce any new life into the talks, and plans for renewed negotiations were cancelled. See *Bridges Weekly Trade News* 12, December 17, 2008.

References

ACWL (2008). Advisory Centre on WTO Law Report on Operations, 2007. Geneva: ACWL, www.acwl.ch.

Adhikari, Ratnakar and Navin Dahal (2003). "LDCs' Accession to the WTO: Learning from the Cases of Nepal, Cambodia and Vanuatu." South Asia Watch on Trade, Economics & Environment (SAWTEE), Kathmandu, Nepal. Accessible at http://www.un ngls.org/SAWTEE.doc.

Anderson, James E. and Eric van Wincoop (2004). "Trade Costs." *Journal of Economic Literature* 62: 691–751.

Anderson, Kym and Will Martin (2005). "Agricultural Trade Reform and the Doha Development Agenda." *The World Economy* 28 (9): 1301–1327.

Arnold, Wayne (2001). "Translating Union Into Khmer: The A.F.L.-C.I.O. Organizes in Cambodia." *New York Times*, July 12.

Auboin, Marc (2007). "Fulfilling the Marrakesh Mandate on Coherence: Ten Years of Cooperation between the WTO, IMF and World Bank." Discussion paper no.13. Geneva: WTO.

Bagai, Shweta and John S. Wilson (2006). "The Data Chase: What's Out There on Trade Costs and Nontariff Barriers?" World Bank Policy Research Working Paper WPS 3899, April. Washington, D.C.: World Bank.

Bagwell, Kyle and Robert W. Staiger (2002). *The Economics of the World Trading System*. Cambridge, Mass. and London: MIT Press.

Barfield, Claude (2009). "The Doha Endgame and the Future of the WTO." Vox EU.org. http://www.voxeu.org/index.php?q=node/2806, accessed January 20, 2009.

Bernstein, William J. (2008). *A Splendid Exchange: How Trade Shaped the World*. New York: Atlantic Monthly Press.

Bhaumik, T.K. (2006). *The WTO: A Discordant Orchestra*. New Delhi: Sage Publications.

Birdsall, Nancy and Robert Z. Lawrence (1999). "Deep Integration and Trade Agreements: Good for Developing Countries?" In Inge Kaul, Isabelle Grunberg, and Marc A. Stern (eds.), *Global Public Goods: International Cooperation in the 21st Century*. New York and Oxford: Oxford University Press.

Blackhurst, Richard (2001). "Reforming WTO Decision Making: Lessons from Singapore and Seattle." In Klaus Günter Deutsch and Bernhard Speyer (eds.), *The World Trade Organization Millennium Round: Freer Trade in the Twenty-First Century*. London: Routledge.

Blackhurst, Richard and David Hartridge (2003). "Improving the Capacity of WTO Institutions to Fulfill Their Mandate." *Journal of International Economic Law* 7 (3): 705–716.

Blackhurst, Richard, Bill Lyakurwa, and Ademola Oyejide (2000). "Options for Improving Africa's Participation in the WTO." *The World Economy* 23 (4): 491–510.

Blustein, Paul (2008). "The Nine-Day Misadventure of the Most Favored Nations: How the WTO's Doha Round Negotiations Went Awry in July 2008." Brooking Global Economy and Development. Washington, D.C.: Brookings Institution. Available at http://www.brookings.edu/~/media/Files/rc/articles/2008/1205_trade_blustein/1205_trade_blustein.pdf, accessed January 25, 2009.

Bosma, Niels, Kent Jones, Erkko Autio, and Jonathan Levie (2008). "Global Economic Institutions, National Regulations, and Entrepreneurship." In *Global Entrepreneurship Monitor: 2007 Executive Report*. Wellesley, Mass. and London: Babson College and London Business School.

Bown, Chad P. (2004a). "On the Economic Success of GATT/WTO Dispute Settlement." *Review of Economics and Statistics* 86: 811–823.

Bown, Chad P. (2004b). "Trade Policy Under the GATT/WTO: Empirical Evidence of the Equal Treatment Rule." *Canadian Journal of Economics* 37 (3): 678–720.

Bown, Chad P. (2005a). "Participation in WTO Dispute Settlement: Complainants, Interested Parties, and Free Riders." *World Bank Economic Review* 19 (2): 287–310.

Bown, Chad P. (2005b). "Trade Remedies and World Trade Organization Dispute Settlement: Why Are So Few Challenged?" *Journal of Legal Studies* 34 (June): 515–555.

Bown, Chad P. and Bernard M. Hoekman (2005). "WTO Dispute Settlement and the Missing Developing Country Cases: Engaging the Private Sector." *Journal of International Economic Law* 8 (4): 861–891.

Bown, Chad P. and Bernard M. Hoekman (2008). "Developing Countries and Enforcement of Trade Agreements: Why Dispute Settlement Is Not Enough." *Journal of World Trade* 42 (1): 177–203.

Broude, Tomer (1998). "Accession to the WTO: Current Issues in the Arab World." *Journal of World Trade* 32: 147–166.

Busch, Marc L. and Eric Reinhardt (2003). "Developing Countries and General Agreement on Tariffs and Trade/World Trade Organization Dispute Settlement." *Journal of World Trade* 34 (4): 719–735.

Business Roundtable (2006). "Expanding Economic Growth through Trade and Investment: A Blueprint for U.S. Leadership in the 21st Century." Washington, D.C.: Business Roundtable. Accessible at: http://trade.businessroundtable. org/news/ttt2.pdf.

Carraro, Carlo, Carmen Marchiori, and Alessandra Sgobbi (2005). "Advances in Negotiation Theory: Bargaining, Coalitions and Fairness." World Bank Policy Research Working Paper WPS3642. Washington: World Bank.

Charnovitz, Steve (2007). "Mapping the Law of WTO Accession." GWU Legal Studies Research Paper no. 237. Washington, D.C: George Washington University.

Chen, Jon-Ren (2004). "Emerging of International Institutions." Conference paper, Center for the Study of International Institutions, Innsbruck, Austria, November.

CIA Handbook, www.cia.gov/library/publications/the-world-factbook/docs.

Cohn, Theodore H. (2002). Governing Global Trade: International Institutions in Conflict and Convergence. Aldershot, U.K., and Burlington, Vt.: Ashgate.

Costantini, Valeria, Riccardo Crescenzi, Fabrizio De Filippis, and Luca Salvatici (2007). "Bargaining Coalitions in the WTO Agricultural Negotiations." The World Economy 30 (5): 863–891.

Cot, Jean-Pierre (1972). International Conciliation. London: Europa.

Curzon, Gerard (1965). Multilateral Commercial Diplomacy: The General Agreement on Tariffs and Trade and Its Impact on National Commercial Policies and Techniques. New York: Praeger.

Dam, Kenneth (1970). The GATT: Law and International Economic Organization. Chicago: University of Chicago Press.

Dam, Kenneth (1971). The GATT: Law and International Economic Organization. Chicago and London: University of Chicago Press.

Das, Dilip K. (2005). The Doha Round of Multilateral Trade Negotiations: Arduous Issues and Strategic Responses. Houndmills, U.K., and New York: Palgrave Macmillan.

Davey, William J. (2005). "The WTO Dispute Settlement System: The First Ten Years." Journal of International Economic Law 8 (1): 17–50.

Davis, Christina L. (2006). "Do WTO Rules Create a Level Playing Field? Lessons from the Experience of Peru and Vietnam." In John Odell (ed.), Negotiating Trade: Developing Countries in the WTO and NAFTA. Cambridge: Cambridge University Press.

De Melo, Jaime and Arvind Panagariya (1993). New Dimensions in Regional Integration. Cambridge, U.K.: Center for Economic Policy Research and Cambridge University Press.

Diego-Fernandez, Mateo (2008). "Trade Negotiations Make Strange Bedfellows." World Trade Review 7 (2): 423–453.

Delcros, Fabian (2004). "Short-Term Organisational Improvements to the WTO." Remarks delivered at the WTO Public Symposium, Geneva, May.

Dornbusch, Rudiger and Holger C. Wolf (1994). "East German Economic Reconstruction." In Olivier Jean Blanchard, Kenneth A. Froot, and Jeffrey D. Sachs (eds.), The Transition in Eastern Europe. Chicago: University of Chicago Press.

Drabek, Zdenek and Marc Bacchetta (2004). "Tracing the Effects of WTO Accession on Policy-making in Sovereign States: Preliminary Lessons from the Recent Experience of Transition Countries." *The World Economy* 27 (7): 1083–1125.

Drahos, Peter (2003). "When the Weak Bargain with the Strong: Negotiations in the WTO." *International Negotiation* 8 (1): 79–109.

Elms, Deborah Kay (2008). "Playing Fair: Unfairness Matters in International Bargaining and Negotiations." Paper presented at the Annual Meeting of the International Studies Association, San Francisco, March.

Evenett, Simon J. (2007a). "Doha's Near Death Experience at Potsdam: Why Is Reciprocal Tariff Cutting So Hard?" 24 June. VoxEU: http://www.voxeu.org/index.php?q=node/317.

Evenett, Simon J. (2007b). "Five Hypotheses Concerning the Fate of the Singapore Issues in the Doha Round." *Oxford Review of Economic Policy* 23 (3):392–414.

Evenett, Simon J. and Bernard M. Hoekman, eds. (2006). *Economic Deveopment and Multilateral Trade Cooperation.* Washington, D.C: World Bank. Copublished with Houndsmills, U.K., and New York: Palgrave Macmillan.

Evenett, Simon J. and Carlos A. Primo Braga (2005). "WTO Accession: Lessons from Experience." Trade Note 22, June 6. International Trade Department, World Bank Group. Accessible at http://siteresources.worldbank.org/INTRANETTRADE/Resources/Pubs/TradeNote22.pdf.

Finger, J. Michael (1993). "GATT's Influence on Regional Arrangements." In Jaime de Melo and Arvind Panagariya (eds.), *New Dimensions in Regional Integration,* Cambridge: Cambridge University Press and Centre for Economic Policy Research.

Finger, J. Michael (2008). "Developing Countries in the WTO System: Applying Robert Hudec's Analysis to the Doha Round." *World Trade Review,* 31 (7): 887–904.

Finger, J. Michael (2005a). "A Diplomat's Economics: Reciprocity in the Uruguay Round Negotiations." *World Trade Review* 4 (1): 27–40.

Finger, J. Michael (2005b). "The Future of the World Trade Organization: Addressing Institutional Challenges in the New Millennium." *Journal of World Trade* 39 (4): 795–804.

Finger, J. Michael (2007). "Implementation and Imbalance: Dealing with Hangover from the Uruguay Round." *Oxford Review of Economic Policy* 23 (3): 440–460.

Finger, J. Michael and Philip Schuler (2000). "Implementation of Uruguay Round Commitments: The Development Challenge." *The World Economy* 23 (5): 511–525.

Finger, J. Michael and John S. Wilson (2007). "Implementing a WTO Agreement on Trade Facilitation: What Makes Sense?" *Pacific Economic Review* 12 (3): 335–355.

Finger, J. Michael and L. Alan Winters (1998). "What Can the WTO Do for Developing Countries?" In Ann Krueger (ed.), *The WTO as an International Organization.* Chicago: Chicago University Press.

Fink, Carsten and Martin Molinuevo (2008). "East Asian Preferential Trade Agreements in Services: Liberalization Content and WTO Rules." *World Trade Review* 7 (4): 641–673.

Fisher, Roger and William Ury (1981). *Getting to Yes: Negotiating Agreement without Giving In*. Boston: Houghton Mifflin.

Fratianni, Michele and John Pattison (2001). "International Organisations in a World of Regional Trade Agreements: Lessons from Club Theory." *The World Economy* 24 (3): 333–358.

Frey, Bruno S. and Beat Gygi (1990). "The Political Economy of International Organizations." *Aussenwirtschaft* 45 (3): 371–394.

GATT Documents Database, Stanford University. Available at http://gatt.stanford.edu/page/home.

GATT (1993). Summary Record of the Second Meeting, comments by Ambassador Yerxa (United States), p. 27. Document SR.48/2. 5 January.

GATT (1994). "Acceptance of and Accession to the Agreement Establishing the World Trade Organization." Meeting at Ministerial Level, Annex I, pp. 14–15. Document MTN.TNC/45(MIN). 6 May.

Gay, Daniel (2005). "Vanuatu's Suspended Accession Bid: Second Thoughts?" In Peter Gallagher, Patrick Low, and Andrew L. Stoler (eds.), *Managing the Challenges of WTO Participation: 45 Case Studies*. Cambridge: Cambridge University Press. Also available at http://www.wto.org/english/res_e/booksp_e/casestudies_e/case43_e.htm.

Goldman Sachs (2003). "Dreaming with BRICs: The Path to 2050." Global Economics Paper No. 99. http://www2.goldmansachs.com/ideas/brics/book/99-dreaming.pdf, accessed January 20, 2009.

Graham, Edward M. (2000). *Fighting the Wrong Enemy: Antiglobal Activists and Multinational Enterprises*. Washington, D.C.: Institute for International Economics.

Grossman, Gene M. and Kenneth Rogoff, eds. (1995). *Handbook of International Economics. Volume 3: International Trade*. Amsterdam: Elsevier.

Hamilton, Colleen and John Whalley (1989). "Coalitions in the Uruguay Round." *Weltwirtschaftliches Archiv* 125: 547–562.

Herrmann-Pillath, Carsten (2006). "Endogenous Regionalism." *Journal of Institutional Economics* 2 (3): 297–318.

Hindley, Brian (1987). "Different and More Favorable Treatment—and Graduation." In J. Michael Finger and Andrzej Olechowski (eds.), *The Uruguay Round: A Handbook for the Multilateral Trade Negotiations*. Washington, D.C.: The World Bank.

Hoekman, Bernard (2002). "Strengthening the Global Trade Architecture for Development: The Post Doha Agenda." *World Trade Review* 1 (1): 23–45.

Hoekman, Bernard and Michel Kostecki (2001). *The Political Economy of the World Trading System*. 2nd ed. Oxford and New York: Oxford University Press.

Hoekman, Bernard and Petros Mavroidis (2000). "WTO Dispute Settlement, Transparency and Surveillance." *The World Economy* 23 (4): 527–542.

Hoekman, Bernard, Aaditya Mattoo, and Andre Sapir (2007). "The Political Economy of Services Trade Liberalization: A Case for International Regulatory Cooperation?" *Oxford Review of Economic Policy* 23 (3): 367–391.

Hoekman, Bernard, Constantine Michalopoulos, and L. Alan Winters (2004). "Special and Differential Treatment of Developing Countries in the WTO: Moving Forward After Cancún." *The World Economy* 27 (4): 481–506.

Horn, Henrik, Petros C. Mavroidis, and Hakan Nordstrom (1999). "Is the Use of the WTO Dispute Settlement System Biased?" CEPR Discussion Paper no. 2340.

Hudec, Robert (2002). "The Adequacy of WTO Dispute Settlement Remedies." In Bernard Hoekman, Aaditya Mattoo, and Philip English (eds.), *Development, Trade and the WTO*. Washington, D.C.: The World Bank.

Hufbauer, Gary Clyde and Matthew Adler (2008). "Why Large American Gains from Globalisation Are Plausible." VoxEU.org, 24 July. http://www.voxeu.org/index.php?q=node/1445, accessed January 25, 2009.

IMF. Listing of transition economies, www.imf.org/external/np/exr/ib/2000/110300.htm#I.

International Labour Organization (1998). Declaration on Fundamental Principles and Rights at Work. http://www.ilo.org/declaration/thedeclaration/textdeclaration/lang—en/index.htm.

Irwin, Douglas (1996). *Against the Tide*. Princeton: Princeton University Press.

Jackson, John (1969). *World Trade and the Law of GATT*. New York: Bobbs-Merrill.

Jawara, Fatoumata and Aileen Kwa (2004). *Behind the Scenes at the WTO: The Real World of International Trade Negotiations*. Rev. ed. London and New York: Zed Books.

Jones, Kent (1981). "Issues of Nonmarket Economy Participation in the GATT." *27th Quarterly Report to the Congress and the Trade Policy Committee on Trade between the United States and the Nonmarket Economy Countries During April-June 1981*. USITC Publication 1188. Washington, D.C.: U.S. International Trade Commission.

Jones, Kent (2004a). "Russia and the WTO: the Long and Winding Road to Accession." In M.L. Bruner (ed.), *Market Democracy in Post-Communist Russia*. London: Wisdom House.

Jones, Kent (2004b). "The Safeguards Mess Revisited: The Fundamental Problem. *World Trade Review* 3 (1): 83–91.

Jones, Kent (2004c). *Who's Afraid of the WTO?* New York: Oxford University Press.

Jones, Kent (2005). "Regionalism and the Problem of Representation in the WTO." Paper presented at the Centre for the Study of International Institutions, University of Innsbruck, Austria, November.

Jones, Kent (2009). "The Political Economy of WTO Accession: The Unfinished Business of Universal Membership." *World Trade Review* 8 (2).

Jones, Ronald W., and Peter B. Kenen, eds. *Handbook of International Economics* (1984). *Volume 1: International Trade*. Amsterdam and New York: North-Holland.

Kaufmann, Daniel, Aart Kraay, and Massimo Mastruzzi (2007). "Governance Matters VI: Aggregate and Individual Governance Indicators." Working Paper Series WPS 4280. Washington, D.C: World Bank.

Kavass, Igor I. (2007). "WTO Accession: Procedure, Requirements and Costs." *Journal of World Trade* 41 (3): 453–476.

Kennett, Maxine: Simon J. Evenett, and Jonathan Gage (2005). "Evaluating WTO Accessions: Legal and Economic Perspectives." Draft prepared for the Independent Development Research Centre, the World Trade Institute, Bern, Switzerland, and University of Oxford. Available at http://siteresources.worldbank.org/INTRANETTRADE/Resources/WBI-Training/Evaluating WTOAccessions_partI.pdf.

Kenworthy, James (2000), "Reform of the WTO: Basic Issues and Concerns." *Trade Trends*, Summer/Fall, 2. www.nathaninc.com/nathan/files/ccPageContentDO CFILENAME000560705546reform_k.pdf.

Khor, Martin (2005). "Mood at WTO Gloomy as Ministerial Green Room Convenes." Third World Network Information Service, 9 November. Accessed June 23, 2008. http://www.europe-solidaire.org/spip.php?article829.

Kindelberger, Charles P. (1973). *The World in Depression, 1919–1939.* 2nd ed. Berkeley: University of California Press, 1986.

Kindleberger, Charles (1981). "Dominance and Leadership in the International Economy: Exploitation, Public Goods, and Free Rides." *International Studies Quarterly* 25: 242–254.

Krueger, Anne O. (1999). "Are Preferential Trading Arrangements Trade-Liberalizing or Protectionist?" *Journal of Economic Perspectives* 13 (4):105–124.

Lacey, Simon (2007). "The View from the Other Side of the Table: WTO Accession from the Perspective of WTO Members." In Jeremy Streatfeild and Simon Lacey (eds.), *New Reflections on International Trade.* London: Cameron May.

Laird, Sam (2007). "Aid for Trade: Cool Aid or Kool-Aid?" G-24 Discussion Paper series, No. 48, United Nations Conference on Trade and Development. Geneva: UNCTAD.

Langhammer, Rolf J. and Matthias Lücke (1999). "WTO Accession Issues." *The World Economy* 22 (6): 837–873.

Lanoszka, Anna (2001). "The World Trade Organization Accession Process: Negotiating Participation in a Globalizing Economy." *Journal of World Trade* 35 (4): 575–602.

Lawrence, Robert Z. (2006). "Rulemaking Amidst Growing Diversity: A Club-of-Club Approach to WTO Reform and New Issue Selection." *Journal of International Economic Law* 9: 823–835.

Lawrence, Robert Z. (2008). "International Organisations: The Challenge of Aligning Mission, Means and Legitimacy." *The World Economy.* 31 (11): 1455–1470.

Leitner, Kara and Simon Lester (2005). "WTO Dispute Settlement 1995–2004: A Statistical Analysis." *Journal of International Economic Law* 8: 231–234.

Leitner, Kara and Simon Lester (2008). "WTO Dispute Settlement 1995–2007: A Statistical Analysis." *Journal of International Economic Law* 11 (1): 179–193.

Levy, Philip (2007). "Do We Need an Undertaker for the Single Undertaking? Considering the Angles of Variable Geometry." In Simon Evenett and Bernard

Hoekman (eds.), *Economic Development and Multilateral Trade Cooperation*. Washington, D.C: World Bank.

M'Bow, Amadou-Mahtar (1978). "The Practice of Consensus in International Organizations." *International Social Science Journal* 30 (4): 893–903.

Marceau, Gabrielle (2001). "When and How Is a Regional Trade Agreement Compatible with the WTO?" *Legal Issues of Economic Integration* 28 (3): 297–336.

Martin, Will and Patrick Messerlin (2007). "Why Is It So Difficult? Trade Liberalization under the Doha Agenda." *Oxford Review of Economic Policy* 23 (3): 347–366.

Maskus, Keith (2002). "Benefiting from Intellectual Property Protection." In Bernard Hoekman, Aaditya Mattoo, and Philip English (eds.), *Development, Trade, and the WTO: A Handbook*. Washington, D.C.: The World Bank.

Mattoo, Aaditya and Arvind Subramanian (2008). "Multilateralism beyond Doha." Working Paper WP 08–8. Washington, D.C.: Peterson Institute for International Economics. Available at www.petersoninstitute.org.

McMillan, John (1988). "A Game-Theoretic View of International Trade Negotiations: Implications for Developing Countries." In John Whalley (ed.), *Rules, Power and Credibility*. London: Macmillan.

Michalopoulos, Constantine (2001). *Developing Countries in the WTO*. London and New York: Palgrave.

Michalopoulos, Constantine (2002). "WTO Accession." In Bernard Hoekman, Aaditya Mattoo, and Philip English (eds), *Development, Trade and the WTO: A Handbook*, 61–70. Washington, D.C: The World Bank, 2002.

Milgrom, Paul and John Roberts (1992). *Economics, Organization and Management*. Englewood Cliffs, N.J.: Prentice-Hall.

Mogilevskii, Roma (2004). "Is Accession to the World Trade Organization Worthwhile? The Experience of Kyrgyzstan." *Problems of Economic Transition* 47 (12): 68–73.

Narlikar, Amrita (2003). *International Trade and Developing Countries: Bargaining Coalitions in the GATT and WTO*. London and New York: Routledge.

Narlikar, Amrita and John S. Odell (2006). "The Strict Distributive Strategy for a Bargaining Coalition: The Like Minded Group in the World Trade Organization." In John S. Odell (ed.), *Negotiating Trade: Developing Countries in the WTO and NAFTA*. Cambridge and New York: Cambridge University Press.

Narlikar, Amrita and Diana Tussie (2004). "The G20 at the Cancun Ministerial: Developing Countries and their Evolving Coalitions in the WTO." *The World Economy* 27 (7): 947–966.

Nordstrom, Hakan and Gregory Shaffer (2008). "Access to Justice in the World Trade Organization: A Case for a Small Claims Procedure?" *World Trade Review* 7 (4): 587–640.

Odell, John S. (2009). "Breaking Deadlocks in International Institutional Negotiations: The WTO, Seattle and Doha." *International Studies Quarterly* 53 (forthcoming).

Odell, John S, ed. (2006). *Negotiating Trade: Developing Countries in the WTO and NAFTA*. Cambridge: Cambridge University Press.

Odell, John S. (2000). *Negotiating the World Economy*. Ithaca, N.Y.: Cornell University Press.

Odell, John S. (2001). "Problems in Negotiating Consensus in the World Trade Organization." Conference paper, American Political Science Association, San Francisco, August.

Odell, John S. and Susan K. Sell (2006). "Reframing The Issue: The WTO Coalition on Intellectual Property and Public Health, 2001." In John S. Odell (ed.), *Negotiating Trade: Developing Countries in the WTO and NAFTA*. Cambridge and New York: Cambridge University Press.

OECD (2005). "Agricultural Policy Reform in China." OECD Policy Brief, October. Available at www.SourceOECD.org.

OECD (2008). "Reporting on Aid for Trade to the Creditor Reporting System: Information Note." Document COM/DCD/TAD(2008)10. 8. September. Paris: OECD.

Ostry, Sylvia (2000). "The Uruguay Round North–South Bargain: Implications for Future Negotiations." In Daniel L.M. Kennedy and James D. Southwick (eds), *The Political Economy of International Trade Law: Essays in Honor of Robert E. Hudec*. Cambridge: Cambridge University Press. Accessible at http://www.utoronto.ca/cis/Minnesota.pdf.

Ostry, Sylvia (2007). "Trade, Development, and the Doha Development Agenda." In Donna Lee and Rorden Wilkinson (eds.), *The WTO After Hong Kong: Progress in, and Prospects for, the Doha Development Agenda*. London and New York: Routledge.

Ostry, Sylvia, Alan S. Alexandroff, and Rafael Gomez (2003) *China and the Long March to Global Trade: The Accession of China to the World Trade Organization*. London and New York: RoutledgeCurzon.

Panitchpakdi, Supachai (2001). "Balancing Competing Interests: The Future Role of the WTO." In Gary P. Sampson (ed.), *The Role of the World Trade Organization in Global Governance*. Tokyo and New York: United Nations University.

Petersmann, Ernst-Ulrich (1997). *The GATT/WTO Dispute Settlement System: International Law, International Organizations and Dispute Settlement*. London: Kluwer Law International.

Prowse, Susan (2002). "The Role of International and National Agencies in Trade-related Capacity Building." *The World Economy* 25 (9): 1235–1261.

Prowse, Susan (2006). " 'Aid for Trade': A Proposal for Increasing Support for Trade Adjustment and Integration." In Simon J. Evenett and Bernard M. Hoekman (eds.), *Economic Development and Multilateral Trade Cooperation*. Washington, D.C.: The World Bank.

Rivera-Batiz, Luis A. and Maria-Angels Oliva (2003). *International Trade: Theory, Strategies, and Evidence*. Oxford and New York: Oxford University Press.

Rose, Andrew (2004). "Do We Really Know that the WTO Increases Trade?" *American Economic Review* 94 (1): 98–114.

Schott, Jeffrey J. (2008). "The Future of the Multilateral Trading System in a Multi-Polar World." Speech delivered in Bonn, Germany. Washington, D.C.: Petersen Institute of International Economics, http://www.iie.com.

Schott, Jeffrey J. and Jayashree Watal (2000). "Decision Making in the WTO." In Jeffrey J. Schott (ed.), *The WTO After Seattle*. Washington, D.C: Institute for International Economics.

Schott, Jeffrey J. and Johanna W. Buurman (1994). *The Uruguay Round: An Assessment*. Washington, D.C.: Institute for International Economics.

Searle, John R. (1995). *The Construction of Social Reality*. New York: Free Press.

Searle, John R. (2005). "What is an Institution?" *Journal of Institutional Economics* 1 (1): 1–22.

Selten, Reihard (1987). "Equity and Coalition Bargaining in Experimental Three-Person Games." In Alvin E. Roth (ed.), *Laboratory Experimentation in Economics: Six Points of View*. Cambridge and New York: Cambridge University Press.

Shaffer, Gregory (2003). *Defending Interests: Public-Private Partnerships in WTO Litigation*. Washington, D.C.: Brookings Institution.

Shaffer, Gregory (2005). "Can WTO Technical Assistance and Capacity Building Serve Developing Countries?" In Ernst-Ulrich Petersmann and James Harrison (eds.), *Reforming the World Trading System: Legitimacy, Efficiency, and Democratic Governance*. Oxford and New York: Oxford University Press.

Sharma, Shefali (2003). "WTO Decision Making: A Broken Process." WTO Cancun Series Paper no. 4. Minneapolis: Institute for Agriculture and Trade Policy. www.iatp.org.

Simon, Herbert (1957). *Models of Man*. New York: John Wiley and Sons.

Smith, Adam (1776) [1976]. *An Inquiry into the Nature and Causes of the Wealth of Nations*. Chicago: University of Chicago Press.

Smith, James McCall (2004). "Inequality in International Trade? Developing Countries and Institutional Change in WTO Dispute Settlement." *Review of International Political Economy* 11 (3): 542–573.

Smith, James McCall (2006). "Compliance Bargaining in the WTO: Ecuador and the Bananas Dispute." In John Odell (ed.), *Negotiating Trade: Developing Countries in the WTO and NAFTA*. Cambridge: Cambridge University Press.

Smith, Murray G. (1996). "Accession to the WTO: Key Strategic Issues." In Jeffrey J. Schott (ed.), *The World Trading System: Challenges Ahead*. Washington, D.C: Institute for International Economics.

Steinberg, Richard H. (2002). "In the Shadow of Law or Power? Consensus-Based Bargaining in the GATT/WTO." *International Organization* 56 (2): 339–374.

Stoler, Andrew (2003). "The Current State of the WTO." Speech delivered at the Workshop on the EU, the US and the WTO, Stanford University, 28 February–1 March. Available at www.iit.adelaide.edu.au/docs/Stanford.pdf.

Sutherland, Peter, et al. (2005). *The Future of the WTO: Addressing Institutional Challenges in the New Millennium*. Geneva: World Trade Organization.

Suwa-Eisenmann, Akiko and Theirry Verdier (2007). "Aid and Trade." *Oxford Review of Economic Policy* 23: 481–507.

Sykes, Alan O. (2003). "The Safeguards Mess: A Critique of WTO Jurisprudence." *World Trade Review* 2 (3): 261–295.

Tang, Man-Keung and Shang-Jin Wei (2008). "The Value of Making Commitments Externally: Evidence from WTO Accessions." NBER Working Paper No. 14582.

Tarr, David G. and Giorgio Barba Navaretti (2005). "Introduction and Summary to Handbook of Trade Policy and WTO Accession for Development in Russia and the CIS." Policy Research Working Paper Series WPS 3726. Washington, D.C: World Bank. Available at http://econ.worldbank.org.

Taylor, Benjamin J. and John S. Wilson (2008). "Trade Facilitation and the Doha Agenda: What Matters for Development." Trade Issue Brief, World Bank, July. Washington, D.C.: World Bank.

Tehrani, Minoo (2008). "European Union and the US Trade Disputes: The Role of the WTO." *Organization Management Journal* 5: 135–148.

Thelen, Kathleen and Sven Steinmo (1992). "Historical Institutionalism in Comparative Politics." In Sven Steinmo, Kathleen Thelen, and Frank Longstreth (eds.), *Structuring Politics: Historical Institutionalism in Comoparative Analysis*. Cambridge: Cambridge University Press.

Tomz, Micahel, Judith Goldstein, and Douglas Rivers (2007). "Do We Really Know that the WTO Increases Trade?: Comment." *American Economic Review* 97 (5): 2005–2018.

Tsai, Meng-chia (2005). "The WTO Negotiations on Trade Facilitation and the Development of Developing Countries." Conference paper, Centre for the Study of International Institutions, Innsbruck, Austria, November.

Tussie, Diana (1993). "Holding the Balance: The Cairns Group in the Uruguay Round." In Diana Tussie and David Glover (eds.), *The Developing Countries in World Trade: Policies and Bargaining Strategies*, Boulder and London: Lynne Renner.

Ullrich, Heidi (2000). "Stimulating Trade Liberalization after Seattle." Conference Paper, New Directions in Global Governance, University of the Ryukus, Okinawa, Japan, July 19–20.

United Nations (2006). List of Member States. Available at http://www.un.org/Overview/unmember.html.

United Nations Conference on Environment and Development (1992). "Rio Declaration on the Environment and Development." UN doc.A/CONF.151/26 (vol.1). 31 *International Legal Materials 874*. New York: United Nations.

United Nations. Membership of Principal United Nations Organs in 2006, Available at http://www.un.org/geninfo/faq/factsheets/FS25.HTM.

United Nations. Comtrade database, http://comtrade.un.org/db.

Wallich, Lori and Patrick Woodall (2004). *Whose Trade Organization? A Comprehensive Guide to the WTO*. New York and London: The New Press.

Watson, Peter (2005). *Ideas: A History of Thought and Invention from Fire to Freud*. New York: HarperCollins.

Wilkinson, Rorden (2006). *The WTO: Crisis and the Governance of Global Trade*. London and New York: Routledge.

Williamson, Oliver E. (1985). *The Economic Institutions of Capitalism*. New York: Free Press.

Wilson, John S., Catherine Mann and Tsunehiro Otsuki (2005). "Assessing the Benefits of Trade Facilitation: A Global Perspective." *The World Economy* 28 (6): 841–871.

Winters, L. Alan (2007). "Coherence and the WTO." *Oxford Review of Economic Policy* 23 (3): 461–480.

Wolfe, Robert (2005). "Decision-Making and Transparency in the 'Medieval' WTO: Does the Sutherland Report Have the Right Prescription?" *Journal of International Economic Law* 8 (3) 631–645.

Worldwide Governance Indicators, http://info.worldbank.org/governance/wgi/index.asp.

World Bank (2008). "Fact Sheet: The World Bank Group and Aid for Trade." Washington, D.C.: World Bank.

World Bank World Development Indicators. database. http://econ.worldbank.org/research.

WTO. (1995). "Accessions: The Mandate Relevant WTO Provisions." www.wto.org/english/thewto_e/acc_e/acc7_3_e.htm.

WTO (1995–1999). *Trade Policy Reviews*, various countries.

WTO (1997). "Leading into the Third Millennium." Press release of Renato Ruggiero speech, 18 November. Available at http://www.wto.org/english/news_e/sprr_e/washin_e.htm.

WTO (1998). "Statement by Mr. William J. Clinton, President." Available at www.wto.org/english/thewto_e/minist_e/min98_e/anniv_e/clinton_e.htm.

WTO (2002). "Accession of Least Developed Countries." Decision of General Counsel, 10 December, WTO Document WT/L/508.

WTO (2003a). Note by the Secretariat, Accession to the World Trade Organization, 28 May. WT/ACC/10/Rev.1.

WTO (2003b). "International Architecture on Trade Facilitation: The WTO and International Organizations and Framework, Communication from Japan." Document G/C.W/465, 10 June.

WTO (2004). Technical Note on the Accession Process (Revision 2). WT/ACC/10/Rev. 2. Available at www.wto.org.

WTO (2005a). Statistics database, http://stat.wto.org/Home/WSDBHome.aspz?language=E.

WTO (2005b). Technical Note on the Accession Process (Revision 3). WT/ACC/10/Rev. 3, 28 Nov.

WTO (2005c). Technical Note on the Accession Process (Revision 6). WT/ACC/11/Rev. 6. Available at www.wto.org.

WTO (2006a). "How to Become a Member of the WTO." Available at http://www.wto.org/english/thewto_e/acc_e/acces_e.htm.

WTO (2006b). "Talks Suspended: Today There Are Only Losers." Press release, 24 July. Available at http://www.wto.org/english/news_e/news06_e/mod06_summary_24july_e.htm.

WTO (2007). "Lamy Welcomes Cape Verde's Accession as Another Sign of Confidence in the WTO." Press release, 18 December. Available at http://wto.az/00073ENG.htm.

WTO (2008a). *Annual Report,* 2008. Geneva: WTO.

WTO (2008b). *A Handbook on Accession to the WTO.* Prepared by the WTO Secretariat. Geneva: WTO.

WTO. International Trade and Tariff Data, www.wto.org/english/res_e/statis_e/statis_e.htm

Yarbrough, Beth and Robert M. Yarbrough (1992). *Cooperation and Governance in International Trade: The Strategic Organizational Approach.* Princeton: Princeton University Press.

Zoellick, Robert B. (2003). Final Press Conference: World Trade Organization Fifth Ministerial Meeting, *The Soy Daily,* September 14, 2003. Available at www.thesoydaily.com, accessed June 15, 2004.

PERIODICAL PUBLICATIONS

Bridges Weekly Trade Digest
Economist (London)
Financial Times (London)
New York Times

WEB SITES

Advisory Centre on WTO Law: www.acwl.ch
Business Roundtable Publications: trade.businessroundtable.org/news/
World Bank: www.worldbank.org
World Trade Organization: www.wto.org
VoxEU.org Economics Blog: www.voxeu.org

Index